Word of God
Bhagavad Gita

notionpress
.com

Word of God
Bhagavad Gita

AJAY GUPTA

notionpress.com

Notion Press

Old No. 38, New No. 6
McNichols Road, Chetpet
Chennai - 600 031

First Published by Notion Press 2016

ISBN 978-93-86009-89-0

BHAGAVAD GITA AS OTHERS SEE IT:

The great Scientist ***Albert Einstein*** said, "When I read the ***Bhagavad Gita*** and reflect about how God created this Universe, everything else seems so superfluous."

Mahatma Gandhi expressed his love for ***Bhagavad Gita*** in these words, "When disappointment stares me in the face, and I do not see a ray of hope, I go back to the ***Bhagavad Gita*** to read a verse here and a verse there and I start smiling."

Sri Aurobindo said, "***Bhagavad Gita*** is a Scripture of the future generations; and Hinduism has acquired a much wider relevance through Bhagavad Gita."

Swami Sivananda said, "***Bhagavad Gita*** is the most precious jewel of Hindu religion, and I suggest its introduction into the curriculum of the Indian schools and colleges."

Swami Chinmayananda said, "The study of ***Bhagavad Gita*** should be undertaken as a Jnana Yajna to worship the Divine Spirit and invoke wisdom. ***Bhagavad Gita*** is a universal Scripture for the mankind irrespective of caste, creed or religion, and its study turns the mind from a state of confusion and agitation into inner contentment, peace of mind and dynamic action."

Swami Vivekananda followed **Bhagavad Gita** in totality. It is said that ***'Bhagavad Gita'*** and ***'The Imitation of Christ'*** were his favourite books. When Swami Vivekananda was travelling all over India as a wandering monk, he kept only these two books with him.

Aldous Huxley, the English writer found ***Gita*** as the most systematic statement of spiritual evolution for mankind. He said, "**Gita** is the most clear and comprehensive summaries of perennial philosophy ever revealed; hence its enduring value is valuable not only to India but to the whole of humanity."

Jawaharlal Nehru, the first prime minister of India said, "***Bhagavad Gita*** deals essentially with the spiritual foundation of human existence. It is a call of action to meet the obligations and duties of life."

Hermann Graf Keyserling, German Philosopher regarded **Bhagavad Gita** as the most beautiful work of the literature of the world.

Hermann Hesse felt that the marvel of the ***Bhagavad Gita*** is its truly beautiful revelation of life's wisdom which enables philosophy to blossom into spirituality.

Indian Prime Minister Narendra Modi is a keen follower of the teaching of Bhagavad Gita. In his maiden visit to the United States on September 29, 2014, Prime Minister Narendra Modi gifted a copy of **'Bhagavad Gita'** to US President Barack Obama during a dinner hosted at the White House.

During ***Prime Minister Narendra Modi's*** visit to Japan on September 3, 2014, he gifted a copy of ***Bhagavad*** Gita to Japanese Prime Minister Shinzo Abe. In addition to the Sanskrit version, a Japanese version of the **Bhagavad Gita** was also presented to the Japanese Prime Minister, Abe.

This book is dedicated to the Spirit of Lord Vishnu who incarnated as Sri Krishna and gave the eternal teaching of Bhagavad Gita to the humanity

and

My late father Dr. Hari Ram Gupta M.A, Ph.D, D.Litt.; Sikh historian and former Pro-Vice Chancellor, Punjab University, Chandigarh (Punjab)

and

My late mother Mrs Uma Gupta

Contents

Preface

The teaching of Bhagavad Gita was given by God incarnate Sri Krishna, more than five thousand years ago. The same truth is as relevant in today's world, as it was in the ancient past. The teaching was given by Sri Krishna as an incarnation of Lord Vishnu, in very compact Sanskrit verses as the 'Song of the God.' Different commentators and writers have interpreted these verses according to their mind and intellectual understanding.

The main verses of Bhagavad Gita in 'Sanskrit' have remained the same like a 'Bible' till date. There are numerous interpretations and various commentaries on these verses. The Scripture of Bhagavad Gita is so sublime and lofty that it has been translated into all the major languages of the world, for the benefit of the humanity.

There is also a possibility that the true essence of Gita may not be understood in the correct perspective, if the verses are not interpreted correctly. Hindu religion is widely known as the religion which worships idols and pictures of God in visual form. On the other hand Christianity and Islam do not permit any form of idol worship.

The teaching of Bhagavad Gita has been grossly misunderstood in Hinduism to propagate the concept of God with manifestation in the form of idol worship only. There are many temples in India, where devotees throng to worship the divinity in the form of an idol. This also serves the purpose to turn the mind to the higher realms of spirituality.

The text and verses of Bhagavad Gita say that the Spirit of God can be realized both in manifest forms as idols or pictures; and also in unmanifest form as One Absolute Spirit of God without form.

Chapter 9 verse 11 of Gita says that deluded people are unaware of My Supreme Spirit of God as the great Lord of the entire Universe. The ignorant consider Me as dwelling in the human form. —Another verse in Chapter 12 of Bhagavad Gita says that the Spirit of God can also be worshiped in unmanifest form, but it is a difficult path for the human beings to follow. All these aspects have been exhaustively explained in my commentary on the verses.

I have presented Bhagavad Gita in this book, as a synthesis of all religions, by linking the Gita verses with moral stories. It is an endeavour to make the lofty teaching easily understandable. This book has been presented with an intellectual grasp of the essence of Gita, and I lay no special claims on spirituality.

The difficult text of Bhagavad Gita has been presented in a simplified manner for reading by both young and old, irrespective of one's caste, creed or religion. Reverence and respect for all religions is the underlying criteria for anyone to assimilate this exalted teaching.

There is however one important injunction in Bhagavad Gita by Sri Krishna; that this lofty Scripture is not to be declared to a person who finds faults or speaks ill of this teaching. This aspect is explained in verse 18:67 of Bhagavad Gita.

I have accomplished the entire task of writing and typing this book on computer, all by myself. This book is dedicated to the glory of God and His eternal Spirit. Verse 18:70 of Gita says that the Spirit of God will be deemed to have been worshipped by all those who study this sacred Gospel of Bhagavad Gita. May all those who have faith and respect for all religions, enjoy reading this book? And may we all prosper together by following the lofty teaching of Gita?

Readers are welcome to send me their comments and queries on my e-mail ajayjalvayu@gmail.com.

Ajay Gupta
A1-214, JAL VAYU TOWERS
SECTOR-56, GURGAON-122011 (INDIA)

CHAPTER 1

THE DEJECTION OF ARJUNA
ARJUNA VISHADA YOGA

Dhritarashtra said to Sanjaya:

O Sanjaya! Gathered together and facing each other on the battlefield of Kurukshetra, eager to fight a war to determine who is righteous; what are the Kaurava warriors on my side, and the Pandava warriors on the other side doing? (1)

Transliteration of the above verse from Sanskrit to English is, "***dharmakshetre...Kurukshetre***: —on the battlefield of Kurukshetra to determine who is righteous (dharma):—***samavetah***: —gathered together: —***yuyutsavah***: —eager to fight: —***mamkah***: —my side (Kauravas):—***pandavah...cha...eva***: —and also the sons of Pandu: —***Kim...akurvata...***O ***Sanjaya***: —what are they doing O Sanjaya!"

Bhagavad Gita is a sacred book on spiritual matters and the path of yoga, but then how does it happen that the book starts with a war scenario to begin with? The treatise of the eternal teaching of Bhagavad Gita was given by Sri Krishna more than five thousand years ago on the battlefield; and what is the relevance of a war scenario from that ancient time to the present modern times of today?

Humanity is constantly at war with each other, whether it was in the ancient past or in the context of the modern world now. The world has seen two World Wars, First World War in the years 1914–1918, and the Second World War in the years 1939–1945. This resulted in a large scale killing of humanity and devastation of property. The conflict virtually involved every part of the world to make it one of the bloodiest wars resulting in a large scale extermination of humanity.

Indian soldiers under the British flag fought the war in other countries. Forty million people including civilian and military personnel died in the Second World War as it was a prolonged war. The dropping of a nuclear bomb on Hiroshima, Japan ended the Second World War due to its devastating effect. The war and terrorism between countries is continuing even today. India has seen two wars with Pakistan in the years 1965 and 1971 and with China in the year 1962.

When all efforts at mediation fail, then war is the only recourse left between the two sides. The war therefore, is as relevant in today's world, as it was in the ancient past. The spiritual discourse on Bhagavad Gita by Sri Krishna starts from Chapter 2 onwards, and those readers who want to hear the spiritual teaching first can go directly to the following Chapters, and later revert back to the first Chapter for description of the warriors on the two sides.

Was there any way that the war between the Kaurava and the Pandava forces could have been averted? A concise summary of the events leading to the start of the Mahabharata war is as follows.

Dhritarashtra is the eldest son in a royal family. Ordinarily he would have become the king, but since he was born blind, his younger brother Pandu took over the throne. In time Pandu had five sons, of whom Arjuna was the second. Dhritarashtra had many sons, of whom Duryodhana was the eldest. The war is between the sons of Pandu called the Pandavas, and their cousins, the sons of Dhritarashtra called the Kauravas. Duryodhana is the leader of the Kaurava army, and Arjuna leads the army of the Pandavas.

Pandu died at an early age and his five sons grew up under the care of their uncle Dhritarashtra, who had usurped the kingdom. All the cousins were brought up together in the same household and had training under the same teachers, the most notable of whom were Bhishma and Drona. Dhritarashtra favoured his sons over his nephews, and condoned all the wicked deeds of his sons including denuding of Draupadi, wife of the Pandavas in full view of the whole assembly.

The sons of Pandu on the other hand had many virtuous qualities and superiority in warfare. Duryodhana was thus always envious of his cousins. Yudhishthira, was the eldest of the Pandavas, and was the rightful heir to the kingdom. Duryodhana conceived many plots to kill his cousins. He built a palace of wax and set fire to it so that his cousins are killed, but they escaped as a divine intervention. There were many other crooked plans devised by Duryodhana, such as to poison his cousins and to entice them into a game of dice. As a result, the Pandava brothers were sent into exile in a forest so that the kingdom is ruled by the Kauravas.

Logically, the kingdom should have been restored to the Pandavas, but to make peace Pandava princes pleaded with prince Duryodhana to give them just five villages out of the entire kingdom, so that they can live there. All pleas and pleadings of the Pandava princes fell on deaf ears, and prince Duryodhana refused to part with any land even of the size of a tip of a needle.

Sri Krishna then approached prince Duryodhana as a mediator to seek justice for the Pandava princes, but it was of no avail. When all the doors to reach an amicable settlement had been closed, then war was the only alternative left.

The two sides approached Sri Krishna to seek his support, as Sri Krishna is a neutral person. As the war could not be averted, Sri Krishna offered his vast army to one side, and he Himself as the charioteer and counsellor on the other side. Arjuna asks for Sri Krishna as his charioteer and counsellor, and Duryodhana was very happy to have Sri Krishna's entire army on his side.

Bible (Romans 8:31) says, "What, then, shall we say in response to these things? If God is for us, then who can be against us?"

At the start of the battle, the two armies are facing each other on the battlefield of Kurukshetra, and the battle is about to begin. Arjuna then asks Sri Krishna to place his chariot in the middle of the two armies, so that he can survey the warriors on both the sides.

The blind king Dhritarashtra is standing on a hilltop with his charioteer and minister Sanjaya, overlooking the battlefield. King

Dhritarashtra turns to his minister Sanjaya to describe the happenings on the battlefield of Kurukshetra. Sage Vyasa temporarily bestows on Sanjaya a divine eye to see all distant scenes on the war front. It is the modern equivalent of television channels these days, to describe the real time events as a live commentary.

Science has made it possible to give live relay of events with the help of communication satellites. But in those days 5,000 years back, the sages did it with their divine powers, which was a portend and forerunner of what the science has now achieved through technology in the modern era.

The first chapter of the Bhagavad Gita narrates the names of the Kaurava and Pandava warriors facing each other, and sets the stage for a spiritual dialogue between Arjuna and his mentor Sri Krishna to begin, from the second chapter onwards.

Sanjaya said:

Upon seeing the Pandava forces drawn up in the battle order; Prince Duryodhana drew his chariot near his Guru and preceptor (Guru Dronacharya), and spoke these words: (2)

Behold O teacher (Dronacharya), the mighty army of the sons of Pandu (Pandavas), marshalled by your talented disciple, and the son of Drupada (Dhrishtadyumna). (3)

In the epic Mahabharata, Guru Dronacharya was the royal preceptor to both the Pandava and the Kaurava princes for training in military arts and divine weapons. His favourite students were Arjuna and his own son Ashvatthama. Dronacharya was a fearsome warrior who was well versed in the art of military warfare. After the fall of Bhishma in the battle, he became the Commander of the Kaurava forces for five days.

Here before me, are the mighty heroes (of Pandava army), the best archers equal in battle to powerful Bhima and Arjuna–the great warriors;–Yuyudhana, Virata and

Drupada; valiant Drishtaketu, Chekitana and the king of Kashi; Purujit, KuntiBhoja and Saibya, the greatest of men; – the powerful Yudhamanyu and the brave Uttamauja; the son of Subhadra and the sons of Draupadi, all of them great warriors. (4-5-6)

O Best of the Brahmins (Dronacharya)! Know also the prominent warrior-chiefs on our side (Kauravas). I describe our mighty warriors for your information and assessment of our strength. (7)

Besides your own-self (Dronacharya); these brave warriors are Bhishma, Karna, Kripa, Ashvatthama, Vikarna, the son of Somadatta; and all these great men are ever victorious in battle. (8)

'Karna' is among the most popular and a complex character in the Mahabharata War, who shows both nobility and nastiness over the course of the War. What was the reason of his bitterness and why did he take sides with Duryodhana? He was a powerful warrior who is projected as bad, because he had bitterness in his life. His bitterness took him into a disastrous life story. He was a noble man with a phenomenal sense of integrity and generosity, but all that was lost.

He was resentful because he did not know whose child he was. His foster parents, Radha and Athiratha, loved him immensely and brought him up lovingly. As a newborn child, he was abandoned and found floating on the waters, and adopted by his foster parents. He was always unhappy and miserable because he could not come to terms, as to why he was being labelled as ***'suta putra'*** or low-born.

All the time, he nourished bitterness within himself about his so-called low birth. He was a great warrior and showed his prowess in different situations, but because of his bitterness in life, he took sides with the Kaurava army. He died in the battle in a foul way.

And there are yet many other warriors of heroic deeds, well-trained in warfare and armed with many different kinds of weapons. All of them are ready to lay down their lives, for my sake. (9)

On the thirteenth day of the War, Kaurava forces challenged Pandavas to break a spiral battle formation known as ***Chakravyuha***. Arjuna's son Abhimanyu was trapped inside this tricky ***Chakravyuha***, and he did not know how to come out of this formation once he had gone inside. ***Abhimanyu*** was thereafter mercilessly killed by the Kaurava forces.

It was a violation of the War rules at that time, to kill a lone warrior. Arjuna was devastated by the death of his son. Thereafter Arjuna killed Jayadratha. It was a battle of no holds barred from thereon, and all fair and unfair means were adopted to kill the opponent. Once the vicious circle of 'tit for tat' had started, there were transgressions of the War rules by both the sides.

Dronacharya was invincible in war and he could not have been killed in a straight fight. He was similarly killed by a clever ploy. He loved his son Ashvatthama so dearly that he would lay down his weapons in grief if his son was killed. An elephant by the name of Ashvatthama was killed and it was announced that Ashvatthama had been killed. Dronacharya thought that his son had been killed and in grief, he laid down his weapons. Dhrishtadyumna from the Pandava forces then beheaded him.

Bible (Matthew) says, "Put away your sword," Jesus told him: "Those who use the sword will die by the sword."

This Kaurava army of ours protected by venerable sire Bhishma (Commander of Kaurava forces) is unconquerable; while the limited Pandava army guarded in every way by mighty Bhima, seems vulnerable and easy to conquer. (10)

Now all our warriors take your respective battle positions, and form a protective ring around our Commander-in-Chief Bhishma, and guard him from all sides. (11)

In order to embolden the Kaurava prince Duryodhana; Bhishma the grandsire of the Kuru dynasty blew his conch-shell triumphantly like a lion's roar to announce the readiness for battle. (12)

In the great battle of Mahabharata, grandsire Bhishma was the Supreme Commander of the Kaurava forces for ten days. Bhishma was one of the most powerful warriors of his time. He was too powerful to be defeated by any warrior of that time. At the beginning of the war, Bhishma had vowed that he will not kill any of the Pandava princes, as he loved them, being their grandsire.

Thereafter, readiness for war was announced by the loud-sounds of conch-shells, kettle-drums, tabors, trumpets and cow-horns from the other warriors of Kaurava army, and the sound was heart-rending. (13)

Then, on the other side of the battle formation, Madhava (Sri Krishna) and Pandava (Arjuna), seated in their magnificent chariot yoked to white horses, blew their celestial conch-shells. (14)

The conch-shell of Hrishikesha (Sri Krishna) named Panchajanya; conch-shell of Dhananjaya (Arjuna) named Devadatta; and the conch of mighty Bhima called Paundra, raised a deafening and tumultuous roar in the sky. (15)

King Yudhishthira, son of Kunti, blew his conch shell Anantavijaya; while Nakula and Sahadeva blew their Sughosha and Manipushpaka conches, respectively. —And the excellent archer, the king of Kashi; and the mighty warrior Shikhandi; Dhrishtadyumna and Virata, and the invincible hero Satyaki; —Drupada and the sons of Draupadi; and the mighty-armed son of Subhadra, each blew their respective conches, to announce readiness for War. O lord of the earth! (16-17-18)

The mighty uproar of the fierce sound reverberated throughout the earth and the sky, causing a fear in the hearts of Dhritarashtra's Kaurava army. (19)

Sanjaya further narrates to King Dhritarashtra: —Then upon seeing the battle array of the two opposing forces, when the war was about to begin, Pandava prince Arjuna

with flag ensign of Hanuman; lifted his bow, and thus spoke to Hrishikesha Sri Krishna. (20)

Arjuna said to Sri Krishna:

O Achyuta! Sri Krishna! Place my chariot in the middle of the two forces drawn up for battle, so that I can see the warriors with whom I have to fight this war. I want to observe the warriors who have assembled here to please Duryodhana, the evil-minded son of king Dhritarashtra. (21-22-23)

Sanjaya said to King Dhritarashtra:

Then Hrishikesha-Sri Krishna, as requested by Arjuna, placed their chariot in the middle of the two battle arrays; while prominently facing Bhishma and Drona and the other Kaurava warriors. —Sri Krishna then said, "O Arjuna! Behold the Kaurava forces assembled here." (24–25)

Standing there, Arjuna saw in the two battle formations, his own paternal uncles, grandfathers, teachers, maternal-uncles, cousins, sons, grandsons, fathers-in-law, comrades and friends. (26)

It was an irony of fate that Arjuna was engaged in a war in which he had to kill his own kith and kin and blood relatives. He had spent the best part of his childhood and youth with them. In a war scenario there are only two options; either the opponent kills you or you kill them. There is no option of a soft corner or mercy once the war is declared.

When Arjuna saw all of his kinsmen and relatives stationed both in his own battle formation, as well as in the opposing battle formation (about to kill each other); he was in a strange predicament, and he was filled with a feeling of deep sorrow and sympathy. In a choked voice filled with compassion, he thus spoke to Sri Krishna.(27)

Arjuna Said to Sri Krishna:

O Sri Krishna! Seeing my nearest and dear relatives and kinsmen, arrayed in battle to kill each other, my limbs fail me, and my mouth and lips are parched dry (due to deep compassion and grief for my close relatives). (28)

My body trembles, and my hair stand on end. My Gandiva bow is slipping out of my hands, and my skin is tingling with a burning sensation. (29)

O Dear Lord! Keshava Sri Krishna! I am unable to stand on my feet, and my head is in a whirl and I have lost my balance of mind. I see evil and adverse omens. (30)

I do not see any worthwhile purpose and good in killing my own close relatives and venerable teachers in this war. I do not long for such a victory, or the kingdom and its pleasures. (31)

O Govinda! O Sri Krishna! Of what avail and of what use are the kingdom and its luxuries, begotten with the blood-shed of one's own relatives; and for that matter, what is the point of living such a life? (32)

These very close relatives and kinsmen for whose sake, and with whom we want to enjoy the pleasures and glory of this kingdom, they themselves are standing here in this battle, ready to die and give-up their earthly possessions. (33)

These close kith and kin are my grandfathers, uncles, fathers-in-law, grandsons, brothers-in-law, teachers and other beloved people. (34)

O Madhusudana! O Sri Krishna! They can kill me, but I do not want to kill my own near and dear relatives, even if I am offered the dominion and empire of the three worlds and heavens, then what to talk the kingship of this earth. (35)

O Janardana! O Sri Krishna! What pleasure can we derive by killing the entire family clan of Dhritarashtra? Only sin can accrue from killing them, even though they are aggressors and are responsible for serious transgressions. (36)

O Madhusudana! O Sri Krishna! Therefore, it does not seem appropriate for us to kill our own relatives and the sons of Dhritarashtra. How can we live happily after killing our own people? (37)

The mind and understanding of our enemy is blinded and overcome with greed and enjoyment of kingly pleasures. They see no sin in extermination and killing of the entire family clan; and of hostility and treason with their own brethren. (38)

O Janardana! Sri Krishna! But why should we not turn away from committing such a heinous sin; when we clearly see evil in the destruction and killing of an entire family clan? (39)

With the destruction of the family, its time honoured family traditions and customs disappear and perish. This results in the destruction of the family virtues, leading to impiety and degradation of the future generations. (40)

O Varshneya! O Sri Krishna! With the growth of lawlessness and rise of sinful-vices; the family women become unchaste and corrupt. With degradation and adultery of women, class and race admixture takes place, thus giving rise to unworthy and foolish progeny. (41)

"***Adharma abhi bhavat***:—from the prevalence of lawlessness and sinful vices:—O ***Krishna***:—O Krishna:—***pradushyanti***:—becoming unchaste and corrupt:—***kula- striyah***:—family woman:—***strishu***:—woman:—***dushtasu***:—becoming evil and corrupt:—***Varshneya***:—O Varshneya:—***jayate***:—leads to or arises:—***varna...samkarah***:—class and race admixture."

Here Arjuna voices his concern, that in a war scenario when the men warriors are killed, it renders their wives as widows. This becomes the cause for the inter-mingling of the classes, when the young war widows either re-marry into lower classes, or have illicit relationships. This gives rise to adultery and caste-admixture.

Adultery or extra-marital relationships, has serious consequences on religious, social, moral, inheritance, and lineage of the race. Strict prohibition of adultery exists in all religions of the world, whether it is Hindu, Sikh, Muslim, Christianity, Buddhism or Judaism. One of the commandments of Christian religion is that 'Thou shall not commit adultery.'

Hell and further downfall is verily the lot of such an adulterated family race, as well as of those who cause such a family destruction. Due to this, the lineage of their ancestors is deprived of their traditional reverence and ritual offerings. (42)

The misdeeds and wrongful doings of those who kill an entire family clan become the cause of inter-mingling of classes and confusion in the family race. This destroys the time-honoured family religious rites, and customs. (43)

O Janardana Sri Krishna! We have often heard that those, whose family traditions and religious-rituals are broken; they dwell in the lower regions of hell for an indefinite period of time. (44)

Alas! What a sin and error we are going to commit, by killing our own relatives and kinsmen, for the sake of greed and pleasures of the kingdom. (45)

Verily, it will be better if the sons of Dhritarashtra, with weapons in hand kill me in this battle, while I am unarmed and offer no resistance. (46)

Sanjaya said to King Dhritarashtra:

Arjuna having thus spoken in the midst of the battlefield; and overwhelmed with sorrow and grief, cast aside his bow and arrows, and sat down on the seat of the chariot. (47)

CHAPTER 2

THE YOGA OF KNOWLEDGE AND WISDOM
SAMKHYA YOGA

Sanjaya said to King Dhritarashtra:

Madhusudana Sri Krishna spoke these words to Arjuna who was thus overwhelmed with sorrow, and whose eyes were drenched with tears of despondency and distress. (1)

Sri Krishna said:

O Arjuna! At this critical juncture (when the war is about to begin), from where has such an unworthy, heaven-barring and disgraceful dejection come upon you? (2)

O Partha Arjuna! It is not worthy of you to yield to this petty weakness. It does not befit you. Cast off this emotional weakness of heart. Stand up and arise, determined to fight this war (O vanquisher of enemies). (3)

Arjuna said:

O Madhusudana Sri Krishna! How shall I fight Bhishma and Drona with arrows on this battlefield? They are worthy of deepest reverence. Is it not better to live in this world as beggars rather than kill our own esteemed and great-souled teachers? Of what use are the enjoyments of wealth and worldly pleasures, tainted with the blood of our respected teachers? (4–5)

I do not know which is better for us: —whether we should conquer them, or they conquer us. But we will not even

want to live this life, after killing the sons of Dhritarashtra, who stand before us in the enemy lines. (6)

My natural mental disposition is overpowered with emotions and compassion for my kith and kin; and I seek Your advice. My mind is confused, and I do not know what my rightful duty is? Tell me for certain as to what is righteous for me, at this critical juncture of war. Kindly instruct me, as I am your disciple and have taken refuge in You. (7)

Even if I were to rule unrivalled the entire kingdom on this earth with all its prosperity or even the sovereignty of all the heavens; even then it does not remove my grief and confusion that is parching my senses. (8)

Sanjaya then spoke to King Dhritarashtra:

After speaking thus, Arjuna then said to Govinda Sri Krishna, "I will not fight this war," and became silent. (9)

O King Dhritarashtra! Then as if smiling Hrishikesha Sri Krishna spoke these words to despondent Arjuna, while positioned in the middle of the two armies. (10)

Sri Krishna said:

You are grieving for a cause which is not truly justified; yet at the same time you are speaking words of wisdom. The wise grieve neither for the dead nor for the living. (11)

There never was a time when either I, or you, or any of these princes here did not exist earlier (as embodied souls on earth); nor it is that we all shall cease to exist in the future. (12)

As the embodied soul in a body experiences childhood, youth and old age; so also the soul passes on to a new body upon death. A wise person has no doubts on this fact. (13)

The body keeps on changing continuously. The newborn is once an embryo in the womb, then a child, a young man or woman, old age and finally death. The cycle keeps on repeating and there are no exceptions, whether one is a king or a poor man. The mind also goes on changing continuously from time to time.

You were happy in the morning, angry with your co-workers in the afternoon, and sad in the evening. The mind goes through different moods, happiness and sorrow, elation and dejection. The clock keeps on ticking and the wheel moves up and down on the periphery. But what is the reference point for measuring all these changes?

There is something which ever remains the same, and which is the reference point to measure all these changes. That which always remains the same and unchanging is the Self-soul in all living beings, as the reference point, and as an Absolute entity.

Everything in the world is constantly changing but the Self-soul is a witness to childhood, youth and old age. The Atman or the Self-soul does not change with time and it is a measuring yard stick to observe the changing world. When the body gets worn out and one has lived the allotted span of life, the soul passes on to another womb to start a new journey once again.

O Kaunteya Arjuna! The contact of the body senses with their respective sense objects; give the sensations of cold and heat, and of pleasure and pain. These sensations come and go, and are of temporary nature. Bear these sensations patiently! O Bharata Arjuna. (14)

That noble person among mankind is fit to attain immortality of Nirvana (liberation), who can maintain his equanimity of mind amidst changing body sensations

and situations; and remains balanced and steady in both pleasure and pain. (15)

That which changes with time is of temporary existence, while the ultimate Reality (Spirit of God) never ceases to be, and does not change with time. The truth of both Real (Sat) and the Unreal (Asat) has been realized by the wise seers. (16)

Know that the all pervading Spirit of God, by which this entire Universe is pervaded, is indestructible. None can cause the destruction of the imperishable Spirit. (17)

The physical bodies of all living beings have an end; while the indweller soul is eternal and indestructible. Therefore O Bharata Arjuna! Fight the war with determination. (18)

One who considers Atman (soul) as killer, and one who considers soul as killed, both of them are ignorant. The soul neither kills nor is killed. (19)

Bible (Matthew) says, "And fear not which kills the body, but are not able to kill the soul: but rather fear him which is able to destroy both soul and body to hell."

The soul has neither birth nor death. Coming into existence at birth and ceasing to exist at death, both do not take place for the soul. The soul is unborn, deathless, eternal, changeless, and ancient from the beginning. The soul is not destroyed when the body dies. (20)

O Partha Arjuna! Having realized that the soul is unborn, deathless, eternal and imperishable, and then who kills whom? (21)

Just as human beings discard worn-out clothes and wear new ones; similarly the embodied soul upon leaving the physical body, enters into others that are new. (22)

Weapons cannot cut the soul, fire cannot burn it, water cannot wet the soul, nor can wind dry the soul. (23)

The soul therefore, is eternal, everlasting, all-pervading, unchanging and immovable and ever remains the same. The soul cannot be cut, burnt, wetted or dried. (24)

It is said that the soul is unthinkable, invisible and does not undergo any modifications and changes. Therefore, realizing that the soul is indestructible, you should not grieve for the perishable body. (25)

O mighty-armed Arjuna! Even if you take the supposition that the soul takes birth and is subject to death, even then you should not grieve. (26)

One who is born is sure to die one day, and all those who die are certain to be born again. One should not therefore, grieve over this inevitable and ultimate truth of life. (27)

Sri Krishna says in Sanskrit, "***Jatasya***:—of the born:—***hi***:—for:—***dhruvah***:—certain:—***mrityuh***:—death:—***dhruvam***:—certain:—***janma***:—birth:—***mritasya***:—of the dead:—***cha***:—and:—***tasmat***:—therefore:—***apariharye arthe***:—over this inevitable fact:—***na...tvam...shochitum***:—you should not grieve."

This story explains the above verse. Veena was the wife of a wealthy man in north India. She had one small son whom she loved immensely and spent all her time playing and looking after her growing child. When her son was old enough to start running around, he fell ill and died. Veena was mad with grief and sorrow. She was unable to accept the fact that her son was dead, and could not be revived and brought back to life.

She became insane and lost her normal composure. She took her dead son in her arms and went all around, asking for some medicine and a miraculous cure to revive her dead son. Everyone whom she met said that she had lost her balance of mind, and has gone mad. Finally, an old man told her that if there was anyone who could help her, it will be the enlightened saint who was sitting under a banyan tree.

In her misery Veena, put the body of her dead son at the feet of the enlightened saint and asked him for the miraculous medicine that would bring her son back to life. The enlightened saint answered, "The child can be brought back to life if she can bring some mustard seeds from a family where no member of their family had ever died."

Carrying her dead son, she went from door to door, to every house asking for a handful of mustard seeds to revive her dead son. At each and every house the reply was the same that in their family; their great grandfather, grandmother or someone else had died in the past.

At last the truth dawned on her that all those who are born, are sure to die one day and that no one can predict death, and she came to the conclusion that, "No household is free from death."—She cremated the body of her son and returned to the enlightened Master who comforted her and taught to her, the tenets of Bhagavad Gita. —She became a disciple of the enlightened Master, and spent the rest of her life in devotion to God and in service of humanity.

You never for a moment think that the incoming breath and the outgoing breath are opposite to each other. The incoming breath is life and the outgoing breath is death. But since it is a continuous process and automatic, we never think about it and take the breathing process for granted. The moving picture on the television is built frame by frame, but the frequency of speed is so high, that it looks like a continuous picture.

Although the mind takes rest during the sleep, but the heart keeps on working without any rest throughout the life cycle of a living being, and keeps on giving the pulses to pump blood and circulate throughout the body. At birth the first breath is life, and at death it is the last breath. The last breath along with the soul goes back to the Cosmic whole. The English phrase says that a person breathed his or her last breath.

O Bharata Arjuna! All beings are unmanifest without a form before birth; and are visibly manifest in the form of a body between birth and death; and are again unmanifest

(without a body) after death. Therefore, what is the point for anguish? (28)

Life is manifest in between the first breath at birth, and the last breath at death. Once a living being is born and manifests in physical form, the final destination is death. The embodied soul is unmanifest again and merges back into cosmic breath. This is an inevitable fact and the ultimate truth of life, then why the anguish and grief?

Where was the baby child before the couple got married? The baby child was unmanifest before the couple got married and was manifest in the form of a body thereafter.

We are born alone and we die alone. Our fortune, wealth, houses, wife and children, will not accompany us after death. At birth we came empty handed with no possessions, and at death one goes back empty handed into dust.

The entire glitter and turmoil of worldly existence is visible between these two points of birth and death. The earth has been in existence for millions of years, and countless have been the births and deaths of the beings, as an evolutionary process.

Bible says, "Then the dust will return to the earth as it was, and the Spirit will return to God who gave it. —All go to the same place. All came from the dust and all return to the dust."

Just a few people ponder over the existence of soul; some describe it as a wondrous puzzle; some others even after hearing about it are ignorant of its existence, but no one can fathom the mystery of the soul. (29)

The meaning of above verse is hidden in the form of a Bija mantra. The verse says that no one can fathom the mystery of the soul. There is no possibility of any scientific discovery on the invisible aspect of the soul as the substratum of all life. The soul is not a matter, and cannot be seen.

The nearest one can explain the soul is in comparison with 'Akasha' or space, which is the fifth element of nature with no physical attributes, and is present both within and without; and hence there can be no scientific instruments to measure space, as it is empty.

God or the Supreme Spirit is both near and far; and this metaphor is used to explain the mystery of God. Space or 'Akasha' can exist both within and outside. No one can fathom the mystery of the soul, and it is so subtle that it cannot be known or seen directly. It can best be explained by means of a story or a parable.

A disciple asked an enlightened master, "How does one seek union with God?"

The master replied, "The harder you seek, the more distance you create between the Spirit of God, and you."

The disciple asked, "So what does one do about the distance? Is the union with God far or near?"

The master said, "Understand that it is not there."

The disciple says, "Does that mean that God and I are one?"

The master replied, "Not one. Not two."

The disciple says, "How is that possible?"

The master said, "The sun and its light; the ocean and its waves; the singer and his song. Not one.... Not two."

Think and meditate over it.

O Bharata Arjuna! The embodied soul in all living beings is eternal, and cannot be killed. Therefore there is no cause for grief. (30)

Even considering your own rightful duty as a warrior-class man, you should not hesitate to engage in this battle; for there is nothing more befitting for a warrior, than to fight a war for a just cause; and uphold justice and righteousness. (31)

O Partha Arjuna! Fortunate are the warriors who get this opportunity to fight a righteous war, which has come of its own accord as an open gateway to heaven. (32)

But if you refuse to fight this righteous war, then abandoning your own duty and honour, you will incur sin. (33)

Besides, people will ever recount your infamy and cowardice; and to one who is highly esteemed and respected, ill-fame is worse than death. (34)

They will think that the great chariot-warrior has fled from the battlefield out of fear, and those who hold you in high esteem will look down upon you. (35)

Your enemies will speak many insulting and unseemly words, and will discredit your powers and capabilities. What could be more painful and insulting than that? (36)

If killed in the battle, you will attain the auspicious regions of the heavens, and if victorious you will enjoy the kingdom of this earth. Therefore O Kaunteya Arjuna! Stand up, and fight vigorously with determination. (37)

Treating with equipoise and equanimity both happiness and sorrow, gain and loss, victory and defeat, you engage in this war. Thus fighting, you will not incur any sin. (38)

O Partha Arjuna! I have declared to you the wisdom of the intellect (Samkhya yoga). Now act endowed with this knowledge. Thus, you will break the bondage of actions. (39)

While practising the teachings of this scripture, no effort is ever wasted and there is never any adverse effect either. Even a little practice and following the tenets of this Scripture in real life, protects one from great fear. (40)

"***na***:—not:—***iha***:—in this:—***abhikramanashah***:—any loss of effort:—***asti***:—is:—***pratyavayah***:—no adverse effect:—***na-vidyate***:—not there:—***svalpam-api-asya***:—even a little practice:—***dharmasya***:—tenets of this scripture:—***trayate***:—protects a person:—***mahatah***:—great:—***bhayat***:—fear."

Swami Paramahansa Yogananda Ji stated in the autobiography of a yogi, "The great Mahavatar Babaji said that mankind should follow Sri Krishna's teachings, and that just a little practice of this Dharma protects a person from great fear; and this practice is always rewarded, and there is never any loss of effort in this."

O Kurunandana Arjuna! To the firm in mind and intellect, there is in this, just one decision. But to an infirm and wavering mind, there are many-branching and endless decisions. (41)

This verse with translation says:—"***vyavasaya atmika***:—firm decision:—***buddhir***:—mind and intellect:—***eke***:—one:—***eha***:—in this here:—***Kuru nandana***:—O Kurunandana Arjuna:—***bahushakkah***:—many-branching:—***hy***:—indeed:—***anantah***:—endless:—***cha***:—and:—***buddhayah***:—of the mind:—***vyavasayinam***:—to the infirm and wavering mind."

A story explains this verse. Suppose a man has been wounded by an arrow smeared with poison, when he went on a hunting trip with his friends. And if he says to his friends, "Look, I will not have this arrow pulled out, nor I will take any medical aid, until and unless I know who is my enemy and who shot this arrow to wound me. Was the man who shot this arrow, a Brahmin, Kshatriya, Vaishya or a Sudra? Was the enemy who shot the arrow tall...short...or of medium height?"

All these arguments are unnecessary at that point of time, since the first priority at that moment is to save the life of the wounded man and rush him for medical help. All other aspects of who shot the arrow, and how the incident happened, can be taken care of, later? To the firm in mind, in these circumstances, there is only one decision as to what is the first priority.

Similarly there are many branching and endless questions on the spiritual path by the spiritual aspirants: whether Sri Krishna, enlightened Buddha or Jesus Christ exist after death. Why do they not come face to face to answer my questions? Where does the soul go after death? What does a soul look like? Is it better to have a body of a handsome male or a beautiful female? Is it better to be rich or poor or just be in the middle class? Which god is more powerful and what if a goddess has more powers? Is there rebirth after death? How to attain Nirvana and so on and so forth?

There are endless questions and the human life will be finished in questions only. To the wavering mind, there are endless questions and decisions. Answers to these endless questions, do not really add to one's spiritual progress. Unnecessary arguments and discussions, on these topics will divert him or her, from the main 'spiritual path' of Self-realization.

The relevant questions on the spiritual path are if human life is a suffering, then what is the cause of suffering? How to destroy this suffering and attain bliss? —How to engage in meditation practice, rather than waste one's precious time in useless discussions and endless questions? The answers to these questions will come on their own in due course of time, with maturity and Self-realization.

We are all moving somewhere, in some direction in our life. The question is whether we are moving in the right direction and on the right path; or away from the desired path? That means one literally creates one's own destiny.

This holy book teaches the 'Art of living' to the mankind. For this reason 'Gita' is called the 'Divine Song of the Lord'; as these teachings are given directly by the God Himself, for the benefit of the humanity.

The foolish and worldly people of little understanding merely indulge in flowery words of the lofty Scriptures. They take delight in unnecessary discussions, arguments and interpretations of the Scriptures, thinking that this is the ultimate in spirituality. (42)

Bhagavad Gita has stated the truth to the humanity in very simple and compact Sanskrit verses. Different writers and commentators have translated these verses according to their mind and intellectual understanding. There are hundreds of interpretations and commentaries on Bhagavad Gita. The Bible in comparison has been translated by the church into more or less the same pattern with little variations.

It has also to be kept in mind that Bhagavad Gita was given by the God incarnate Sri Krishna, more than five thousand years ago. The same truth is as relevant in today's world, as it was in the hoary past. There was a perfect harmony between the teacher and the disciple at that time, and there was no communication gap.

The lofty Scripture of Bhagavad Gita is so sublime, that its teaching has been acknowledged all over the world as a lofty Scripture. It has been translated into all the major languages of the world and it is revered as a Book of Wisdom.

The Scripture contains knowledge and wisdom to enable the mankind to live a purposeful life, and gives solutions to the complex problems of life. It enables human beings to perform their work efficiently and skillfully with awareness and consequences of actions; and thus get liberated from the bondage of actions. A story below explains the wisdom of life.

A philosophy professor stood before his class with some items on the table in front of him. When the class began, he quietly picked up a large empty glass jar, and proceeded to fill it with rocks, about 2 inches in diameter. He then asked the students if the jar was full. They agreed that it was full. The professor then picked up a box of small pebbles and poured them into the jar. He shook the jar lightly. The pebbles, of course, rolled into the open areas between the rocks.

He then asked the students again if the jar was full. They all said that it was now full up to the brim. The professor then picked up a box of sand and poured it into the jar. The sand filled up the remaining open spaces in the jar. He then again asked the students if the jar was full. All students responded with a unanimous "Yes."

The professor then carefully poured water on the sand and the water simmered into the sand; and he asked the students again, if the jar was full now. The students were hesitant and quiet now, as their previous answers were all wrong. Seeing the silence, the professor put some salt over the water, and the salt dissolved into the water and disappeared. The professor once again asked the students, "Is the glass jar full now." There was a hushed silence, and the students looked at the professor in suspense.

"Now" said the professor, "I want you to recognize that this jar represents your life. Each one of you will have different interpretations of the above experiment according to your own understanding and mind." Some students said that the rocks represent the important things in one's life like one's religious faith and belief in God, spiritual practices, education and knowledge, health, job and family, etc.

The pebbles are the other things—like your material possessions, your friends circle, your car, your mobile phone, etc.

The professor continued, "If you put the sand into the jar first, then there is no space for the pebbles or the rocks. The same goes for your life. If you spend all your time and energy on small and trivial issues of life, then you will not have time for the bigger things in your life. Pay attention to the things that are most important to you. Take care of the rocks first—things that really matter in your life. Set your priorities. The rest is just sand."

Bible (John) says, "In the beginning was the Word, and Word was with God, and Word was God. —And the Word was made flesh, and dwelled among us."

Words are important as they convey the quality of the intellect of the writer or the person who is talking. When you read a book, you get in touch with the mind of the writer, and you come to know if it contains any useful and knowledgeable contents for assimilation or not.

Science and Engineering has both theory and practical classes in the laboratory. One needs practical experience in addition to the theoretical knowledge. A menu will not satisfy your hunger. A formula of Hydrogen and Oxygen for water will not quench your thirst. And yet words form the basis of theoretical knowledge; but the void has to be filled with practically following the teaching of the Scriptures.

Scholars and pundits engage in lengthy discussions and arguments on lofty Scriptures to show their knowledge and mastery on the subject. Empty vessels make a lot of noise. Whereas an enlightened or a real saint, will go into silence and meditation; as he has no necessity for arguments on the words of Holy Scriptures to prove that he knows. The enlightened saint has nothing to gain by arguments with ignorant people, as this will waste his time and energy.

They perform many rituals of different kinds to enjoy worldly pleasures, and to attain heavenly regions, hereafter. But as a result of their deeds (karmas), they merely take rebirth back on earth. (43)

People, who lack discrimination, get carried away by the sensual enjoyments and the glitter of the worldly prosperity. They lose fixity of mind, and are unable to practice deep meditation, for union with the Supreme Spirit of God (Samadhi). (44)

The Vedas describe the three Gunas of Prakriti, O Arjuna! You go beyond the influence of these three Gunas. Be free from the conflicts of the pairs of opposites, ever-balanced; remain ever established in the purity of Truth, free from materialistic acquisitions and preservation, and ever centred in the Self-soul. (45)

To an enlightened sage (Brahmana) who has become one with God-consciousness, and who sees the Spirit of God everywhere, all the Vedic scriptures are as useful as a little water in a small tank, at a time when there is a flood and abundance of water all around. (46)

This verse is in the form of a metaphor. First the distinction between these two Sanskrit words 'Brahmana' and 'Brahmins' must be known, to understand the text of Bhagavad Gita. In the olden days 'Brahmins' were priest class people, who performed their duties as temple priests or as wise men, and they were supposed to be well-versed in the Scriptures.

In the modern times, there is no strict separation of classes in the human society. In the new generation, money over-rides all classes. The world has now only two classes, the rich and the poor. Wealth is the hallmark to determine one's status in society these days. If a poor man becomes rich, then he rules over all other classes as he can now employ the educated and learned Brahmins to do service for him.

The word 'Brahmana' as used in Bhagavad Gita is for a person who is enlightened and has become one with God consciousness. The word 'Brahmana' in Sanskrit means one who has attained union with God Consciousness. An enlightened sage who has attained to 'Brahmana' means one who has arrived at the final goal of Self-realization or Nirvana liberation.

Once a person has reached the final goal of enlightenment, then he is not dependent on the knowledge of the Scriptures anymore, as these have become a part of his being and wisdom. His actions are then based on the intellectual illumination within his being.

It is like a person who is going from one city to another, and he needs a route map and the confirmatory signs on the way to reach his destination. Once he has reached his final place of destination, then he can discard the route map, as there is no further need for this. The above verse says that similarly for an enlightened and a wise sage, further knowledge of Vedic Scriptures is of no or little use, as he has reached his final destination.

Your right is to perform your work and duties only, and not for the results and fruits thereof. Let not getting the fruits of your actions be your motive to perform work; and yet you should not lean towards inactivity in life. (47)

This is a famous verse of Bhagavad Gita where Sri Krishna propounds to the world the secret of action. The verse says: — ***karmani***: —in work: —***eva***: —only: —***adhikarah...te***:—your right:—***ma***:—not:—***phaleshu***:—in the fruits and the results thereof:—***kadachana***:—never, at any time:—***ma***:—not:—***karma ...phala...hetuh...bhuh***:—let not the fruits of action be your motive:—***ma***:—not:—***te***:—your:—***sangah***:—attachment:—***astu***:—let:—***akarmani***:—inaction (no-action).

Not only in India but Bhagavad Gita is a universal Scripture for the world, and even other countries have adopted mottos from this lofty Scripture. The motto of Special Forces of the Indonesian Air Force is, "***adhikaraste...ma...phaleshu...kadachana***" which means, "You have no rights to the fruits of your actions."

It seems a little strange at first, that one has the right (***adhikarah***) to perform one's work only, but no rights on the results (***phaleshu***) thereof. The results will come as a Universal law of action and reaction, but you cannot demand results. The first part of the verse is: 'you have the right to perform your work and duty, but you have no claim to the results thereof.'

Demanding immediate results will not help, because there are many other things beyond our control. The results will come in due course of time, but the results may or may not be as we had expected.

One may sow the seed, but it is not in our hands whether the seed will sprout or not, as there are many factors involved. One has to choose the right soil, water the soil, the soil has to get adequate sunlight, and it has to be in the right season and timing for the plant to grow. And we need not dig the ground everyday to see what is happening to the seed; otherwise we will destroy the seed. One has to wait, and the results will automatically come, one need not demand.

The second part of the verse is: "Let not getting the rewards of your work be your motive in life; and neither you should become inactive." We may or may not see the rewards of our work. The trees we planted will mature in due course of time, but we cannot be sure that we will eat their fruits.

The fruits we are eating now are from the trees, which someone else had planted. And who knows who will eat the fruits of the tree which you have planted. If you started a business, it cannot be certain that you will reap the profit out of this venture. It may even happen that your children or relatives will later reap the fruits and profit of this business, when it grows and gives returns later.

One has every right to put in one's best efforts in all undertakings and work, and accept whatever results follow. One can do the necessary corrections wherever required. It implies that we should not give up our efforts, and neither should we lean towards inactivity (no-action), irrespective of whether the results are favourable or unfavourable.

Do whatever is needful, and do it wholeheartedly with awareness and alertness. If one dedicates all acts to God, then one need not worry about the results and rewards. Many a big business entrepreneurs were a failure in the beginning, but with persistent efforts, they ultimately succeeded. The initial failures were a stepping stone to success later on.

O Dhananjaya Arjuna! Perform all actions, ever remaining balanced, renouncing attachments; keeping evenness of mind in success and failure. This equipoise and equanimity is verily known as 'Yoga.' (48)

The word 'yoga' and 'yukta,' is used by Sri Krishna in Bhagavad Gita many times repeatedly. Sanskrit language was in usage in India, five thousand years ago and Arjuna as a disciple understood the meaning of the word 'Yoga' instantaneously, and no explanation was required.

With the passage of time, the real meaning of the word ***'yoga'*** was lost to the world. The world now has a shallow understanding of the word ***'yoga,'*** to imply bodily postures, and physical and mental fitness. The meaning of the word ***'yoga'*** is very complex, with a wide range of connotations.

With the benefits of ***'yoga'*** at the body and mental level, yoga has spread everywhere from Delhi, Mumbai, to America, to Europe and all over the world. But the word ***'yoga'*** as conveyed in Bhagavad Gita means 'union' of the individual soul with the Spirit of God. However in the modern world it is understood as mere physical postures (Asanas) and breathing exercises (Pranayama).

The modern world has immediate requirement of physical fitness, and undertaking further steps of higher spirituality by the majority of the population are rare. The definition of '***yoga***' is deeply spiritual, but the modern world has lost the true meaning of the word '***yoga***' to its fullest extent, which is to reach the state of '***Samadhi***' or '***Moksha***' or liberation. The full connotation of '***yoga***' has eight limbs or eight steps.

Bhagavad Gita is the most ancient text on 'Yoga.' The other texts of Yoga-sutras by Maharishi Patanjali were added later on. These are complementary texts to 'Bhagavad Gita.'

There is a complete harmony between the Gita verses, and the Patanjali's Yoga-sutras. Both Lord Sri Krishna, and sage Patanjali emphasize on the fact, that one must transcend all false conceptions and notions of 'I' and 'Mine' and develop true love for God; which Patanjali calls '***Ishvara-pranidhana***' or dedication of all acts to God. Patanjali wrote the text in third century CE, but little is known about his life.

The ashtanga yoga-path formulated by Maharishi Patanjali's Yoga-sutras, consists of eight 'limbs' or eight parts as follows:–1.–***Yama***; 2.–***Niyama***; 3.–***Asana***; 4.–***Pranayama***; 5.–***Pratyahara***; 6.–***Dharana***; 7.– ***Dhyana***; 8.–***Samadhi***. The first two limbs of Yama and Niyama are like the Ten Commandments of Bible.

Yama—as a discipline of the mind has five disciplines to be followed. These are (i) non-violence to others (physical, verbal or mental); (ii) truthfulness (both mental and verbal); (iii) non-stealing (non-possession of anything which does not belong to oneself); (iv) Brahmacharya or celibacy; (v) Non-greed.

Niyama—has five habits and observances to be followed (i) ***Austerity*** (***Tapa***)—(austerity here implies living a simple life with moderation in eating, sleeping, recreation and not indulging in luxuries); (ii) Study of Scriptures on a regular basis (***Svadhayaya***); (iii) Contentment—(***Santosha***) which implies not comparing yourself with others, and to be satisfied with what one has; (iv) Purity of body (both internal and external) ; (v) ***Ishvara-pranidhana***: devotion and surrender to the Lord (dedication of all actions to God).

Asana—is a proper and comfortable sitting posture, wherein the spine is kept straight to enable full circulation of energy. The seat has to be comfortable where a person can sit for a long time, without the necessity of any physical movements. This is described in Bhagavad Gita Chapter 6.

Pranayama—is basically control of breath and life-energy; which forms the basis of all existence in all living beings. Bhagavad Gita describes the basic techniques of ***Pranayama*** which are used in meditation, for realization of spiritual goal in chapter 4 and chapter 5. There are several other variations of Pranayamas.

Pratyahara consists in training the mind to detach itself at will from external worldly sense-objects. By means of pratyahara, a person can check the outward flow of the mind and free the senses from any distractions and attachments. This is an important and essential requirement for deep meditation and its spiritual benefits. Bhagavad Gita makes reference to this, in chapter 2 verse 58 by giving an analogy of a tortoise, who can withdraw its limbs within its shell at will.

The last three limbs of '***ashtanga yoga'*** are the higher steps of '***yoga practice,***' for advanced spiritual attainments. These last three steps are the final stages of yoga meditation.

Dharana (concentration) consists in keeping the mind focussed on a particular thought to the exclusion of all other thoughts. Sri Krishna explains this method to focus the entire attention on the tip of the nose, and not allow the mind to drift away on any other thoughts, but only upon the incoming and outgoing breaths as explained in Chapter 4 and Chapter 5.

Although it looks very simple prima facie, since it does not require any other external support or equipment, yet it is most difficult to keep the thoughts pivoted on a particular point. Arjuna says to his teacher Sri Krishna that mind is so powerful and restless, that it is like controlling the mighty wind. Sri Krishna replies that although it is very arduous and difficult, yet by constant practice or 'Abhyasa' and Dispassion, the mind can be controlled.

Meditation (dhyana) is the next step after concentration (dharana), and it implies a constant and uninterrupted flow of thoughts towards a chosen object or union with the energies of a chosen object, (in manifest or unmanifest aspects), without interference of any other thoughts.

Samadhi or ***Nirvana*** is the total absorption in the Spirit of God, in which a yogi rejects all other objects of name and form, and is so absorbed in meditation in a blissful manner that he and the object of his meditation become one and the same. This means there is no duality between the two. This is called the ultimate 'union of Spirit,' in which the subject and the object merge together and become one and the same.

In this state there is no desire for any worldly objects, or fleeting sensual delights, and there is no attachment with anyone. This is described as the biggest gain and after having achieved this, there is nothing higher than this.

It is like a person who is watching a very interesting and an absorbing movie on the cinema screen, and the man gets so engrossed in the movie, that he even forgets that he is sitting in the theatre, and only the movie remains. The absorption in this case also is total as in meditation, but in this case it is absorption on the external objects outside like the hero and the heroine, and the associated story projected in the movie.

On the other hand, in the process of meditation the object and the subject are both within, and all outside worldly thoughts and objects have to be totally rejected and kept away.

O Arjuna! Mere performance of actions is far inferior as compared to the performance of actions with knowledge and wisdom. Seek to attain wisdom of the intellect. Those who seek the results of their actions are miserable and unhappy in life. (49)

In this world we see that everyone is acting for some personal motive or some self-interest. Practically everyone is working with the idea of getting some personal benefit from his work and activities. Everyone is working to maintain and support his family, and he or she needs money for that, and no one is working without some self-interest and personal gain.

The world is moving with a clockwork precision because everybody has some selfish interest in whatever he or she is doing. Otherwise, it will not be possible to maintain orderliness in the world. But a yogi and a real saint is above all personal self-interest as his goal is to achieve union with God-consciousness.

On the spiritual path perfection in Krishna-consciousness means to act without any desire to enjoy the fruits of one's work, and without any personal benefit or for fame.

Endowed with this wisdom, one goes beyond the effects of both the good and bad 'karma' in this very life itself. Therefore strive on this 'yoga path' to achieve oneness with the Universal Spirit. Work performed skilfully to perfection is verily called 'yoga.' (50)

"***Buddhi yuktah***:—endowed with this wisdom:—***jahati***:—goes beyond:—***iha***:—in this very life:—***ubhe***:—both:—***sukrta dushkrte***:—good and bad:—***tasmat***:—therefore:—***yogaya***:—to yoga:—***yujyasva***:—strive and devote yourself:—***yoga- karmasu-kaushalam***:—work done skilfully to perfection is called yoga."

The motto of the Indian Naval establishment INS Shivaji; a training establishment for Naval engineers is, "***yoga...karmasu...kaushalam***"—meaning skill in action is verily called '***yoga.***' The word '***yoga'*** in Bhagavad Gita has different meanings in different contexts.

The wise perform actions with evenness of mind, giving up the fruits of their actions. They are thus freed from the bondage of birth and death, and attain merger with the Supreme Spirit. (51)

When your mind and intellect goes beyond all confusion and delusion, then you will not be influenced by the conflicting interpretations of the Scriptures that you heard in the past, and will again hear in future. (52)

A story best explains this verse. —Two monks came out of a hall after listening to a lecture on the Bhagavad Gita by their spiritual Master. Outside the hall, they had a heated argument on the interpretation of a Gita Verse given by the Master. To settle the dispute, they decided to go to the Master and ask him directly, as to who is right and who is wrong.

After hearing the arguments put forth by the first monk, the Master said, "You are correct!" The monk was overjoyed and casting a winner's glance at his fellow monk, he left the room. The second monk was very upset, and he put forth his own arguments on the subject to the Master. After he had finished, the Master looked at him and said, "You are also correct!" Upon hearing this, the second monk felt that he was the real winner and with a proud look, he left the room.

A third monk who was also in the room was greatly puzzled by what he saw. He said to the Master, "The positions of the two monks on the subject were totally opposite and conflicting. They both cannot be right! How could you say that both of them are correct?" The Master smiled and looked into the eyes of this third monk and said, "You are also correct."

Everyone has his own understanding and interpretation of Scriptures according to his mind and intellectual discrimination. Many of the Scriptural verses become clear later on, in due course of time with repeated readings and intellectual clarity. Mere arguments when the mind is not yet fully mature, is a waste of effort.

And when your intellect becomes steady and firm after reflection upon different Scriptural interpretations, and gets fully absorbed in meditation; then one attains union with this 'yoga path.' (53)

The spiritual path of 'yoga practice' does not encourage putting up a show of any supernatural and miraculous powers for public display or for personal gratification and recognition.

One day a Holy saint was waiting to go across the river bank by a ferry boat. An ascetic passed by, and proudly showed off his miraculous powers by crossing the river back and forth by walking on the water.

The Holy saint smiled, and asked him, "How long did it take you to attain such powers to walk on the water?"

"It took me thirty years!" said the ascetic proudly.

The Holy saint replied, "Oh! Thirty years of precious life wasted? Well, I can cross the river any time safely, by using the ferry boat. It just costs ten rupees!"

Arjuna said:

O Keshava Sri Krishna! How can one identify a man who is firmly established and absorbed in Divine Consciousness? In what manner does an illumined soul speak? How does he sit? How does he walk? (54)

Sri Krishna said:

O Arjuna! When one gives-up all desires of the heart, and is contented within his Self-soul by the self; then one is said to be firmly established in steady wisdom. (55)

One who is not hankering for happiness and is not shaken by heaviest of sorrows. Free from passion, fear and anger; such a person is then said to be a person of steadfast wisdom. (56)

One who is free from the desire to receive affection from others (bonds of flesh are broken), who neither rejoices at

receiving good fortune nor hates when getting misfortune, then one is said to be poised in steady wisdom. (57)

Just as a tortoise can completely withdraw its limbs from all sides (within its hard shell at will); similarly a person who can fully withdraw one's senses from their sense-objects at will, is a person of steady wisdom. (58)

The translation of this important verse is: " ***yada***:—just as:—***samharate***:—withdraws:—***cha***:—and:—***ayam***:—this:—***Kurma***:—tortoise:—***angani***:—its limbs:—***iva***:—like:—***sarvashah***:—from all sides:—***indriyani***:—the senses:—***indriyarthe...bhyah***:—from the sense-objects:—***tasya***:—of him (yogi):—***prajna***:—wisdom:—***pratishthita***:—of steady wisdom."

A tortoise can withdraw its limbs at any time within its outer hard shell for safety, whenever the tortoise perceives any danger from outside objects and other creatures. This is called ***'Pratyahara'*** or withdrawing from outer sense-objects.

Similarly human beings while moving in the outside world are subjected to the temptations and dangers of so many sense-objects in their day to day life. Beautiful sights, alluring smells of perfumes, relishing food, sound of lovely music, and the delights of a sensual touch with the opposite gender, are all different sense-objects for the human senses. There are also harmful objects in the outside world, such as bad odour, putrefied food, ugly sights of violence, toxic air and many other things, which one needs to avoid.

The mind is drawn to various sense-objects in the outside world, and the intellect as the decision maker has to decide what actions to perform and which actions to refrain from. As in the case of a tortoise, a man can also withdraw his or her senses within himself, as a safety shield from the outside world by ignoring unwanted things.

To succeed in life, a man has to overcome all temptations and dangers, or else he will be diverted from his path and he will not be able to achieve the purpose of his life. That person is successful who can withdraw his senses from the dangers of the outside sense-objects, similar to a tortoise, who can withdraw its sense organs within its outer hard shell at will.

In the spiritual practice similarly, during meditation, the senses of seeing, hearing, smell, taste and touch, are required to be withdrawn from the outside world and have to be directed inwards to one's own Self-soul. This will avoid all outside distractions and focus the entire energy to a single point of concentration.

As the desire to enjoy sense-objects, turns away from a starving person; but the taste and the longing to enjoy these sense objects later still remains. But the desire and the longing to enjoy worldly sense-objects also ceases and comes to an end, when one is bestowed with the grace of God and Oneness with the Spirit of God. (59)

This verse is pregnant with meaning to explain the deep truth of the spiritual path. Unless a striving person is following the eightfold path of '***Ashtanga yoga***'; it is difficult to restrain the sense enjoyments. There has to be a goal, otherwise it is difficult to keep away from the allurements of sensual enjoyments.

It is like a doctor restricting a sick patient from certain types of pungent and oily foods during sickness. The poor health of the patient temporarily takes away the desire for sensual enjoyments; but the taste for these enjoyments still remains to be enjoyed later on. When he or she regains health, the desire to enjoy exotic food, sex and material wealth will again catch up, as and when the opportunity arises.

To give up the lower sensual pleasures, one has to experience the higher taste of bliss through the yoga path of meditation. Otherwise, no matter how much austerity and body-senses denial one practices; the desire for sense gratifications will still remain in one's heart in a dormant form. When a suitable temptation arrives, one will again fall into the trap to satisfy the sensual urges. The desire to enjoy the company of this or that beautiful girl will still remain. One thus falls and deviates from the spiritual path, and again descends to the transient and temporary joys of the material world.

The above verse says that due to one's devotion and grace of God, the taste to enjoy lower sensual objects falls away and ceases on its own; because one has tasted the higher bliss. The lower sensual pleasures then hold no further attraction.

O Kaunteya Arjuna! The excited body senses forcibly carry away the mind of even a vigilant person, striving hard for spiritual perfection. (60)

Therefore, keeping body-senses under control, one should sit in meditation on My Supreme Spirit. One, whose senses are fully under control, is established in perfect wisdom. (61)

Constantly thinking on the objects of the senses, one develops attachment to them; and from attachment arise the desire to possess them; and desires give rise to anger (when desires are unfulfilled). (62)

From anger springs up delusion of mind; and the deluded mind gives rise to confused memory; and the confused memory leads to decay of intellectual reasoning; due to decay of reasoning, one is ruined. (63)

A thought has an existence of its own. A person is continuously dispersing his thoughts all around him into the environment. When you talk, you throw your thoughts into others. But while you are silent, then also you convey your subtle thoughts. Unnecessary thoughts are like a leakage in your being, as thoughts also consume energy. Useless thoughts are like a water pot with holes, resulting in wastage of energy.

When there are no thoughts, then the energy is contained within, and the level of energy starts to rise higher and higher. Then the words are not just empty words, but they have a soul to them. The above verse says that constantly thinking on a particular sense object, one develops attachment to it and the further sequence of events starts with that.

Take care of your thoughts because they become your words. Take care of your words because they become your actions. Take care of your actions because they become your habits. Take care of your habits because they form your character. Take care of your character because it forms your destiny. And your destiny is the sum total of your life on this earth.

But the disciplined yogi, moves among sense-objects with senses under control; free from attraction and aversion, and thus gains in tranquillity. (64)

With tranquillity and peace of mind, all sorrows come to an end. This leads to a joyous mind, and the intellect is thus firmly established in equilibrium. (65)

There is no wisdom for a person who is not in union with the Supreme Spirit. To the unmeditative mind, there is no peace. And then how can a restless mind enjoy bliss and happiness? (66)

Just as the force of the wind pushes a boat away from its path on the waters; similarly the discrimination of a person whose mind yields to the roving senses, is carried away from its path. (67)

Therefore, O mighty-armed Arjuna! That person's wisdom is firmly established whose body-senses are completely under control from their respective sense-objects. (68)

That which is like darkness to all human beings (awareness of God Consciousness), to that the disciplined sage is ever awake; and to that in which all human beings are ever awake (material wealth and sensual pleasures), is like darkness to the soul-cognizing saint. (69)

Transliterated from the Sanskrit to English, "***Ya***:—which:—***Nisha***:—darkness or night:—***sarva...bhutanam***:—to all beings:—***tasyam***:—to that:—***jagriti***:—is awake:—***samyami***:—self-controlled:—***yasyam***:—in which:—***jagriti***:—awake:—***Bhutani***:—all beings:—***sa***:—to that:—***Nisha***:—like darkness or night:—***pashyatah***:—is cognized:—***Muni***:—realized saint."

When literally translated from Sanskrit, the verse reads as, "That which is night to all beings, in that the disciplined man is awake; and that to which all beings are awake, is night to the Atman-cognizing Muni."

I once asked a lady who was reading Bhagavad Gita, as to what she understood from this verse. She said that it means that while all worldly human beings sleep at night; the yogi meditates at night and sleeps during the day time. She was far from the truth as the real meaning of such an intricate verse is discernible to only a few.

Sri Krishna is talking here in the form of a metaphor, which contains a deep truth in a veiled form. Such verses with hidden meanings are meant to be known to only those who have a quest for knowledge, and not for mere curiosity. Different commentators will impart different meanings to a metaphor, and will interpret according to their own intellect and understanding. This verse of just two lines contains great spiritual truth, and has to be pondered over again and again to decipher its real meaning.

The above verse does not imply that while the whole world sleeps at night; the yogi keeps awake at night and meditates. Everybody whether a realized saint or a worldly person gets tired, and needs sleep to rejuvenate the body and mind. The soul is a witness to all things from birth to death, and at all times during day and night. The soul is a hidden aspect and worldly people are asleep and unaware of this aspect.

A realized saint has awareness of this and is always awake to the Self-soul and consciousness of God. The worldly people are always awake to name, fame, power, prestige, wealth, houses, cars and bodily pleasures of sex. The realized saint is asleep to all these material objects and sensual pleasures.

The yogi has awareness and a witnessing soul even in sleep. Awareness and dreaming cannot be together and for the yogi there is no dream state. Dreams are unfulfilled desires and a yogi is beyond any desires. Just a few hours of dreamless sleep is enough for the yogi to get refreshed.

Bible says, "No one can serve two masters. Either you will hate the one and love the other; or you will be devoted to one and despise the other. You cannot serve both God and worldly wealth."

Spiritual texts in the form of sutras have been interpreted in hundreds of ways, because the sutra is so small, so condensed, and so full of meaning, that you can take any viewpoint. Its meaning opens in all the dimensions; and the real purport and meaning is hidden in the form of a seed. Sometimes it goes on until one Sutra has been interpreted into twelve or fifteen different ways, and no one can claim that only his interpretation is correct.

A lady asked an enlightened Master, "What is your daily activity in your spiritual path of Self-realization."—The Master replied, "When you are hungry, eat; when you are tired, sleep."—The lady said, "Is that not what everyone else is doing, by the way?"

The enlightened Master replied, "No! No! Most people entertain hundreds of thoughts when they eat, and scheme over many plans, when they sleep."

Just as the water of the rivers finally merge into the oceans, and the oceans ever remain full and undisturbed; similarly that person attains peace, whose desires merge into one's own Self-soul, and not the person who hankers and runs after desires. (70)

Therefore, only that person attains abiding peace who has given up all desires; and who is untouched by any kind of craving; and who is without egoism, and sense of ownership of worldly possessions. (71)

Sri Krishna gave the lofty Scripture of Bhagavad Gita to the humanity as an incarnation of the Spirit of God. What Sri Krishna teaches to Arjuna while clad in human form, is from an exalted state of mind, which is in union with God-consciousness. It may seem difficult for us human beings to grasp and understand the Truth in the beginning, as we are looking at it from our own egoistic mind with a limited vision.

We are on earth, and God is in heaven and how can the twain meet, and have the same thinking instantaneously. It will take time for the Truth to sink in slowly and gradually; as our intellect gets more and more refined, and becomes purer and purer.

The difficulty is that Sri Krishna has to use the same linguistic "I" as we all human beings do, but there is a tremendous difference of connotation between His "I" and ours. Arjuna as a human being, would have said, "What are you saying? Why on earth should I surrender to you?"

The ego of Arjuna would have been hurt. – When we say 'I' it means the deluded embodied soul in our physical body with all human impurities and ego. The embodied 'Jivatma' or the individual soul is a prisoner in the human body. When Krishna says 'I' or 'Me' it means the Consciousness which permeates the whole Cosmos. Therefore Sri Krishna says to Arjuna, "Give up all doctrines and dogmas, and take refuge in My Krishna-consciousness; and I will take away all your sins, do not grieve."

But Sri Krishna's "I" as incarnation of God is absolutely free from all traces of egoism, and for this reason he could tell Arjuna to surrender to Him. Here, 'Surrender to Me' in this linguistic form, really means surrender to the Whole; to the primordial and mysterious Spirit that permeates the whole cosmos.

Egolessness is inherent in Krishna-Consciousness; Buddha-consciousness; Christ-Consciousness, and Mahavira too. But it may not be achievable for most of their followers, as they may have to take many rebirths yet, to attain refinements and purity of their individual souls, and clear their karmic debts. So the followers may or may not achieve enlightenment in one life-time. Sri Krishna is talking of renunciation and Nirvana, from the beginning itself, for the seekers who are in the advanced stage of spirituality.

O Partha Arjuna! Upon attaining this divine state of Oneness with the Cosmic Spirit, a person is never deluded again. Being established in this state, even at the last hour and before final moments of death, a person attains union with the Spirit of God. (72)

CHAPTER 3

THE YOGA OF SELFLESS ACTION
KARMA YOGA

Arjuna Said :

O Keshava! O Sri Krishna! If you consider, that the path of knowledge and wisdom is superior to the path of action; then why do you urge me to engage in this terrible act of war? (1)

You are puzzling my mind by these seemingly conflicting statements. Tell me conclusively that path, by following which I can attain the highest good. (2)

Sri Krishna Said:

O Sinless Arjuna! The twofold path of yoga was declared by Me to the world in the ancient beginning. The path of knowledge (Jnana yoga) for those endowed with a contemplative and a meditative mind; and the path of selfless work (Karma yoga), for those who are active in the worldly work. (3)

One does not reach the state of mind beyond actions, by merely abstaining and giving-up work; nor can one rise to perfection in yoga path, by renunciation of prescribed duties. (4)

None can remain inactive (in thoughts, words and deeds) even for a moment; for everyone is helplessly driven to activity perforce, by the Gunas born of Prakriti. (5)

A deluded person of foolish intellect outwardly controls his 'body organs of action'; but inwardly in his mind, he or she dwells and relishes the enjoyments of sensual-

objects. Such a person is called a pretending 'hypocrite' (mithyacharah). (6)

The above verse with transliteration from Sanskrit says, ":— ***Karmendriyani...samyama***: —controlling the organs of action: —***yah...aste...manasa...smaran***: —who inwardly dwells in his mind: —***Indriyarthan...vimudhatma***: —the deluded person enjoys the sense objects: —***mithyacharah...sa...uchyate***: —he or she is called a pretending hypocrite."

'Mithyacharah' in Sanskrit means a person who is a hypocrite, one who deceives, and pretends to have virtues, moral or religious beliefs that he or she, actually does not possess. It is just an outward show to fool others.

Bible (Job 8:3–8:8–8:9) says, "God never twists justice; he never fails to do what is right.—Look for a moment at the ancient wisdom; consider the truths our fathers learnt—Our life is short, we know nothing at all; we pass like shadows across the earth."

Bhaja Govindam text says, "One ascetic has matted locks of hair, other has shaven head, one has all hair pulled out one by one, yet another is parading in the guise of ochre robes; all these deluded fools do not see the truth, although they have eyes. Different disguises of these hypocrites are only for the sake of their belly....One may go on a pilgrimage to Ganga Sagar, where the Ganga water finally discharges into the sea, or observe vows, or do charity but if he is devoid of the experience of Self-realization, then one will not get liberation even after hundreds of lives."

A group of novice teenage monks were visiting Varanasi, with their respected Guru for the first time. There were many young girls living in that area, who used to come to the bathing Ghat for a dip in the cool water and wash their clothes. Their Guru told them, "If you are disturbed by the sight of beautiful young girls and you cannot control your mind, then you just chant the mantra with closed eyes, Govinda! Govinda! Govinda!–Meditating in this way, your mind will be controlled."

The Guru then left, to attend to some other important work. After some time, one among the young monks yelled, Govinda! Govinda! Govinda!–The rest of the monks asked in chorus! Where? Where? Where?

A '***Mithyacharah'*** or hypocrite is a person, who forcibly controls his organs of action like for example sex organs; but inwardly in his or her mind, relishes the enjoyment with the opposite sex. This is suppressed sexuality and not celibacy. In life, many things and events happen to all of us, but the only thing that truly matters is how we choose to react to it.

Even an unpleasant happening can be a stepping stone to success, when we learn lessons from such mistakes. Life is all about learning, adapting and converting all struggles that we experience into something positive.

O Arjuna! But that person excels who controls his body senses by the mind; and remaining unattached with the worldly objects, engages his organs of action to the path of work. (7)

Engage yourself in your allotted and obligatory work; for action (work) is superior to inaction (no-action). If one remains totally inactive, then even the mere maintenance of the body will not be possible. (8)

Actions are a cause of bondage in this world except for those actions which are performed as dedication to God in a spirit of Yajna sacrifice. Therefore O Kaunteya Arjuna! You earnestly perform actions without any attachment, dedicating as a Yajna sacrifice to the Supreme Spirit. (9)

Having created mankind in the beginning along with the spirit of Yajna sacrifice, the Lord blessed mankind and said, "You shall propagate by this; and may this Yajna (sacrifice) yield prosperity and the enjoyments you seek like a milch-cow (Kamadhenu)." (10)

Kamadhenu is understood as a mythical cow residing in heaven that fulfils all desires. ***Yajna*** is an offering to ***Kamadhenu***. When you work in a spirit of service and sacrifice towards a higher goal, then all your desires get fulfilled. Rise above personal desires and the object of your desire will come to you. Chase after desires and your cherished objects will go far away.

Perform the Yajna-sacrifice to the Devas and may those divine spirits be gracious unto you. Thus mutually cherishing one another, you shall reap the supreme good. (11)

Fostered by the Yajna spirit, gods will fulfil your desires. One who enjoys the worldly prosperity without offering gratitude to the gods in return, is verily a thief. (12)

The virtuous first offer their food to the Lord, and then eat only what is remnant, they are thus said to perform Yajna-sacrifice even for eating, and are freed from all impurities. But the person, who partakes of food without first offering to the Omnipresent Lord, eats only sin. (13)

All living beings are sustained by food, and rains cause the production of food crops and plants; rains are caused by the bounty of Yajna spirit; and Yajna is born of karma. (14)

Know that karma has its origin in the Vedas, and the Vedas proceed from the imperishable Word of God. Therefore all-pervading infinite spirit of God is always present in the acts of Yajna sacrifice. (15)

O Arjuna! One who does not become aware of the ever changing 'Wheel of life' thus rotating in the world, leads a useless life of no consequence whatsoever. A person who perpetually remains addicted to the lower realms of sins and sensual enjoyments of senses, wastes one's precious life." (16)

Translated from Sanskrit to English the verse reads as: —"***Evam... pravartitam...chakram...na...anuvartayati...iha***:—One who does not follow the wheel of life thus changing and rotating in the world here:—***aghayuh...indriyarama...mogham... Partha...sah...jivati***:—O Partha Arjuna! Sinful of life rejoicing and addicted to the pleasures of senses only; he or she waste's one's precious life."

The verse says that the wheel of life keeps on moving continuously and it is never stagnant in one place. Everything in life is constantly changing. Nothing is permanent. When life energy builds up then the reference point is at the top of the wheel, and with depletion of energy the wheel moves down again to the bottom of the circumference point.

The centre of the wheel axle remains unaffected and unmoved. Similarly the ups and downs of life are at the outer circumference of life, while the Self-soul atman remains the same from childhood to youth and to old age.

The focal point of the body is the embodied soul, which is the substratum of all living beings, and it always remains the same and unmoving. The more one remains centred in one's Self-soul, and not in the outer physical body, to that extent one is not affected by the joys and sorrows of the world.

A story explains the above phenomenon. A villager came to a big city for the first time in his life. He was amazed by the glitter of the Shopping Malls and the display of modern household items, electronic shops, restaurants, and beauty parlours all under one roof. He wanted to buy something from the city, to take back to his village.

Most of the items needed electricity supply and his village had no electric supply, and these items were of no use to him. He was delighted when he found a battery operated flashlight, which did not require any external power supply. He bought the flash light, and it fascinated him a lot that every time he pushed the switch, the bright light came on.

As he went around the shopping Mall, he noticed a crowd of people waiting in line at a multiplex Movie theatre. Upon enquiry he was told that they were purchasing tickets for the movie being screened in the theatre. He had no idea what it was like to see movie in a theatre. He also purchased a ticket and was ushered into the dark Movie hall.

After a while the movie started, and he was fascinated to see beautiful scenery of the hills, and the hero and heroine singing around the trees and bushes. He was mesmerized by the dazzle of the alluring short skirt of the heroine who was holding hands with the movie hero and singing.

Suddenly he remembered his newly acquired possession of flash light. He thought, "The cinema hall is in darkness, and if he will point his flashlight on the screen then he will see the face and legs of the heroine with more clarity." He took out his flashlight and pointed the beam of light on the theatre screen, but to his amazement the picture on the screen faded away and lost the clarity.

People from all sides shouted at him to switch off the torch light! He hurriedly told the person sitting next to him, "But I only wanted to have a better view of the picture." His next seat neighbour replied, "Do not you know that in a theatre, we see more clearly in the dark."

The message of the story is that our life is like a movie in a theatre. We are all living in spiritual darkness. Our worldly pleasures and joys which we pursue and upon which we place such an exaggerated high value, is due to our spiritual darkness.

When we bring the light of God into our lives, all these false pleasures and inflated values fade away on their own. These sense pleasures and enjoyments are fleeting, and are of temporary nature and become a cause of suffering and turbulent ups and downs in life.

But a person who is joyous in one's Self-soul; satisfied in one's own self, and is centred in his own Self-soul, for such a person there is no obligatory duty to perform. (17)

Such an illumined person has nothing to gain or lose by either doing an action, or by not doing an action. Neither is he dependent on anybody for anything. (18)

The joy and bliss of a person who is in union with the Spirit of God comes from within one's own Self-soul, and not from the outside world or the people around him. Such a person is not a sad or a serious person, as he does not sink into the negative world of darkness. A saint has no obligation to please the world and the people around him by becoming sad and serious.

A real spiritual person has no lust, and he does not get ensnared into the temptations of the world. He is not dependent on the outer world for his happiness or else the people around him will exploit him. One has to be a master of oneself and not a slave of the world to cater to the whims and fancies of others. There is a saying that a saint who is sad is no saint at all. What is the point of following the spiritual path, if one is going to be sad and miserable? The world is contrary to the spiritual path, and will try to bring him down to their level of misery.

How can a person be happy when there is so much misery all around? A meditative person is at ease in all kinds of situations, and listens to his inner voice, on what actions to perform and what actions to refrain from.

Therefore always perform your obligatory duty without any attachment; for by performing work without attachment, one attains the highest good. (19)

King Janaka and others indeed attained perfection through selfless actions. You should also act similarly for the guidance and welfare of the humanity. Whatever a great man does is followed by the humanity; people go by the example he or she sets up. (20–21)

An old monk was sweeping the open yard in a monastery, in the scorching heat of the Sun. A young monk passed by and asked him, "How old are you?" The old monk replied, "I am ninety-five years old."—The young monk said, "And why are you still working so hard? Why?–Why?–tell me."

The old monk replied, "Well, because I am here." The young monk asked, "But even then, why do you work so hard in the scorching heat of the summer Sun?"

The old monk replied, "Because the Sun is there."

The moral of the story is to perform one's actions without looking for rewards, and to strive for excellence in whatever work you do. The old monk was setting an example for the others to perform selfless work, even if they are of a menial nature like sweeping the house or some other earthly work.

One may not get medals or monetary rewards for selfless service. But if you put your heart into doing even the simplest chores of daily life, then life becomes worth living, and the ego is dissolved. Selfless actions without expecting any rewards for work, is pleasing to the God as well.

O Partha Arjuna! There is nothing in the three worlds which has not been attained by Me; nor there is anything which is yet remaining to be attained; but I still engage in work. If I do not relentlessly engage in work, people will always follow My path in every respect. The worlds will perish if I did not do action, and I will become the cause of confusion and destruction of the living beings. (22-23-24)

O Bharata Arjuna! The ignorant engage in action due to attachment and for rewards of action. But the wise and the enlightened should act without any attachment and without seeking the fruit of actions for the guidance of the people. (25)

Even a European country like Germany follows Sanskrit as an optional subject with great interest. The great scientist Albert Einstein who made great scientific discoveries said, "When I read the Bhagavad Gita and reflect on how God created the Universe, everything else seems so superfluous. I have made Bhagavad Gita as the main source of my inspiration and guide for the purpose of scientific investigations and formation of my theories."

However, the wise should not unsettle and confuse the minds of the ignorant people attached to work; but instead inspire others by joyously performing selfless work themselves, while united with the spirit of God. (26)

All actions are induced by the Guna attributes of Primordial Prakriti Nature. But due to egoism and ignorance, a person thinks, "I am the doer." (27)

O mighty-armed Arjuna! One with intuitive insight of karma and Gunas (modes of Prakriti) knows that the Gunas as senses and mind, interact with Gunas as objects, and therefore one does not get entangled therein. (28)

Due to the delusion of the Gunas of Prakriti, one gets attached to the functions of the Gunas (which gives rise to false-identification with the body, thus creating bondage with the world). The wise man of perfect knowledge should not unsettle the minds of ignorant people attached to the material world for the fruits of their actions. (29)

A woman complained about her destiny to the Master. The Master said, "It is you who make your destiny."

The woman said, "But surely, I am not responsible for being born a woman?"

The Master said, "Being born a woman is not destiny. That is fate. Destiny is how you accept your womanhood, and how you shape your life for a useful purpose."

The moral of the story is: raise the quality of your actions and not your voice; it is rains which give the bounty of flowers, and not the thunder storms.

Surrendering all actions to My Spirit of God (Krishna-consciousness), with thoughts centred on Self-soul; free from all expectations and egoism of ownership of possessions, thus engage in the battle, without any fear and anxiety. (30)

Arjuna at the back of his mind had so many questions, "But to kill these people– just for the sake of kingdom;–to kill so many people, so much violence, so many murders on his head, so much bloodshed– how can that be right? Killing all his relatives and friends, just to enjoy the pleasures and glory of the kingdom, did not make any sense to him. He would rather prefer to renounce and retire to the serenity of the forests, and become a monk."

Once you have dedicated all your actions to God, never look back and have any fear or anxiety, whether you have done the right thing or not. If you do things out of fear you cannot do them wholeheartedly. The mind is very cunning, and it will find ways and means to escape from unpleasant situations.

Neither should you have any worry of tomorrow, as to from where I will get my food and clothing. Bible says in this context, "Therefore I tell you, do not worry about your life, what you will eat or drink; or about your body, what you will wear. Is not life more than food and the body more than clothes? Look at the birds of the air; they do not sow or reap or store away in barns, and yet your heavenly Father feeds them. Are you not much more valuable than they? Can any one of you by worrying add a single hour to your life?"

Those who always abide and follow this Scriptural teaching with full faith and without indulging in fault-finding; they too are released from the bondage of actions. (31)

But those who criticize and do not follow the tenets of this teaching, know them to lack discrimination, and deluded in all aspects of spiritual knowledge. (32)

The teaching of Bhagavad Gita should not be linked with the stories and incidents of Puranas, as it will divert the mind from the real path of Self-realization. This Scripture is just seven hundred verses out of a total of one lakh verses of Mahabharata. It is the essence of all the Vedas, and it is complete and whole on its own.

Even the wise act according to their own inherent nature; and all beings follow their own natural tendencies, and then what shall forcible restraint do? (33)

Attraction and repulsion of the body senses for their respective sense objects are natural in the world. Let none come under their influence and dominance, as they are verily one's enemies. (34)

One's own allotted duty (Dharma) even if tinged with faults, is better than the duty of another even if well performed. Better death in the performance of one's own duty, as the duty (Dharma) of another person is fraught with evil and danger. (35)

The motto of the Indian Navy is ***'Shano Varuna'***—a Sanskrit verse taken from 'Taittriya Upanishad,' which means 'May the god of the oceans be auspicious unto us.' Transliteration of the above verse from Sanskrit to English reads as, "***shreyaan***:—better:—***svadharmah***:—one's own allotted duty:—***vigunah***:—even if tinged with faults:—***para dharmat***:—than the duty of another:—***svanushthitat***:—well performed:—***svadharme***:—in one's own duty:—***Nidhanam***...***Shreyah***:—death is better:—***paradharmah***...***bhayavahah***:—the duty of another is fraught with evil and danger."

Madras Regiment of the Indian Army has adopted this motto, 'Svadharme Nidhanam Shreyah' (It is glory to die doing one's duty). It does not matter whether one dies at the war front or while carrying out one's duties in peacetime. All that matters is that the individual carried out the lawful and the allotted duty. If one dies during the performance of such a duty, then it is a meritorious death, as an open gateway to heaven.

The above verse has practical utility in day to day human endeavours. Everyone should perform one's respective duty even if it is accompanied with faults and demerits, as doing the duty of another in which one is not an expert, is fraught with dangers. Work done to perfection is verily yoga, and life itself is a battle and risks are part of life.

Arjuna said :

O Varshneya Krishna! Then impelled by what forces does a person commit sinful acts even against one's own will, as if driven by powerful external forces? (36)

Sri Krishna Said :

It is anger and insatiable lust, arising from the quality of Rajas Guna, which is all-sinful like a raging fire; understand these to be your greatest enemies, here on the earth. (37)

As fire is covered by smoke, as a mirror by dust, as an embryo by the womb; so is the knowledge of Self-soul covered by sinful lust and anger. (38)

O Kaunteya Arjuna! Lustful desires cover the knowledge and carry away the intellectual discrimination of even a wise man. It is a constant enemy of the wise. It is like a raging fire which can never be satisfied. (39)

The senses, the mind and the intellect are said to be the seat of these lustful desires, which delude the wisdom of human beings. (40)

O Bharata Arjuna! Therefore, first mastering your body-senses, destroy this sinful enemy in the form of lustful desires; which obstructs wisdom and Self-realization. (41)

The senses are said to be superior to the body; the mind is superior to the senses; the intellect is superior to the

mind; and understand that which is superior and above the intellect, is the Self-soul. (42)

O mighty-armed Arjuna! Thus knowing Self-soul as superior and above the intellect, restraining the self by the Self-soul, kill this enemy in the form of desire, which is very hard to overcome. (43)

The above verse says that desire for mere sensual gratifications is like an enemy for human beings, and extremely difficult to conquer. The world of human beings has pair of opposites such as man and woman, night and day, riches and poverty, happiness and sorrow, and so on.

The masculine and feminine energies can either uplift each other or can become hostile to each other on the downward path. The war is fought not only on the battlefront, but there is constant war by the human beings to conquer their senses and overcome the enemy in form of lustful desires.

The world is invaded with sex as the motive force which can be either good or bad. Sex as a bodily pleasure overrides all other pleasures and it becomes the centre around which life revolves. There is a deep natural instinctive urge for the seed within the man and woman to unite for propagation of the species. It is inbuilt in the biology of all living beings, in their hormones and genes. Nature wants to reproduce its own kind and propagate the species, and the pairs of opposites are attracted to each other like the opposite poles of a magnet.

The Bible (genesis) says, "God created male and female in His own image. God blessed them and said to them, be fruitful and multiply."

If sexual union is followed as per God's commandments to beget offspring, then there will be no perversions, no incest, no rapes and no sexual crimes. Sex has the possibility of becoming a sin, and also the potential to raise the consciousness to higher levels. But then how to keep sex as the 'good thing'?

One needs to keep a watchful awareness as to what happens during the sex act itself. These fleeting moments of orgasm also open a momentary glimpse into one's own soul which is a part of cosmic consciousness. In the final moments of sex; time disappears, identification with the body and mind vanishes and ego disappears.

It is a state of no-desires, no-thoughts for a few seconds. This momentary bliss gives a desire to repeat the experience. But this momentary bliss also results in a loss of vital energy. Can this state of bliss be prolonged at will, without any loss of vital energy?

The experience of deep meditation or 'Samadhi' where one's Self-soul is united with cosmic consciousness is similar to the state of no-thoughts, no-mind and is beyond the realm of the body. It is the same experience which is glimpsed during sex. But in deep meditation there is no limitation of time and it is invigorating for the body, and it is bliss from the beginning to the end and the other person is not involved in this.

In the present day society, one cannot escape from the invasion of sexual stimulus in subtle forms on the television, media and advertisements. Sex is exploited and commercialized in the world to sell anything from cars, furniture, clothes and other household items with pictures of beautiful, half-dressed, seductive women. The internet has made cybersex and pornography into a multi-billion dollar industry, which projects sex with a huge inflated value for instant self-gratification.

Sex is not limited to sexual organs only, but there is mind at the other end. And a man or woman can never have enough of it. Age is not a bar for sexual lust, and the desire if not sublimated can continue up to old age.

Bible says, "The spirit is willing, but the flesh is weak."—Over indulgence in sex has bodily limitations; and the other partner just acts like a catalyst in the process. It is like pouring ghee (clarified butter) into the fire, and the fire blazes even more.

Sri Krishna says in verse 3:39, "O Arjuna! Lustful desires cover the knowledge and carry away intellectual discrimination of even a wise man. It is a constant enemy of the wise. It is like a raging fire which can never be satisfied."

The paradox is that sex is a sensation of intense pleasure in the beginning, and a deep sadness in the end. It is a climb to the peak of momentary bliss and then a sudden drop to the valley of sadness. The joys which one experiences from bodily sense contacts are a source of deep human suffering later on.

Adi Shankara, the eighth century mystic saint composed a bouquet of very piercing verses in a poetic form called 'Bhaja Govindam,' for the benefit and welfare of the humanity. Adi Shankara says, "Upon seeing the seductive breasts and navel button-hole of a young woman; do not come under the grip of maddening delusion. This is just a modification of body flesh and fat. O man! Reflect on this again and again.–Remember and always chant the Holy name of Govinda Krishna again and again, to come out of the delusion and mire of this Maya."

How much pleasure a person expected out of the sexual experience; how much he or she waited for it to happen; and what all difficulties one endured to experience this bodily sensation? And finally nothing is left in one's hands, just a memory. And why is sex such a powerful and a tempting force to reckon with? Read this story.

Once, two holy men went on a pilgrimage together. They reached a river and they had to go to the other side of the shallow river. There, they saw a beautiful young girl in tears, because she could not cross the river, as the water level of the river had risen due to continuous heavy rains. Seeing her difficulty, the elder holy man volunteered to pick her up and carry her across the river.

After crossing the river the elderly holy man set the young girl down. The younger holy man looked at the entire situation with disgust and consternation. The young girl profusely thanked the elderly holy man, and went on her way to the village where she lived.

Thereafter, both the holy men proceeded on their pilgrimage. They reached a night shelter and decided to sleep there. The elder holy man quickly fell asleep, while the younger holy man was restless and tossed around in the bed and was unable to sleep.

He could not calm down his mind, and finally woke up the elder holy man and said, "We are holy men, and we are not supposed to touch women. I am really ashamed that when you picked up that young girl for crossing the river, her breasts and other parts of the body were touching you. That is indeed shameful."

The elder holy man looked at his friend in the eyes and broke into laughter and said, "Oh! Oh! So that is what is troubling you, and therefore you are not able to sleep. You are still thinking about that incident. Brother, I did my duty to help that young girl as a human being, and left the girl on the river bank, but why are you still carrying her in your mind?"

The story drives home the point that lust and pleasure are seated in the mind and intellect of an individual. If the mind is pure, then it does not matter whether one touched a male or a female body as a part of one's duty.

The above verse is translated as, ":—***evam...buddheh... param...buddhva***:—thus knowing that the Self-soul is superior to the intellect:—***samstabhya...atmanam...atmana***:—restraining the self by the Self-soul:—***Jahi...shatrum***...***mahabaho***:—kill this enemy in the form of desire...O mighty-armed Arjuna:—***Kama... rupam....durasadam***:—desire in the form of lust is very hard to conquer."

Lust for money, lust for sex, lust for name and fame or lust in other forms, is the biggest enemy of human beings on the spiritual path. The embodied Self-soul is higher than the intellect and the mind. The intellect and the mind have to be purified from all sinful thoughts to reach the inner portals of Self-soul, and thus achieve victory over lust.

CHAPTER 4

THE YOGA OF WISDOM THROUGH ACTION
JNANA KARMA SANYASA YOGA

Sri Krishna said:

I declared this knowledge and wisdom of imperishable yoga to Vivasvat (presiding deity of Sun); Vivasvat further taught this yoga to Manu (the Hindu law-giver); and Manu imparted this knowledge to Ikshvaku (founder of Solar dynasty). (1)

Transliteration from Sanskrit to English of the above verse is, “: ***imam***:—this:—***vivasvate***:—to Sun god:—***yogam***:—-yoga:—***proktavan***:—taught:—***aham***:—I:—***avyayam***:—imperishable:—***vivasvat***:—Sun god:—***manave***:—to Manu:—***praha***:—further passed on:—***manu***:—Manu:—***Ikshvakave***:—Manu the Hindu law-giver taught to Ikshvaku:—***abravit***:—taught.”

The Sun has been an object of veneration in many cultures and religions throughout the human history. Humanity’s most fundamental understanding of the Sun is as a luminous disk in the sky, whose presence above the horizon creates day and whose absence causes night.

In many prehistoric and ancient cultures, the Sun was thought to be a solar deity. Worship of the Sun was central to many ancient civilizations as the main life-giving source of heat and light. No life on earth whether human life, animal life or plant life is possible without the Sun.

The Sun is a main-sequence in the solar system informally referred to as a yellow dwarf. It formed approximately four and a half billion years or 45,00,000,000 years ago from the gravitational collapse of matter. Scientists estimate by calculation that it will carry on pretty much as it is now for another four and a half billion years yet–and hence there is going to be no surprises in our lifetime and for the future generations to come for the time being.

Most of this matter gathered in the centre, whereas the rest flattened into an orbiting disk that became the Solar System. The central mass became increasingly hot and dense, eventually initiating nuclear fusion in its core.

The Sun is roughly of middle age now, and has not changed dramatically for the last four billion years, and will remain fairly stable for a period of another four and a half billion years. The Sun has finished half of its life and the remaining half life of the Sun is nourishing the world now.

A star's life cycle depends upon its mass. Stars like the Sun spend most of their lives, eating up the hydrogen in their centre. The German scientist Albert Einstein, read Bhagavad Gita as an inspiration, to understand the phenomenon of the Universe. He understood that the Sun is giving out energy in the form of heat and light due to nuclear fusion in its core. This gave rise to the invention of the scientific theory that Energy is equal to mass multiplied by the square of the speed of light.

Sun will grow old much the same way as we humans do. When the Sun is about eight to nine billion years old, it will start to change and will become bigger and cooler.

By the time it is about ten billion years old, it will change into a red giant and its atmosphere will stretch out to near where the earth is now and it will finally swallow the earth planet. This is as per the calendar of the Universe which is gigantic extending to millions of years as compared to the very small human calendar.

The age of the Sun is estimated using computer models of stellar evolution, by the scientists and astronomers. However, after hydrogen fusion at its core stops, the Sun will undergo severe changes and become a red giant. It is calculated that the Sun will become sufficiently large to engulf the current orbits of Mercury, Venus and Earth.

The Sun therefore also has a finite life, although in billions of years. The life of the earth is linked with the life of the Sun. But human life span of 90 to 100 years is too small and just a small bubble in the vast ocean. Millions of generations will yet come and continue to inhabit this planet earth before the final extinction of earth takes place.

But finally all life will come to an end at some point, but that happening is yet very far away as per the scientific calculations. It is not just a religious prediction or blind faith but computer calculations on the remaining life of the Sun which is linked to earth's life as well. The present generation need not have any concerns on that account though.

That is what Sri Krishna says about the time span of Brahma's Cosmic day and Brahma's Cosmic night, and the beginning and end of Yugas. The calculation of time span of the Universe is mind boggling.

The enormous effect of the Sun on the Earth has been recognized since prehistoric times, and the Sun is considered as a deity in Hindu culture. Earth's movement around the Sun is the basis of the solar calendar, which is the predominant calendar in use today.

Sri Krishna as an incarnation of God is talking of an era even before that. It is not possible for human beings, to comprehend the enormity of the Universe; neither do we have any memory of our earlier births. Jesus Christ says in Bible, "Very truly I tell you; before Abraham was born, I am!"

O Arjuna! Thus transmitted in regular succession the royal sages knew this 'Yoga knowledge' (union of individual soul with cosmic Spirit). Due to long efflux of time in the intervening time period; this knowledge of 'Yoga path' was lost to the world. (2)

The same ancient science of yoga knowledge, is now being declared to you by Me; for you are My devotee and a friend, and this knowledge is indeed a profound secret, and of utmost benefit to the humanity. (3)

Arjuna said:

The manifestation of Vivasvat (Sun god) was earlier, and later was Your birth. How then am I to understand that You declared this knowledge in the ancient beginning? (4)

Sri Krishna said:

O Arjuna! Many are the births taken by Me and you from the ancient past; while I remember them all, you do not have memory of past births. (5)

Though I am unborn and of imperishable Cosmic Spirit and the dwelling soul in all living beings, yet I manifest as a human incarnation, by presiding over My own Maya (Prakriti). (6)

Sri Krishna says in the above verse, that I take incarnation in this world as an 'Avatar,' by presiding over My own 'Maya and Prakriti.' The purpose of Prakriti is to produce duality in this world and ensnare human beings in the net of elusive and transitory sensual pleasures, and material wealth.

It is invisible and beyond our perception. Maya is like darkness, and only the light and effulgence of the Spirit of God can dispel the darkness. God is not bound by Maya, just as a magician is not deluded by his own magic tricks.

O Bharata Arjuna! Whenever there is a decline of righteousness (Dharma) and rise of wickedness (Adharma) in the world; then I bodily manifest Myself as Divine incarnation. (7)

This verse became very popular during the television telecast of ***Mahabharata*** episodes, where it was sung as a chorus in Sanskrit pronunciation as,—"***Yada-yada***: —whenever:—***hi***:—surely:—***dharmasya***:—righteousness:—***glanir***:—decline:—***bhavati***:—is:—***bharata***:—O

Bharata:—***abhyuthanam***:—rise:—***adharmasya***:—of unrighteousness:—***tada***:—then:—***atmanam***:—Myself:—***srjami***:—manifest:—***aham***:—I."

For protection of the good and for destruction of the wicked and for the establishment of Dharma; I appear as incarnation of God in human form from age to age. (8)

God Vishnu incarnates on earth from time to time (from Yuga to Yuga), to eradicate evil forces and to restore the Dharma and save the righteous. Lord Vishnu in His full avatar as Sri Krishna speaks in Bhagavad Gita to deliver the 'Word of God' to the humanity. Human beings have a free will to act as they want, and even God cannot impose any restrictions on the acts of men and women.

The incarnations and messengers of God take manifestation on earth in different ages and Yugas, to give teachings to the mankind for their highest good and deliverance from evil. Human beings ought to discriminate between vice and virtue and between what is right or wrong, and hold the Scriptures as a guide.

The first four avatars of Lord Vishnu appeared in Satya or Krita Yuga, the first of the four Yugas, is also called 'The Golden Age.' The next three appeared in Treta Yuga, the eighth and ninth in Dwapara Yuga, and the tenth is yet to appear later in Kali Yuga. The time till completion for Kali Yuga is estimated to be 427,000 years.

In the Vishnu Purana and the Bhagavata Purana, the Kali Yuga is described as ending with the appearance of the final Kalki avatar, who will defeat the wicked and liberate the virtuous to initiate a new Satya Yuga. Lord Vishnu as the One Primal Spirit of the Universe for all moving and nonmoving beings, and the Supreme Soul, takes birth as God-incarnate to protect the principles of Dharma and righteousness.

O Arjuna! One who understands the true essence of My manifestation as Divine birth and actions; and acts on the tenets of my teachings, does not take further rebirth, but comes to My Supreme Being. (9)

Freed from passion, fear and anger, having taken refuge in Me and uniting with My Divine Spirit; having burnt all impurities in the fire of knowledge, many purified souls have attained to My Being. (10)

O Partha Arjuna! In whatever manner and form, people approach and worship My Divine Spirit, I fulfil their desires accordingly; for people always follow My path in all the ways. (11)

Longing for worldly success; people worship many heavenly deities; for quick is success born of actions in this human world. (12)

Translation of the above verse is ":—***kankshantah***:—longing:—***karmanam***:—of actions:—***siddhim***:—success:—***yajante***:—worship:—***iha***:—in this world:—***devatah***:—deities:—***kshipram***:—quick:—***hi***:—because:—***manushe loke***:—in the human world:—***siddhih***:—success:—***bhavati***:—is attained:—***karmaja***:—born of actions."

The above verse says that in this human world, quick is success born of actions. And the short-cut and the easiest way to explain this verse is by means of a story.

This is the real life story of Dashrath Manjhi; the man who moved a mountain, so that his village folks could reach civilization with the basic amenities of water supply, electricity, a school, and a medical centre. It was the year 1960 and Dashrath a landless labourer, who lived amid rocky terrains of Gaya in Bihar, a state of India. He was regarded as the lowest of the low, and the poorest of the poor, in a caste-ridden Indian society.

A 300-foot tall mountain loomed between him and the civilization. Like all poor men, Dashrath Manjhi, worked on the other side of the mountain. At noon, his wife Phaguni would bring his bare lunch of wheat chappatis. As they had no road, the trek took long hours over the mountain. Dashrath tilled the fields for a landlord on the other side. He would quarry stones. In a few hours of strenuous physical labour, he would be tired and hungry. He would then watch and wait for his wife Phaguni.

One of those days, his wife came to him empty handed and injured. As the harsh summer sun was beating down, Phaguni tripped on the loose rocks and stones. Her water pot shattered. She slid down several feet, injuring her leg. Hours past noon, she limped back to her husband. He rushed to chastise her for being late. She said, 'look at the mountain, and the distance I had to travel on foot to reach you.' On seeing her tears, he took a decision to cut the mountain and make a path in the mountain for a short-cut to the other side.

He could not bear the tears of his wife. Dashrath sold his goats, and bought a hammer, chisels and a crowbar with that money. He climbed to the top of the mountain, and started chipping away at the mountain. Years later, he would recount, "That Mountain had shattered so many pots and claimed so many human lives. I could not bear that the mountain had hurt my wife. If it took all my life now, I would carve a road for the village people through this mountain."

He quit his wage based job, and his family often went without food. Then, Phaguni fell ill. The doctor was in Wazirganj, a distance of 75 kilometres, around the mountain and he was unable to make the journey, as he had no money for the bus fare. Phaguni died but her death, further spurred Manjhi in his determination to make a road in the middle of the mountain.

It was not easy. Unyielding, the mountain would cascade rocks at him, while he dug into the mountain. He undertook this massive and daunting work all alone, without any help from others. He got hurt many times while breaking the rocks manually with a hammer, but he would take rest and start again.

It was an impossible task to do single-handed, but he was determined.....In 1982, Manjhi finally broke through a thin wall of the remaining rock and walked out into the open space at the other side of the mountain.

What a historic moment for Dashrath? After 22 years, Dashrath Das Manjhi, the outcast landless labourer had conquered the mountain. He had carved out a path 360 feet long, 30 feet wide single-handed without any assistance from anybody.

Wazirganj, with the facility of a hospital, jobs, and a school, was now only 5 kilometres away from the village through this short-cut path. People from 60 villages in Atri could use this road. Children had to walk only 3 kilometres to reach the school. Grateful, they began to call him '***Baba***,' the revered man.

But Dashrath did not stop there. He began knocking on the doors of government, asking for the road to be tarred and to be connected to the main road. He walked along the railway line all the way to New Delhi as he had no money to pay for the train fare.

He submitted a petition there, for a hospital for his people, a school, and water supply. In July 2006, '*Baba*' went to the then Bihar Chief Minister, Nitish Kumar's 'Janata Durbar.' The Minister was overwhelmed and got up to offer to the '*Baba*' his chair, his Chief Minister's seat; a rare honour for a man of Manjhi's background.

The Indian government rewarded his efforts with a plot of land; Manjhi donated the land back to government for a hospital. They also nominated him for the 'Padma Shree' award, but forest ministry officials fought the nomination, calling his work illegal as he had not taken approval from the department. "I do not care for these awards, the fame and the money," he said, "All I want is a road, a school, and a hospital for our people. They toil so hard. It will help their women and children."

It took the government 20 years to tar this road, and this is an example of how the bureaucracy works. Self effort is the best help, when one has the determination to accomplish even a huge task against all odds.

On August 17, 2007, Dashrath Manjhi, the man who moved the mountain, died in a hospital. Manjhi's legacy, his inspiration, though lives on. It lives on among the thousands of Indians who are making a difference to their fellowmen, fighting new battles and overcoming challenges.

The battle of ***Mahabharata*** was not only fought on the grounds of ***Kurukshetra***, but it is fought even now in the lives of human beings in the day to day living. This time, the battle of Dashrath Manjhi was with a mountain and he won the battle against all odds single-handed. It lives on in many of you who are moving your own mountains. Manjhi showed us that the real hero lies inside you. It is you who can rise up to meet the challenge.

Self-less work without seeking the rewards of actions; is pleasing to God; and the above verse says that, for quick are the results born of actions in this human world.

Bible (Matthew) says, "Jesus said to them, because of the littleness of your faith; for truly I say to you, if you have faith even as small as a mustard seed, you shall say to this mountain, 'Move from here to there,' and it shall move; and nothing shall be impossible for you."

The four fold caste division for human beings was propounded by me, in accordance with the inherent attributes and individual karma of human beings (for efficient governance of the world). But understand My divine Being as a non-doer and changeless spirit. (13)

If your work in life is humble, do not apologise for it. Be proud that you are fulfilling the duty given to you by God. He needs you in a particular place, in a particular job; all people cannot play the same role. As long as you work to please God, all cosmic forces will harmoniously assist you. An engineer, a doctor, a plumber, a peon, a Prime Minister, a nurse, and for that matter, everybody has to do their respective work, so that everything works for the betterment of humanity. If people do not perform their respective duties, then there will be utter chaos in the world.

Once, Rukmini wife of Lord Sri Krishna said to her husband, "Dear Lord! It would be great, if every house in our Kingdom of Dwarka is prosperous and has a big bungalow and mansion like ours. I find so many huts and slums, where there are not even basic amenities of toilets, water and electricity. These slums are not worth living for human beings."

Sri Krishna replied, "My dear, if everyone was rich and had beautiful houses; then from where you will find the labourers, masons, tea-shop vendors and sweepers to do the menial jobs; who work for a mere survival on a day-to-day basis? Everyone has to reap the fruit of one's karma of the previous births, as well as the deeds of the present life. God has created good trees, poisonous plants, and weeds which grow alongside together. Among the animals there are wild animals and domestic animals as well–all kinds of creatures. A lion eats the dog; the dog eats the cat; and cat eats the mouse, and so on. You need everything to make it a world."

My Spirit of God does not take part in anyone's karma (in thoughts, words and deeds), nor the fruits thereof. One, who thus understands My Spirit, is not bound by actions. (14)

Knowing the nature of karma thus; the ancient seekers performed the righteous deeds for liberation. Therefore you should also perform righteous actions, as the ancient seekers did in the past. (15)

Once, a man was walking along a beach. The Sun was shining and a cool breeze was blowing. In the distance he could see a woman going back and forth between the surf's edge and the beach. There were so many starfish stranded on the sand due to low tide. The woman was picking up the struggling starfish on the sand, one by one, and throwing them back into the sea water.

The man was struck by the sheer futility of such a task in hand; as there were thousands and thousands of starfish, stranded on the sand due to low tide. The man came up to the woman and said, "You must be crazy, this long beach stretches into miles, and you cannot possibly make a difference with this single-handed, small effort of yours."

The woman then bent down to pick up one more starfish on the sand and threw it back into the sea. She turned back to the man and said, “It sure made a difference to that one!”

Even the wise are perplexed as to what constitutes an action, and what is inaction (no-action). Therefore I shall explain to you what is action, after knowing which you shall be freed from their evil-effects. (16)

There was once a person who was so devoted to Lord Krishna, that he will spend his whole day chanting the name of the of the God like a parrot. He used to tell the villagers that whenever he will be in dire need of help, God himself will come to help him. He had a blind faith, but no true knowledge or wisdom; nor had he read any of the Holy Scriptures. He just used to chant the name of the God mechanically, and he considered himself a very wise person.

It so happened that during the rainy season, there were continuous heavy rains for many days; and the whole village was flooded with water all around. Rains kept pouring with all the fury, and there was no sign of abating. The water level continued to rise and entered the houses on the ground floor. He started praying fervently and called God for help.

A boat man came and asked him to jump into the boat to go to the higher lands. But he refused and said in pride that people did not know his faith in God. The boat man went away. The water level still kept on rising, and he climbed to the first floor of his house. A second boat came but he again refused to go in the boat, and said that God has got to help him under all circumstances, and he is sure of that.

The water level further rose and he went to the second floor and started praying to God furiously. A third boat man came and asked him to please come into the boat. He refused and said he had full faith in God. Finally the floods swept away all the houses along with him, and he died.

His soul sought an audience with God and said, “Oh God! I had total faith in You Sir, and still you did not come to rescue me in the floods when I was drowning. You know God; you are almighty and powerful, and I did not miss a single day, when I did not chant Your Holy name, and offer my ritualistic prayers."

God replied, "I came to help you but you refused my help. Not only once, but I came three times in the form of a boat man, but you did not recognize Me. You were so full of pride and arrogance of your devotional chanting that you did not listen to anyone."

The moral of the story is that you cannot be so ignorant to think that only your ritualistic chanting is the best and the devotion of all others is useless. God helps those who help themselves.

That man was counting on God for help, and God was counting on him to take the necessary 'action' to save himself.—'Action' was required in this case and not 'Inaction.' The above verse says that one must know when action is required, and when no-action is required. The wise man knows when to act and when to refrain from actions.

It is needful to understand and discriminate as to what is 'desired action'; what is 'prohibited and forbidden action'; and what is 'inaction.' Indeed complex and mysterious indeed are the ways of actions. (17)

The above verse talks about the consequences of three types of actions: —***karmanah***: —action: —***vikarmanah***: —forbidden action: – ***akarmanah***: —inaction; —which ought to be known and understood: —***Gahana...karmanah...gatih***: —for mysterious are the ways of karma.

There is no escape from the effects of one's deeds and karma done in the past. The effects of past deeds can somehow be nullified, by performing righteous and good deeds in the present. A cause produces an effect, which in turn becomes a new cause. The retribution of tit for tat in this way becomes endless. It is like a vicious circle and getting stuck in a vortex, and then it becomes increasingly difficult to come out of the effects of one's deeds. Our motive good or bad is what finally determines the fruit of actions.

Bible (Ecclesiastes) ruminates on the meaning of life and says, "There is a time for everything, and a season for every activity under heaven; a time to be born and a time to die, a time to plant and a time to uproot; a time to kill and a time to heal, a time to tear down and a time to build; a time to weep and a time to laugh, a time to mourn and a time to dance, a time to scatter stones and a time to gather them, a time to embrace and a time to refrain, a time to search and a time to give up, a time to keep and a time to throw away, a time to tear and a time to mend, a time to be silent and a time to speak, a time to love and a time to hate; a time for war and a time for peace. What does the worker gain from his toil?"

One, who has intuitive discrimination to perceive inaction while in the midst of action; and perceive action in inaction, is a wise person and a yogi, who can accomplish all work. (18)

You cannot judge a person from the outer appearance whether he is wise or foolish, because sometimes acts of the wise and the foolish may just be the same. The result and fruit of actions, performed by human beings, are indeed very mysterious and complex. An action which is done at the right time and right place, bears good results; while the same action done at the wrong time and wrong place; bears unfavourable results. A plant sapling sown in the right season, and in the right soil, bears a healthy tree; while the same plant sapling, sown at the wrong time of the season and in wrong soil, does not sprout.

Existence is not making a judgment about what is good or bad. It is the society of people in which we live that tries to judge others, as good or bad. And society has selfish people to grind their own axe. It is only other human beings, who try to judge you as good and bad. Existence never judges, one thing which is good under some conditions, becomes bad under another set of conditions and circumstances.

If you do the right things at the right time, the right results happen. That is perfectly fair. Society may not be fair, but the existence is perfectly fair. Unless you do the right things, the right results will not happen. If existence was not like this, there would be no value for doing the right thing. Nothing that we value in our life would be valuable, if you could do wrong actions and still get good results.

One whose undertakings are devoid of all selfish-motives and the desire for results; and who has burnt all actions in the fire of knowledge; he is called a wise person. (19)

"***Yasya***:—whose:—***sarve***:—all:—***samarambhah***:—undertakings:—***kama...samkalpa...varjitah***:—devoid of selfish-motives:—***Jnana...agni...karmanam***:—whose actions have been burnt by the fire of knowledge:—***tam***:—him:—***ahuh***:—is called:—***panditam budhah***:—a wise person."

A person who has gone beyond the vicious circle of desires; by understanding that one desire leads to another, and there is no end to human desires; is a wise man or woman.

The moment one desire is fulfilled, another desire raises its head; and only a wise person who has burnt all desires in the fire of knowledge, is a liberated man. The journey is to move inwards towards the bliss of your own Self-soul; and not to the outer world of desires and sensual gratifications of the flesh. A story below explains the nature of desires.

A King once went out of his palace for a morning walk, and came across a beggar outside. He asked the beggar, "What do you want?"–The beggar laughed and said, "You are asking me as if you can fulfil my desires!"

The king was offended. He said, "Of course I can fulfil your desires. I am the king here with all the wealth of the treasury and resources of men at my command. What is your desire? Just tell me."–And the beggar said, "Think twice, before you promise me anything." The beggar was no ordinary beggar, but an enlightened man; who was a king himself in his past life. He had promised to this man that, "I will come and wake you up from the slumber of delusion in your next life. In this life you have missed the spiritual goal, but I will come again and meet you."

The king had no memory of his past life. The king said to the beggar, "I will fulfil anything you ask. I am a very powerful king and you do not know my powers. What can you possibly desire that I cannot give you? Your desire must be for woman and wealth?"

The beggar said, "It is a very simple desire. You see this begging bowl. Can you fill it with something?"

The emperor said, "Of course!"–He called one of his assistants, and told him, "Fill this man's begging bowl with money and gold." The assistant went to the palace, and got some gold and poured it into the bowl, but all the gold disappeared in a moment. And he fetched more money and gold, and poured in the begging bowl. Again and again, it would disappear from the bowl in a moment as if by a magic. And the begging bowl was empty again.

The whole palace and people gathered around to see the strange phenomenon. By and by, the rumour spread throughout the city, and a huge crowd gathered. The prestige and honour of the king was at stake. He said to his assistants and helpers, "I am ready to lose all the wealth of this entire kingdom, but I cannot be defeated by this beggar."

Diamonds, pearls and emeralds and all the money of the treasury was poured into the beggar's bowl but it became empty, the moment anything was poured into the bowl. The begging bowl seemed to be magical. Everything that was put into the bowl disappeared mysteriously!

The king could not solve the mystery and everyone was stunned into silence. The treasury of the king was empty. The king dropped at the feet of the beggar and admitted his defeat. He said, "Just tell me one thing. You are victorious...but before you leave, just answer my curiosity. What is this begging bowl made of?"

The beggar laughed and said, "There is no secret of this begging bowl. It is made up of the human desires which are never ending. The moment you satisfy one desire, another desire arises."

The moral of the story is that desires are hydra- headed and when one desire is fulfilled, another ten desires raise their head. How does fulfilment of desires function? First there is a great excitement, great thrill and great satisfaction.

You feel at the top of the world. Now you will be recognized by the world. Something is going to happen, and you are on the verge of your ultimate goal. And then you buy the big car, you buy a lovely house, you fulfil your sensual desires with beautiful women; and then suddenly everything is meaningless again. Your life is empty again, as everybody who came in your life, enjoyed your wealth and disappeared. You are again the same lonely man, but now even more lonely, as everybody exploited you.

What happened? The big car is standing in the driveway, but there is no excitement anymore. The excitement was only in getting it. You momentarily became so drunk with the desire that you forgot your inner emptiness. Now all your desires have been fulfilled, the big car is in the garage, the beautiful woman is in your bed but you are drained out, big money is in your bank account, but yet all the excitement is gone.

All this has left you nothing but worries and anxieties. The people and relatives, who came to your house, enjoyed your hospitality and said bye-bye and left. The emptiness is still there which is causing you anxiety and trouble. Again you have to create another desire, to escape from this emptiness.

This is how one moves from one desire to another desire. That is how one remains a beggar throughout one's life. And you again go to the temples and churches, to ask this god and that god, to fulfil your desires. Until and unless one goes beyond these desires, it will be an endless cycle of birth and death, and being reborn again in the womb of a woman; to grow up and enjoy other women and wealth, and it is a vicious circle.

Every desire frustrates, and you want to fulfil these by hook or crook, by any means. And when this desire is fulfilled, you will need another desire; and finally at death the soul goes back to its primal source with unfulfilled desires, and a person again takes rebirth.

Giving up attachment to the results of one's actions, ever content within oneself, not depending upon the outside world; though performing actions, one is not bound by the effects of karma. (20)

This verse of Gita says that without looking for rewards and fruits of one's actions, and without depending upon the outside world; ever content in one's Self-soul, one is not bound by the effects of one's karma and actions, and thus achieves the supreme good.

In the olden times, a King asked his men to place a boulder of rock on a highway road. Then he hid himself behind a tree to see if anyone will remove the huge rock or just pass on and circumvent the boulder. Some of the king's wealthiest merchants and courtiers came and simply passed around the boulder, without doing anything. Many loudly blamed the king for not keeping the roads clear; but nobody did anything to remove the roadblock out of the way.

Then, a farmer came along carrying a load of vegetables. Upon approaching the rock boulder, the farmer laid down his load of vegetables; and started pushing the stone boulder to the side of the road, all by himself. The farmer thought that self-help is the best help, and in the world everybody thinks that the other person will do the needful, and finally nobody does anything. After much pushing and jostling, he finally succeeded in removing the roadblock.

After that, the farmer picked up his load of vegetables to proceed further, but he noticed a purse lying on the road, where the boulder was previously blocking the road. The purse contained many gold coins, and a note from the king saying that the gold is for that person, who will remove the boulder from the highway road.

The farmer never expected any rewards for his action of removing the boulder from the road, and he thought it was his duty to do so. He decided that he will return the purse to the king. The king, who was hiding behind the tree came out, and the farmer returned the purse back to the king. The king in return rewarded him with a huge plot of land to grow vegetables and fruits, as a token of his selfless work and motivation.

The moral of the story is whenever a person does some selfless work, he is rewarded sooner or later, and every obstacle presents an opportunity to improve one's life. The above verse says that not expecting anything as the fruit of one's actions, and not depending upon others; one, who is ever content, is not bound by the effects of one's deeds.

Relinquishing all expectations and worry of the future, with mind and Self-soul in harmony with the Universal Spirit; giving up all possessions, one who performs sheer bodily actions does not incur sin. (21)

Content with whatever one gets of its own accord, free from the duality of the pairs of opposites, without any envy, balanced in success and failure; though performing actions, one is not tied down to the evil effects of karma. (22)

That is our problem too. We make unnecessary comparisons with others and feel inferior. We do not value what God has given us. This leads to unhappiness in life. It is better to be happy with whatever one gets of its own accord, as a fruit of one's labour and hard work, instead of looking at what others possess. There will always be someone, who has more or less of material things than what you have.

A person, who is satisfied with what he or she has, is a happy person. He neither begs nor borrows but manages with what he has. Material things are meant to be used to make life easy; and people are to be loved and respected. But the problem in the modern world is that people are being used; and material things are being loved.

One who is free from all attachment, with mind liberated from all entanglements and firmly established in knowledge and wisdom of Self-realization; and performing all work as dedication to the Spirit of God; for such a person the effect of entire karma melts away. (23)

The above verse with translation from Sanskrit says: '***gatasangasya...muktasya***:—one who is free from all attachment:—***jnanavasthita...chetasah***:—with mind firmly established in knowledge and wisdom:—***yajnaya...acharatah***:—dedicating all actions to the Spirit of God:—***karma...samagram... praviliyate***:—entire karma melts away':—which translated into English means, "one who is free from attachment, with mind firmly established in knowledge and wisdom; performing all work as a dedication to the Spirit of God, the entire bondage of karma for such a person is dissolved."

In the performance of a sacrificial Yajna, the constituent elements, the fire; the clarified butter; the act of offering the oblation into fire; are all sacred. Unto to the Spirit of Brahman (Spirit of God) verily it goes, when all these acts are recognized and performed as a dedication to the Supreme Spirit. (24)

Fire is one of the sacred elements of nature without which no life is possible. In the ritual of Yajna worship (***Havan***), the fire into which the offering is made; such as clarified butter and grains; and the person who makes the oblation, are all considered as part of divinity. When all these acts are performed as a sacrifice to the Supreme Spirit, then it becomes a Yajna sacrifice.

The same connotation applies to the human body; as it is the internal heat of the body which keeps the body alive. Eating daily food is obligatory for all living beings, whether one is an enlightened saint or just an ordinary person.

The sage makes the act of eating as a Yajna sacrifice. The digestive heat and energy of the body is divine; the food that is offered to the body for eating is divine; and the act of eating by the person, is also divine. When all these acts put together are performed in dedication and as a sacrificial offering to the Supreme Spirit of God, then this act becomes a divine Yajna.

The above verse of Bhagavad Gita is recited in Hindu culture before partaking of food to express one's gratitude and thankfulness to God for the food one is going to eat to keep the body alive. The food is thus considered as a gift of divine grace, as there are so many hungry and thirsty people on this earth, who do not get even one square meal a day.

Similar grace and thanksgiving is said in Christian religion to thank God for the food one is going to eat. We cherish God by thanking Him, and God similarly cherishes us by giving us good health and well being. Sanskrit is not a language in daily use in India now; and majority of the Hindus also do not know the full significance of the above verse as a thanksgiving prayer before eating food.

The Christian prayer being in English language is far more easy and simple to understand. The Bible prayer says, "Our Father who art in heaven, hallowed be thy name. Thy kingdom come. Thy 'will' be done on earth as it is in heaven. Give us this day our daily bread, and forgive us our trespasses, as we forgive those who trespass against us, and lead us not into temptation, but deliver us from evil."—A simple prayer which asks for daily bread for this day only, is said as a grace by Christians all over the world, before partaking of food.

Some devotees offer acts of Yajna rituals to the heavenly deities only; others offer their Self-soul spirit as Yajna sacrifice for purification in the fire of Brahman. (25)

Some offer restraints on senses like hearing, seeing and other senses as sacrifice in the fire of self-control. Yet others offer restraint on speaking and other sense-objects as a sacrifice in the fire of self-control. (26)

Few others kindled by knowledge; offer all the actions of the senses and functions of the life-energy breath, as a sacrifice into the fire of self-control. (27)

Some offer wealth as charity, few undertake penances, some follow eightfold Yoga path, few undertake self-study of Scriptures for knowledge and wisdom; and some others take up strict vows as sacrificial Yajna. (28)

Few yogis offer as sacrifice the outgoing breath into the incoming breath; and the incoming breath in the outgoing breath; restraining the flow of the outgoing and the incoming breaths, thus fully absorbed in the conservation of life-energy. (29)

Still others of regulated food habits offer in the prana the functions thereof. All these seekers are performing various Yajna sacrifices, and by their continuous practice they redeem their karmic sins. (30)

O Arjuna! Those who eat the purified food and the remains of a Yajna sacrifice, follow the path of Brahman Spirit. This world is not for the non-sacrificer, then how the next world? (31)

Various sacrificial Yajnas as these are stated in the vast Scriptures of the Vedas. Know that these yajnas are born of karma and the practice thereof results in liberation. (32)

O Parantapa Arjuna! Jnana Yajna (knowledge sacrifice) is superior to wealth sacrifice (charity). All karma deeds in its entirety, finally lead to knowledge and wisdom. (33)

Seek this spiritual wisdom by prostrating, by asking questions, and by rendering service to the enlightened saints, who will instruct you in this knowledge. (34)

O Pandava Arjuna! Having gained this spiritual knowledge, you will not again fall into the snare of worldly delusion. You will then perceive the oneness of the entire Creation in your Self-soul, and also in My Supreme Spirit of God. (35)

Even if you be the most sinful of all sinners with heinous crimes; yet you shall cross-over all sin by the bridge of this knowledge and wisdom. (36)

O Arjuna! Just as a blazing fire turns all wood into ashes; similarly the fire of this divine knowledge, burns all karmic deeds into ashes. (37)

Once there was an enlightened Master, who wanted to train two of his disciples on the spiritual path, by giving them practical example of how to live a good life. The Master said to his disciples, "Take 900 rupees, each of you, and use it to buy whatever you can with this money, for your living room. In five day's time, I will return back to inspect your rooms."

When he returned and visited the room of his first disciple, he saw that it has been filled up with rags and discarded clothes, and there was no place in the room even to sit. This disciple had a tough bargain deal with a rag dealer to purchase the entire lot, and the rags and the worn out clothes were the cheapest items available in the market. The enlightened Master was shocked to his horror.

And then the Master went to inspect the room of his second disciple and he found that in the middle of the room there was a lighted ghee lamp along with some lighted incense sticks. Light and fragrance had filled the entire room and there was a Holy book of 'Bhagavad Gita' on the table, to study and absorb its sublime teachings.

The Master was immensely delighted and said, "You have truly understood the art of living. Life is very much like an empty room and it ought to be filled up with the light of knowledge and the fragrance of selfless service in dedication to the Lord. Life cannot be wasted with discarded and filthy things of the world."

The message of the story is that one should not fill up one's mind with the filthy and worthless things of the world, and carry ugly memories. Be in the world, but do not allow the filth of the world to get inside you. Discard all hatred, jealousy and cunningness of the world as junk; and surround yourself with divine thoughts and company of good people.

Verily, there is nothing more purifying in this world like knowledge. One, who is perfected in this yoga knowledge, realizes it in one's own heart in due course of time. (38)

Bible proverb says, "Gold there is, and rubies in abundance, but lips that speak knowledge are a rare jewel. —Wise men store up knowledge, but the mouth of a fool invites ruin."

Those who have absolute faith, full devotion, total control over their senses; they attain knowledge along with Self-realization. Upon attaining this knowledge they quickly reach the state of abiding peace. (39)

"***Shraddhavan***:—people with faith:—***labhate***:—attain or gain:—***jnanam***:—Knowledge:—***tatparah***:—devotion to the Supreme Spirit:—***samyate...indriyah***:—one who has controlled his senses:—***jnanam***:—knowledge:—***labdhava***:—having attained or gained:—***param***:—supreme:—***shantim***:—to peace:—***achirena***:—at once:—***adhigacchati***:—goes."

The motto of the Indian Navy Establishment, INS Hamla is: —"***Shraddhavan...labhate...jnanam***" meaning, 'Those who have faith attain knowledge.'

The ignorant, the faithless and those with inner conflicts and doubts, go to destruction. Such doubting people have no happiness either in this world or in the next. (40)

It is essential that one is free from all doubts and mental conflicts to make a progress on the spiritual path. Swami Chinmayananda used to say that all those who go naked, with matted hair, mud-splattered; who fast and sleep on the ground; and smear their body with ashes, and sit in endless meditations;–so long as he or she is not free from doubts, one will not find freedom. All these rituals that people follow are empty rituals, but they believe them to be holy.

O Arjuna! Actions cause no bondage for a person, whose doubts have been removed by knowledge and Self-realization; those who dedicate all actions to the Spirit of God are ever poised in awareness of Self-soul. (41)

Therefore cut all doubts in your heart born out of ignorance, with the sword of this Self-soul knowledge. Be firmly established in this Yoga path, O Bharata Arjuna! Stand up and arise to perform your duty as a warrior in the battle field. (42)

Translation of this verse from the original Sanskrit says:—***tasmat***: —therefore:—***ajnana...sambhutam***:—born out of ignorance:—***hritstham***:—residing in the heart:—***jnanasina***:—by the sword of Self-soul knowledge:—***atmana***:—of the Self:—***chittva***:—having cut:—***enam***:—this:—***samshayam***:—doubts:—***yogam***:—yoga:—***atishtha***:—firmly established:—***uttishtha***:—stand up and arise:—***O Bharata***:—O Bharata Arjuna!

Prime Minister of India Shri Narendra Modi, while delivering the Independence Day address to the nation from the ramparts of Red Fort, New Delhi on 15 August 2015 said, there is a new modernisation programme for India by the name of 'Start up or Stand up' but it sounded like 'Stand up.'

Those who were listening to his speech as an audience at the Red fort were suddenly jolted to attention by the word 'Stand up' to mean that national anthem is about to begin, where everyone is duty bound to stand up as a mark of respect for the national anthem.

Nobody could link up as to why the Prime Minister said, 'Stand up ' in the middle of the speech. Little did the audience know that this, 'Stand up' has come up from the inspiration of this verse 4:42 of the Bhagavad Gita, where Sri Krishna tells Arjuna to 'Stand up' to perform your duty as a warrior on the battlefield.

The audience did not know that late Swami Dayananda was the teacher of Shri Narendra Modi. —Shri Narendra Modi, in his earlier days as a young man, used to roam around in the Himalayas, and he became the disciple of Swami Dayananda while he was in Rishikesh.

The television media channels later showed the meeting of Swami Dayananda with the Indian Prime Minister at the Prime Minister's Office. The Prime Minister Narendra Modi also hurriedly visited Swami Dayananda at Rishikesh when he got the news that his teacher is about to die due to illness at the old age of 85 years.

In the years 1952–53 Swami Dayananda as a youth, when he was a journalist became involved with Chinmaya Mission and worked there in various capacities. At one point of time he wanted to become a fighter pilot, and joined the Indian Air Force, but left after six months due to strict regimentation in the Armed Forces.

Later he went to Uttarkashi and met Swami Chinmayananda's Guru Swami Tapovan Ji Maharaj. In the year 1962 he was given Sanyasa by Swami Chinmayananda, and given the name of Swami Dayananda Saraswati. In the subsequent years Swami Dayananda established his own religious institutions by the name of 'Arsha Vidya Peetam Gurukulam' with its Headquarters at Rishikesh.

Swami Dayananda was an erudite scholar of Bhagavad Gita, and he used to give ten days lectures on Bhagavad Gita as 'Gita Jnana Yajna' programmes, in different cities in India. I had the opportunity to associate with Swami Dayananda personally and talk to him, when I attended his lectures, and listened to his erudite explanation of Bhagavad Gita way back in the year 1985 at Kochi in South India, while I was serving in the Indian Navy.

Indian Prime Minister Narendra Modi is a keen follower of the teaching of Bhagavad Gita. In his maiden visit to the United States on September 29, 2014, Prime Minister Narendra Modi gifted a copy of 'Bhagavad Gita' to US President Barack Obama during a dinner hosted at the White House. Also during the Prime Minister Narendra Modi's visit to Japan on September 3, 2014, he gifted a copy of Bhagavad Gita to Japanese Prime Minister Shinzo Abe. In addition to the Sanskrit version, a Japanese version of the Bhagavad Gita was also presented to the Japanese Prime Minister, Abe.

Isha Upanishad says, "Unillumined indeed are those worlds clouded by the blinding darkness of ignorance; unto death sink all those who destroy their Self-soul."—Human life on this earth is the only place where one can work out the cycle of one's karma. One can either live in ignorance or gain the virtue of wisdom and knowledge. By living the ignorant life of lust, anger and greed, one is harming one's own Self-soul, which bars the entry to the gates of heaven.

CHAPTER 5

THE YOGA OF RENUNCIATION
SANYASA YOGA

Arjuna said:

O Sri Krishna! You praise renunciation of actions (sanyasa yoga), and at the same time you recommend performance of selfless actions (karma yoga). Of these two, which one is better? Tell me that conclusively. (1)

Transliteration from Sanskrit to English of the above verse is: "***samnyasam***:—renunciation:—***karmanam***:—of actions; O Krishna!:—***punah***:—again:—***yogam***:—yoga:—***samsashi***:—You praise or recommend:—***yat***:—which:—***shreya***:—is better:—***etayoh***:—of these two:—***ekam***:—which one:—***tat***:—that:—***me***:—to me:—***bruhi***:—tell:—***sunishchitam***:—conclusively."

Arjuna here asks Sri Krishna very soul searching questions. It is really difficult to grasp how these two paths which look so divergent finally converge at the same point. In the path of renunciation (sanyasa yoga) all bondage and attachment with the world is broken, while the path of karma yoga means performing all duties of the world with no selfish motives.

It is easy to understand that by retiring and renouncing from all hassles and attachments of the world, a person can find peace in seclusion; but it is really difficult to comprehend that one can also find peace while in the thickest of market place while performing selfless actions in the path of karma yoga. How can one remain unattached and innocent while in the very midst of relationships and attachments? How can one remain calm and peaceful while living in the very centre of a cyclone?

There is no difficulty in accepting that the flame of a candle will remain steady and still, in a place which is well secluded from winds and storms; but how can you believe that a candle can still keep burning steadily even in the midst of raging storms and hurricanes? Sri Krishna gives the logic and answers to all these questions.

Sri Krishna said:

Renunciation of actions and performance of selfless actions both lead to the highest good. But of the two, performance of selfless actions is superior to renunciation of actions. (2)

O mighty-armed Arjuna! That person should be known as a steadfast renunciate who neither hates nor desires anything and who is free from the conflicts of the pairs of opposites. Such a person easily breaks the shackles of bondage. (3)

Sri Krishna tells his disciple Arjuna, and through him to the entire mankind; to go beyond the dualities of the pairs of opposites, and thus transcend all suffering in life and attain freedom from the grip of Maya. One has to go beyond the dualities of masculine and feminine energies; riches and poverty; joys and sorrows; heat and cold, and so on.

The impure mind has a lot of weight due to hundreds of unfulfilled desires and ambitions to achieve recognition in the world. The unfulfilled thoughts have subtle undercurrents, which pop up again and again, seeking to be fulfilled. The mind moves between the duality of the pairs of opposites, both positive and negative. The pairs of opposites of likes and dislikes do not allow the mind to settle down.

Hate goes very deep and love is also bondage of Maya. The so-called worldly love is skin deep. Everything in life is constantly changing, and is in a state of flux. The friends and well-wishers of today can become enemies tomorrow. It can happen that the woman or the man you love today can become a source of suffering in later years. Nobody can predict which way the things will finally turn out.

The best one can do is to perform one's duty without any expectations from others and without undue dependence on the world. Having faith in higher consciousness of God will take away the fears of the future. Seasons change, the summer will change into winter; the clear and sunny days will change into stormy and rainy days. The cycle repeats, but the mind clings to pleasant memories of the past.

The pure mind which is merged in cosmic consciousness has no worries, no expectations and no ambitions. The above verse of Bhagavad Gita says that for a happy living, one has to go beyond the pairs of opposites of love and hate, joys and sorrows; as these come and go, and are temporary and transient. One has to perform one's obligatory duty and follow the middle path of moderation in eating, sleeping and recreation.

A story best explains the functioning of the pairs of opposites. Once, a very beautiful and gracefully attired woman visited a house. The owner of the house asked her who she was; and she said that she was the goddess of wealth. The owner of the house was delighted and greeted her with open arms. She had all the freedom in the house to do whatever she wanted.

Thereafter another woman came who was ugly looking and dressed in rags like a beggar. The owner of the house asked her who she was, and she said that she was the goddess of poverty. The house owner was frightened and tried to drive her out of the house, but the woman refused to depart from the house saying, "The goddess of wealth is my sister. There is an agreement between the two of us that we cannot live apart from each other; and if you chase me out, then the other beautiful lady who is goddess of wealth will also depart with me."

As soon as the ugly woman was driven out of the house, the other beautiful woman also disappeared.

Birth and death are the two sides of a coin. Fortune goes with misfortune; bad things follow good things. Foolish people dread misfortune, and cling to good fortune; but those who seek enlightenment must transcend all pairs of opposites, and freedom from of all worldly dualities of riches and poverty.

Ignorant, not the wise consider the path of wisdom (Samkhya) and the path of selfless actions (karma yoga) as divergent. But being truly established in one of these, one obtains the rewards of both. (4)

The state reached through Jnana yoga (knowledge) is also attained by karma yoga (selfless-actions). One, who has true vision, realizes that both these paths finally converge to become one and the same. (5)

O mighty-armed Arjuna! Total renunciation of actions is very hard to attain without first performing selfless service (karma yoga). Purified by selfless service together with meditation on the Supreme Spirit, a person soon attains the final goal. (6)

More advanced souls who have the calling of God, may go directly to the renunciation stage of life. For the majority of the people life is divided into four stages. The first stage is called 'Brahmacharya,' the years of youth in school and college life, which require a certain discipline, guidance and purity. The second stage is called the 'Grihastha' stage or the house holder phase of life. This is the time to get married and raise children.

The third stage is 'Vanaprastha' or the hermitage stage which is the time for contemplation and gradual withdrawal from the family encumbrances and worldly activities. The fourth and the last stage of life is 'Sanyasa' or renunciation phase. The person now old and full of wisdom no longer partakes in social and political activities and engages full time on the 'yoga path of renunciation' to cross over to the next world. In this last stage of renunciation one has to give up all attachment with family, lust, anger, greed and wealth.

There are different seasons in human life as in creation. What grows in the spring time will not grow in autumn. The action which is appropriate in spring season is out of place in the fall time. Life is like a journey gathering experiences on the way to reach the final destination.

One ought to remember that one is like a traveller in the journey of life and this world is not a permanent home. The final destination is returning back to the Primal spirit of God, and the breath which once was life goes back to its original source as the last breath. Isha Upanishad also reiterates the same truth that both selfless actions of karma yoga and renunciate life of meditation should be combined to attain the highest good. Just pursuing one path is lop-sided.

Isha Upanishad says, "In darkness live those, for whom the world outside alone is real. In still bigger darkness live those, for whom the world within, alone is real. The first leads to a life of action, the second to the life of meditation. One who knows these two together; through selfless action leaves death behind; and through meditation gains immortality."

The above Gita verse emphasizes that both selfless work and meditation should be joined together to reap the best results and achieve the final goal.

With the union of one's soul with the Supreme Spirit through karma yoga, one is not tainted by the performance of one's actions. Becoming the master of one's senses with a purified Self-soul, one perceives the universal soul as the substratum of all living beings, and material manifestations. (7)

A realized saint who knows the ultimate truth, understands that the body senses move among sense-objects, and does not consider himself as the doer of actions while seeing, hearing, touching, smelling, eating, moving, sleeping, breathing, speaking, emptying bowels and bladder, holding objects and the involuntary opening and closing the eye-lids. (8—9)

A person of self-realization is just a witness of all the activities that takes place in the body, mind and intellect. He considers himself as a non-doer as he identifies himself with his Self-soul which is actionless. One is thus freed from the sense of 'egoism' and as the doer of actions.

One who gives up all worldly attachments, and dedicates all deeds to the Supreme Spirit of God, is not touched by sin as a lotus leaf by water. (10)

The above verse with transliteration says:—***brahmani***:—in the spirit of God (Brahman):—***adhaya***:—having placed:—***karmani***:—actions:—***sangam***:—attachments:—***tyaktva***:—having given-up:—***karoti***:—acts:—***yah***:—who:—***lipyate***:—is touched:—***na... sa***:—not he:—***papena***:—by sin:—***padma...patram***:—lotus leaf:—***iva***:—like:—***ambhasa***:—by water.

The lotus plant grows and gets all nourishment from the water in which it grows. It withers away and dries up if taken out of the water. While growing in the water, the lotus leaf is so slippery that water drops do not wet it, and water just slips off. Similar to the lotus leaf, a person who remains unattached with the world, and dedicates all deeds to the spirit of God is not touched by the effects of karma deeds.

A karma yogi performs work with the body, mind and intellect without attachment, considering them as mere instruments for self purification. (11)

A yogi, who attains Oneness with the Supreme Spirit while giving up the fruits of one's actions, gains abiding peace. The non-yogi on the other hand devoid of Oneness and being attached to the results of actions, gets into karmic bondage and in vicious circle of cause and effect. (12)

Both the yogi and bhogi (non-yogi) perform actions. Nobody can remain actionless as Prakriti will force him or her to do work. For that matter even sitting idle and just thinking also consumes energy and constitutes a mental activity. Although the same activity is performed by both the yogi and bhogi, yet there is a huge difference in the outcome.

The yogi dedicates all actions to God and is free from all worries and the effect of karmic deeds. The bhogi with the sense of doership is worried whether he will get the required results or not, and gets into karmic bondage.

Mentally renouncing all activities, the indwelling soul of a self-controlled yogi happily resides in the body of nine gates, neither a doer himself nor driving others into action (Nine gates of the body are two eyes, two ears, two nostrils, one mouth, genital organs and anus for bowel evacuation). (13)

The Spirit of God neither causes actions in the world nor is affected by the results thereof. It is Cosmic Prakriti which induces all actions. (14)

The Omnipresent Spirit of God is not involved in the sins and virtues of living beings. The real Knowledge is veiled by ignorance, and the beings are thus deluded. (15)

For those whose ignorance has been removed by Self-realization; for them the ultimate reality of Supreme Spirit is revealed like a shining Sun. (16)

With their sins burnt by the fire of Self-knowledge and with the intellect and soul ever merged with the Supreme Spirit, there is no further rebirth for them on this earth. (17)

An enlightened person, by perceiving the same spirit of God in all; looks with equal vision and is same-sighted on a humble learned priest; a cow; an elephant; a dog; and an outcaste member of the society, they being expressions of the same infinite Spirit of God. (18)

Transliteration of the above verse from Sanskrit to English is, "***Vidya***...***vinaya***...***sampanne***:—one who is endowed with learning and humility:—***brahmane***:—man of Self-knowledge:—***gavi***:—a cow:—***hastini***:—an elephant:—***shuni:***—a dog:—***cha***:—and:—***eva***:—even:—***shvapake***:—an outcaste:—***cha***:—

and:—***panditah***:—a sage or an enlightened person:—***sama... darshinah***:—with equal vision."

This verse says that the same Spirit of God exists in all living beings whether they are human beings, animals, birds, or underwater creatures in the sea. All life is sustained and is possible because of the presence of soul within living beings. Human beings are the highest in the ladder of evolution, as they have the capacity to think and an intellect to distinguish between right and wrong.

God created mankind in his own image. Animal kingdom and other living creatures are lower in hierarchy of evolution, and they function by the instinct for survival and propagation of their own species, and are subservient to human beings. The sameness of the Spirit of God is perceived in all by the enlightened saint; whether one is a Brahmin priest, an out-caste Sudra member of society, a cow, a dog or an elephant. One has to be compassionate towards all living beings and perceive the sameness of spirit in all.

Bible (Genesis 1:26) says, "Then God said, Let Us make man in Our image, according to Our likeness; and let them rule over the fish of the sea and over the birds of the sky and over the cattle and over all the earth, and over every creeping thing that creeps on the earth."

Sri Krishna was a cowherd boy in childhood, and he used to take his herd of cows to graze in the fields. Sri Krishna used to call his cows with lovely music on his flute and the cows will respond by gathering around him, and listen to his music with love and affection.

Overwhelmed by the affection, Sri Krishna would pat and caress the cows with his hands. Similarly the owner of a pet dog will lovingly feed and caress his or her dog. The mahout of an elephant will take care of his elephant and shower his affection and love. This is known as having an equal vision for all living beings with love and compassion for all. The Spirit of God resides in all creatures and life of everyone is precious.

Having an equal vision and being same-sighted on all implies that there is no ego inside you and that you are not superior to others.

We are simply a part of the same existence. The ego in human beings creates different categories and we think that we are someone special. The existence needs everything to make it whole.

True friendship does not distinguish between high and low status or between rich and poor. Therefore, even today after thousands of years, the childhood friendship between Sri Krishna and Sudama is remembered, as a symbol of true friendship and treating everyone as same irrespective of one's status in society.

Sudama was from a very poor family and he lost contact with Krishna over the years. Meanwhile Krishna became the King of Dwaraka city. Sudama was so poor that he did not have enough money to feed his children. His wife Kalyani reminded him of his childhood friendship with Krishna, and told him to meet his childhood friend.

Though initially reluctant to go to his friend for help, Sudama finally agrees to do so. He goes to meet Sri Krishna with the gift of just some rice tied in a piece of cloth as a present. He remembers that beaten rice is Krishna's favourite, and decides to give this as a gift to his friend.

Sri Krishna is overwhelmed with love and affection to meet his old childhood friend, with whom he used to play as little children. He treats Sudama royally and with great respect and honour. While in the midst of the splendour and opulence of Sri Krishna's palace, Sudama did not ask for any material favours. But Sri Krishna realizes the plight of his friend and knew what his friend needs.

On his return journey, when Sudama finally reaches his home, he is surprised to find a palatial mansion instead of the dilapidated hut where he previously lived, and he is greeted by his wife and children at the main door.

Those with equanimity of mind, conquer the illusions of the world in this very life. The Supreme Spirit is without any impurities and present all around; therefore they attain Oneness with the Supreme Spirit. (19)

One who is neither dejected nor elated with either unpleasant or pleasant happenings is a wise person of balanced intellect with no delusion; firmly established in Supreme Consciousness. (20)

With the mind detached from external outside objects, one realizes bliss within one's own Self-soul. Such a person merged in meditation of union with the Supreme Spirit enjoys constant bliss. (21)

O Kaunteya Arjuna! The pleasures and joys which arise from the contact of senses (eyes, ears, smell, taste and touch) with external sense-objects are a source of deep human suffering. These temporary joys have a beginning and an end, and are fleeting (short-lived). A wise person does not indulge in these fleeting sense pleasures. (22)

Transliteration of the above verse says:—***Ye...hi***:—which verily:—***samsparshajah***:—contact-born:—***bhoga***:—enjoyments:—***duhkha.. yonayah***:—source of human suffering:—***eva...te***:—only they:—***ady...anta...vantah***:—have beginning and an end:—*O* ***Kaunteya***:—O Arjuna!:—***na***:—not:—***teshu***:—in them:—***ramate***:—rejoice and indulge in these:—***budhah***:—the wise person.

The above verse very clearly enunciates the causes of human suffering and points out the way to overcome suffering and pain while living in this world of dualities. The shortest distance for the human mind to understand the deep truths of the Scriptures, is by means of a story.

A man living in the big city of Delhi, India suddenly became rich when he got a huge government contract for building overhead bridges. Earlier when he was poor, he used to get up early in the morning and make tea for himself and his family.

While making tea he used to read a few verses from the Holy book of Bhagavad Gita. He had imbibed this habit of reading Bhagavad Gita verses from his late father during his early childhood days, and he continued with the practice of reading the Holy Book.

His college going young daughter wanted to follow the example of her father in every way. The father purchased a new copy of Bhagavad Gita and gifted to his daughter so that she could read it in her own time as convenient. After a few days the daughter said, "Father, I try to read Bhagavad Gita like you do, but I do not understand most of it, and whatever little I do understand, I forget as soon as I close the book. So what good is the reading of the Book doing to me?"

The father smiled and said, "Girl, you are still very young, and one day when you will be in total despair and disappointment stares at you from everywhere, then you will understand the importance of reading a few verses of the Holy book, here and there."

Time passed on and the girl now had a lot of money to spend with her friends, as she could get money from her rich father on some pretext or the other. The girl got into a circle of boys and girls who used to go for late night disco dances and enjoy bodily pleasures in all the ways.

The wheel of destiny took a turn. She along with her friends met with a car accident and each blamed the other for the mishap, and there were heated arguments among them. She and her boy friend fell apart and broke-off the relationship. To add to her woes, she failed in the annual college examinations.

The girl was in total misery, and there was no ray of hope for her. She could not face her parents, and she thought of committing suicide to put an end to her suffering and agony. Before committing suicide, she thought, "Let me read a few verses from Bhagavad Gita as a grand finale to life." She came upon the above verse 5:22 of the 'Bhagavad Gita,' and she understood that the bodily sense pleasures which she was seeking from external sense-objects like disco dances and other sense-objects, was the cause of her downfall and suffering.

These were temporary pleasures, and in any case her boyfriend had ditched her and there was nothing more for her to look forward to in life. She thought that since she was now aware of the root cause of her problems, why not turn a new leaf in her life, and make amends for her earlier mistakes? She made a firm resolve to devote all her time to her studies and pass the college examinations next year with high percentage of marks, and prove to her parents that she is capable of excelling in academics.

Sure enough she passed her college annual examinations with distinction, which made her parents proud of her. From there on, she understood the significance of reading a few verses of 'Bhagavad Gita,' here and there.

One who is able to overcome the powerful urges of lust and anger in this very life, before casting off the body at death, is a happy person of unified consciousness. (23)

One whose happiness is within, whose joy is within; whose illumination of wisdom is within one's own Self-soul, such a yogi united with the universal Spirit attains liberation (Nirvana). (24)

With sins wiped away, doubts and dualities removed by the knowledge of Self-soul; the self controlled men and women, delighting in the welfare of all beings, attain the state of Brahman (Nirvana). (25)

Translation of the above verse from the original Sanskrit verse given by Sri Krishna is:—***labhante***:—obtains or attains:—***brahma...nirvana***:—Absolute freedom or Nirvana:—***rishaya***:—the Rishis:—***kshina...kalmashah***:—whose sins have been wiped away:—***chinnadvaidhah***:—whose doubts and dualities have been removed:—***yatatmanah***:—the self-controlled men and women:—***sarva...bhuta...hite***:—in the welfare of all beings:—***ratah***:—delighting.

The saints and sages down the ages realized that life is a struggle, and encompasses suffering from childhood to old age and then death. The struggle in life never ends, and it continues throughout life. Then what is the way out of this misery? The sages wanted to find a way out to attain Moksha or Nirvana and go beyond the cycle of birth and death. With that the suffering of life ends forever, and the soul can rest in eternal bliss of union with the cosmic Spirit.

Sri Krishna in Bhagavad Gita is talking to his disciple Arjuna, on how to come out of the worldly misery and attain everlasting bliss! Maintenance of body requires food and shelter, for which one has to constantly work and struggle. There is a hierarchy of needs from bodily survival to mental and emotional needs, and finally the spiritual needs of the soul.

The fulfilment of spiritual needs can take place only after the physical and mental needs have been met. It is not possible to meditate on an empty stomach and the need for food has to be met first. Once the bare minimum earthly needs of food and shelter have been met, then one can take the flight of weightless meditations to the heavens above.

It is possible only if there are no worldly desires to weigh the soul down. It is like an aircraft where the final all-up-weight of the aircraft has to be within the specified limits as per the aircraft design, otherwise the aircraft will not be able to take off even with the engines at full throttle. The weight of the worldly desires has to be dropped for the soul to take off to the heavens above. Going beyond the body and mind, one can soar to the freedom of the skies.

The path of renunciation means you have no weight of attachment to earthly material possessions; you are then ready to take off beyond the gravitational pull of the earth to the regions of spiritual sky. It means the pull of the opposite sex of beautiful women and youth, the luxury of houses and the latest models of the cars have no further attraction for you. Then you have broken the bondage of earthly attractions and the downward pull of gravity, and you get the required upward lift to soar into space of freedom and bliss.

The theory of aircraft aerodynamics states that when the upward lift of the aircraft provided by the wings and the forward speed by the engines, is more than the downward pull due to the weight of the aircraft, then the aircraft will lift off from the runway. The same phenomenon applies in the spiritual domain as well.

Bible says, "And he lifted up his eyes on his disciples, and said: Blessed are you who are poor, for yours is the kingdom of God. Blessed are you who are hungry now, for you shall be satisfied. Blessed are you who weep now, for you shall laugh."

The implied meaning of the 'poor' here is a renunciate who does not own anything and has broken all earthly shackles of bondage. In spiritual parlance, the soul of a poor renunciate is lighter as it does not have the weight of earthly possessions to tie him down. At the same time, the life of a renunciate is not a bed of roses, as having given up everything one does not know from where his next meal will come from.

Renunciation is the ultimate step for a person, who has seen life in all its dimensions, and now he cannot be lured with the enticements of wealth and young women, as he is finished with these forever. It is not a coincidence that the enlightened Masters like Sri Rama, Sri Krishna and Gautama Buddha, were all from royal families and later they renounced.

If one is mentally sound, then there is no need of alcohol, drugs and sex. A house holder fulfils one's emotional requirements by bringing up his children and later on when the children are grown up and are on their own; he takes up the life of retirement to fulfil his or her spiritual needs.

Self-soul realization is the ultimate peak to be conquered. It is an upward and arduous climb as one has to leave the valleys behind in the quest of the final goal. It is then a solitary journey of the alone to the peak of consciousness, to the lasting bliss of Self-soul. One has to then break all bondages and dependence on others, and it is a journey of the alone to the Spirit of God. You cannot take others along with you on this quest as everyone has to reap one's own karma.

The span of human life is very small, and the step of renunciation is a direct highway as one does not get entangled in the by lanes and diversions. Renunciation is not wearing ochre robes, but of the mind and heart. Real life is simple, natural and spontaneous. Worldly life is phony, plastic and people think they are smarter than others, but in ultimate reality it is all false. Worldly life is hypocrisy with artificial masks, and pretending to be what one is not.

Be in the world yet do not be of it. Live in the world but do not allow the world to live in you. Be in the crowd, yet be yourself. One has to be centred in Self-soul, and not get carried away by others. Sri Krishna talks about the wheel of life, which has many ups and downs on the periphery and circumference, but the centre and axle of the wheel always remains unaffected by the roughness of the road.

The bliss of Oneness with the Supreme Spirit is both here in this world and hereafter, for those who have shed lust and anger; and are self-controlled and Self-realized. (26)

Shutting out thoughts of all external worldly objects from the mind, directing the gaze in the space in-between the eyebrows, equalizing the outward and inward moving breaths in the nostrils–; one who has thus controlled one's senses, mind and intellect, having cast away desire, fear, and anger, intent on liberation (Moksha) as the final goal, such a sage is ever free and liberated. (27—28)

The above verse is an important and a key verse, as it is the basis of an easy and comfortable method of meditation practice. This method of meditation is used in Kriya Yoga practice for an accelerated progress on the spiritual path, and is shrouded in secrecy and not revealed to all.

Bible (Genesis) says, "Then the LORD formed man of dust from the ground, and breathed into his nostrils the breath of life; and man became a living being."

Knowing My Supreme Spirit as the receiver of all sacrifices (Yajnas) and austerities; as the Ruler of all the worlds, and as the friend of all beings; one attains abiding peace. (29)

CHAPTER 6

THE YOGA OF MEDITATION
DHYANA YOGA

Sri Krishna Said :

That person is a true renunciate and a yogi who performs one's dutiful and prescribed work, without expectations of any rewards for one's efforts. It is not possible to become a renunciate by merely giving up activities and the sacrificial fire. (1)

O Pandava (Arjuna)! What is called in the Scriptures as renunciation (Sanyasa), know that to be also Yoga (uniting one's Self-soul with the Supreme Spirit). Nobody becomes a renunciate yogi without first renouncing the desires of the heart. (2)

For a striving aspirant who is still in the process of seeking perfection on this path of yoga, performance of righteous selfless actions without any selfish motives is said to be the way. But for a yogi, who has already reached the final goal of union with the Supreme Spirit, total quietitude and termination of all worldly thoughts and activities, is said to be the way. (3)

One is said to have reached the ultimate heights on this 'Yoga path,' when there is no trace of any worldly thoughts; no attachment or bondage with any worldly objects or beings, nor any inclination to undertake any further work to fulfil desires. This meditative state of union with the Cosmic Spirit of the Universe is called as being firmly established in the 'yoga path.' (4)

Bondage is just the opposite of liberation. Freedom and liberation is what everyone seeks. What is 'bondage' then? When one becomes a slave of one's habits; and the body and the mind become the master; and the Self-soul becomes the slave, then it is bondage.

It is a very unnatural state of affairs when a servant becomes the master of the house and dictates terms to the owner of the house. Self-soul who is the owner of this body has been forgotten, and the physical body which is perishable is decorated with fine clothes to look beautiful. Bondage means you are carrying out actions out of obsession and out of unconsciousness. It is as if some outside force is acting against our own will, and we are a slave of our habits.

If our Self-soul is the master, then we are beautiful as God created us with special features of our body as they are; whether they look beautiful or ugly to others. There is no need to decorate our body as per the fashion and dictates of the world. We are not a slave of the world, but our own master. It is 'godlike' to be a master of our own inner kingdom. When we have complete control over the body, senses and the mind, then we are not a slave to thousands of desires.

If we are rooted in the objects outside, then our slavery is infinite because the objects are infinite. A desire is slavery. When we reach the core of our being, then there are no desires and others cannot manipulate us. When the Self-soul is the master, then the senses and mind are the slaves. The bondage is broken, and the mind cannot dictate terms to us.

Bible proverbs say, "Like a city whose walls have been broken, and is open to attack; is a man who lacks self control."

Let a person raise and elevate oneself by one's own mind and intellect; let one not lower or debase oneself. For one is one's own best friend, as well as one's own worst enemy. (5)

One who cannot control one's mind lives with the enemy within himself, and such a person cannot achieve anything worthwhile in life. Bhaja Govindam text says, "Do not waste your time and effort in the outside world to make friends or fight against your enemy, friend, son or relatives. See the Self-soul everywhere and lift the sense of difference and plurality, born out of ignorance."

When one has conquered one's lower self (comprising of body-senses and mind) by one's higher Self-soul, then one's own self becomes like one's friend. But for the one who is a slave of one's senses and mind, one's own self becomes like an enemy. (6)

It means we have to accept the responsibility of our actions, and the consequent results of our actions. Human beings have a tendency to always throw the blame on others if something bad or undesirable happens to them. In this way a person will go on committing the same mistakes again and again, and he or she will never change for the better. If someone degrades himself or herself due to lust, anger, greed and attachment, then one should not blame others for one's actions.

By falling into the temptations and snares of the world, one becomes one's own enemy. Even if someone has committed a mistake; he should lift himself by his own efforts to correct that mistake and listen to his own inner voice. Human beings have a free will to act, and whatever they do is their own decision, and they should not allow others to impose their will on them.

Righteousness means you take the responsibility for the pattern of life you have chosen, as it is your choice. Society is man-made, and its values are different in different cultures, different places and in different countries. We have no obligation to please others, but we have an obligation to our own Self-soul to follow the righteous path, and live a harmonious life, without harming others.

The above verse says that when one who has conquered one's lower self of body, senses and mind, then one's own Self-soul becomes one's own friend. One is not then dependent upon the opinion of others. One can be blissful in a miserable world. Nobody is hindering you except your own self, and the false values you assign to the outer world. We create our own obstacles and later we waste our life to remove these obstacles.

If we change our own self, we have started changing the world. Do not bother about what the other people in the society will think of you, as there are many trouble makers in the society who will want to drag you down to their level of thinking. The world will continue as before, and one has to uplift one's own mind and thinking, and not be a slave of other people's opinions.

The composure of a self-controlled and serene-minded person always remains undisturbed and unaffected while moving among the pairs of opposites, such as heat and cold; happiness and suffering; honour and insult. (7)

Translation of this verse reads as:—***jitatmanah***:—self-controlled:—***prashantasya***:—serene-minded:—***paramatma***:—the Supreme Self:—***samahitah***:—undisturbed and balanced:—***shitoshana...sukh***...***duhkheshu***:—in cold and heat, and happiness and suffering:—***manapamanayah***:—in honour and insult.

The above verse says that one should treat as same, the pairs of opposites like heat and cold, suffering and joy, honour and dishonour. Human beings get inflated when someone praises him or her and gets angry when someone insults them. It is the normal response of a human being. How to respond to honour and insults in this world? Read the story below.

Once a disciple asked his learned Master, in what way he should follow the teaching of Bhagavad Gita. The spiritual Master replied, "Go to the cremation Ghat and insult the dead." That was a weird command from the Master but the disciple had to carry out the instructions of his Master, as he knew there must be some hidden teaching in that.

The disciple went to the cremation Ghat and found a dead body, which was being prepared for cremation. Then he insulted and offended the dead body by saying, "You worthless man. You wasted your entire life and it was of no consequence. In your lifetime you never remembered and meditated on the eternal Spirit of God. What is the use of telling you now, since you are dead? Life gave you so many opportunities to lead a life of selfless service and do virtuous acts, but you were always immersed in sensual pleasures with different women. None of those ladies are now present here with your dead body to mourn your death." In this way he insulted the dead body and came back.

When he returned, his spiritual Master asked him, "So what did the dead person say?"–The disciple was surprised by this question and answered, "Respected Sir, the dead person did not give any reply."—The spiritual master said, "Good! Now you go back to the cremation Ghat again and praise a dead body!"

The disciple went back to the cremation ground and this time he found the dead body of a woman, who was being prepared for cremation and he praised her by saying, "Oh! You virtuous woman, you did so many good acts of charity, sacrifices and reading the Holy Scriptures and keeping the company of holy people in your lifetime. It is difficult to count so many of your good deeds. In your lifetime you were a woman of self-controlled senses and mind, and you never digressed from the virtuous path, even when you faced the wrath of other people."—After that he returned back to report to his spiritual teacher.

The Master asked, "And! What did the dead body say this time?"—The disciple said, "Sir, they are dead bodies, and they do not respond to praises and insults."

The Master then said, "Just as the dead bodies did not answer your praises and insults, similarly when you hear praises or insults from other people, you should not become inflated with vanity, nor should you feel insulted when you are abused. Thus, you will be content in both happiness and sorrow, while you keep your mind fixed on the Lord. In this way you can best follow the teachings of Bhagavad Gita."

Firmly rooted in knowledge and Self-realization, ever content within oneself, master of body-senses and remaining unmoved in the ever changing circumstances of life. United with the Cosmic consciousness; one who views a lump of clay earth, a stone and gold, as one and the same, and of equal value; is called a 'Self-realized yogi.' (8)

That person stands supreme, who treats everybody on an equal basis and with the same vision, whether one is a well-wisher, friend, indifferent, enemy, neutral, jealous, a relative, a saint or a sinner. (9)

Life is continuously changing, as change is the law of life. Life is a play of light and shade. Now there is light here and shade there; the next moment this light and shade will be somewhere else. In life from morning to evening, you will find that everything is constantly changing; morning turns into evening, day into night and light into shade. The flowers that bloom now will wither away with time.

He is wise who is neither anyone's friend nor enemy. One who is aware that a friend can turn into an enemy and an enemy into a friend, as it all depends on the circumstances. But, we as human beings take things for granted. We are friends with some, and enemies with others. And when the circumstances change, we find ourselves in a great difficulty. Then we try to carry on with our old relationships and suffer. The world is a game of strange bed fellows.

Friendship and enmity is not something permanent or static; they are fluid. From a higher standpoint if a person has no axe to grind and has no selfish motives for personal favours, then why worry if a person is a friend, enemy, arbiter, relative, a saint or a sinner. All these factors come into consideration only if one has to gain some material wealth, power, or some influential position or favours from others. The above verse says that one, who is same to all, stands supreme.

Free from the desire for material possessions; without any expectations from others; with body and mind self-controlled; the aspiring yogi should meditate alone in a secluded place (away from all distractions); fully absorbed in meditation with one's Self- soul merged in the Supreme Spirit. (10)

The mind is tethered to our material possessions and to our near and dear ones. The above verse says that one has to free oneself from all desires to attain fixity of mind during the meditation practice.

Meditation is a journey within, and others will be a source of hindrance on this inner journey. When you are with others, they start encroaching on your space and your freedom. The others impose conditions on you and they will start demanding attention from you.

On the spiritual path, freedom and being alone is of immense value. Being alone in spiritual parlance does not mean lonely. Loneliness is different from being alone. Loneliness means you are missing the others, wife, husband, children, friends, and the attractions of the world. Being alone with yourself means you are happy with your own being. A happy person wants to be left alone to savour his happiness. It is in sadness and grief, that you need the company and sympathy of others.

In the worldly affairs, the majority of the humanity has settled for mutual love of convenience. Man has reduced woman into a slave to meet his own requirements, and woman likewise has reduced the man into a slave for her needs. Both hate the slavery, and there is a constant friction and fights due to encroachment on each other's privacy. The real fight is for freedom, and nobody wants others to meddle in his or her affairs.

If someone goes on living with the memory of good old times of the past, then it is a wrong way of living. Past is useful to the extent that one need not repeat the mistakes of earlier days. The thought of having a good time in the future is also futile and a figment of imagination, as the future has not yet arrived. The past is no more and the future is yet to arrive. Between these two one should not waste the present moment of time, which is the real moment of time available for useful work.

One should sit for meditation in a clean place, on a seat neither too high nor too low, with grass, deer skin and a cloth, spread one over the other. (11)

Sri Krishna gave this Scripture of Gita five thousand years ago, and people at that time used to meditate while sitting under a tree or in a forest; where insects or wild animals could encroach. Hence these instructions for a suitable meditation seat were stated for comfort in those circumstances.

In the modern word while one is meditating in one's room, there is no such fear of wild animals or insects encroaching. One can have any comfortable seat which is stable and firm, whether on a blanket or a rubber mat on the ground, but not a moving or a rocking chair. The seat should be firm and stable for the mind to be stable.

One should see one's convenience in this regard, and not worry too much about the formalities and requirements of an ideal seat. What finally matters is how good the meditation practice is. If someone is unwell, one can even meditate while sitting in a chair with back straight.

Sitting on this seat, making the mind one-pointed, completely stilling the senses, mind and all thoughts; one should engage in 'Yoga meditation' for self-purification. (12)

Firmly holding the body, head and neck erect and motionless, let one gaze at the front of one's nose with unseeing eyes, not allowing the eyes to wander around in other directions. (13)

With the mind under one's control, calm and fearless, following celibacy (free from all sexual defilements). One should thus meditate, fully absorbed on My Super-consciousness, considering this as the highest goal in life. (14)

Fearlessness is an essential requirement on the spiritual path, as well as in all undertakings of life. Fear does not allow you to perform the task to your fullest potential and live fully. It means you make a half-hearted attempt in your task. Fear will keep your mind divided, and will not allow full intensity of your participation in the chosen work.

With fear you will soon be exhausted and you will lose the battle of life. It is said that fortune favours the bold, because if you had given that last bit of extra push to your work, you would have won. It is the last bit of final push without fear that finally matters and decides the excellence in your work. The verse says that one should engage in meditation with a calm mind, which is under control and without any fear or worry.

Be sure you are doing the right thing, and do it wholeheartedly without any fear. If someone is doing something which is illegal, for example robbing, stealing or impersonating, then there is always fear in one's heart that he will be caught. A thief runs in fear although nobody is chasing him. But when you are sure that you are doing the right thing, then there should be no question of any fear or anxiety.

Thus always united with My Spirit (Krishna-consciousness), the Yogi living a disciplined and an austere life; attains abiding peace, culminating in 'Nirvana,' and goes to My supreme abode. (15)

"Yunjan...evam...sada...atmanam...yogi: —the yogi thus always united with the Spirit of Krishna-consciousness... ***niyata...manasah...shantim...nirvana...paramam... matsamstham...adhigacchati***: —living a disciplined life of self-control, attains abiding peace culminating in Nirvana and goes to My supreme abode."

Nirvana or liberation is the ultimate goal, when one has gone beyond all desires for material wealth, sense gratifications and lust etc. Then there is nothing more to be gained in this world. Nirvana means no more birth and death. In the modern world, the word 'Nirvana' is merely used as a buzzword, without knowing its true meaning.

Wife tells her husband that I want Nirvana, and daughter tells her father, "Wow! Nirvana is great."—Nirvana is not a commodity which can be purchased in a shopping Mall. Nirvana is an ultimate happening, as a result of many life-times of spiritual discipline and meditation practice on the 'yoga path.'

A hermit was meditating by a river, when a young man came to him, "Master, I want to become your disciple." said the man. The hermit asked, "Why?"

The young man said, "Because I want to get Nirvana." The Master jumped up, grabbed him by the scruff of his neck, dragged him into the river, and plunged his head under the water. After holding him there for a minute, while he was kicking and struggling to free himself, the master finally pulled him out of the water.

The young man coughed up water and gasped for breath. When the man had finally regained his composure and became normal, the master said, "Tell me, what you wanted the most, when you were under water." The man answered, "Air, for my survival!"—

The Master said, "Very well! Go home, and come back to me, when you want 'Nirvana' as much as you wanted the breath of fresh air for survival."

O Arjuna! This yoga of union with the Divine Spirit is neither for the person who eats too much or too little; nor for the person who sleeps too much or too little. (16)

One has to follow the middle path; which does not lean to either of the extremes. Living a disciplined life of self-control has immense virtue in itself. Do not move from one extreme to another like a pendulum. The above verse says that one should be controlled in eating and not fast too much; nor sleep too much or be awake too much; moderation in recreation and allotted work. One has to be very alert because small things can lead one away from the desired path and direction. Very small and harmless desires can lead one astray.

If you eat too much, you will feel heavy and lethargic as the entire energy is diverted towards the digestion of food. If you eat too little or fast too much, then you will have no energy to move into meditation. If you sleep too little or oversleep then you will not be alert in your work.

Moving from one extreme to the other is like getting into a vicious circle and the pendulum will go on oscillating. Just the 'golden mean' like a finely tuned guitar is necessary for a meaningful life. Very tight guitar strings will break, and loose strings will give no music. In meditation one has to go beyond the body and mind to reach the inner portals of Self-soul. It requires alertness and just the 'golden mean' of a disciplined life and not the extremes.

When a person is hungry and starved then he or she needs food and not meditation. When a person is sick, he needs medicine and rest. Only a healthy person can become aware of the higher possibilities of life which come with meditation. Meditation is the ultimate luxury, when all other basic needs have been met.

One has to be comfortable and relaxed to go beyond the realm of body and mind. If one has a worried and a tense mind, then all the thoughts will be tethered to that. If one has bodily pain then all the attention will be diverted to that part of the body, and one will not be able to meditate.

The practice of this 'yoga path' ends all suffering for a person, who is regulated in food and recreation; skilful in performing actions and who does not over-exert in work, and is regulated in one's sleep and wakefulness. (17)

One is said to be firmly established in this 'Yoga path,' when one's mind is under firm control and one is not touched by any worldly desires, and one's mind rests in the Cosmic Spirit of God alone. (18)

As the flame of a candle placed in a windless place does not flicker, similarly the thoughts of a yogi absorbed in meditation on the Divine Spirit do not flicker. (19)

The mind thus attains stillness of total quietitude by regular practice of this yoga meditation, and beholding the Self-soul by the self, one is content in one's own self. (20)

Wherein one experiences the bliss of the Supreme Spirit, which is beyond the grasp of the human senses but is perceived by the purified intellect; and being established in this Self-realization, one never moves away from the Absolute Reality of God. (21)

Having experienced this bliss, one is convinced that there is no greater gain than this, and being established in this, one is not perturbed by even the heaviest of sorrows and afflictions. (22)

Let this spiritual path, where all suffering comes to an end; be known by the name of 'Yoga.' This spiritual path needs to be practised with a firm determination and a single-pointed mind. (23)

One should give up all desires arising from thoughts of the world by controlling the mind and the whole group of senses from all sides. (24)

With regular practice, one should gradually attain stillness of mind little by little. With steady intellectual wisdom and mind fixed on God-consciousness, let him not think of anything else. (25)

Due to whatever causes the restless and unsteady mind wanders away in meditation, let one pull back the mind from these objects, and repeatedly bring it back under one's control. (26)

Abiding bliss comes to that yogi whose mind has become serene; whose passions have been exhausted, and who has gone beyond all temptations; and who has become free from the impurities of sins, and has attained Oneness with the infinite Spirit of Brahman (God). (27)

There is a Biblical saying, "Everything is permissible; but not everything is beneficial."—Bible (Matthew) says, "Unless you change and become innocent 'like' children, you shall not enter the kingdom of heaven."– The implied inference here is that one has to once again regain the lost 'innocence' of a child, which was taken away due to the manipulations and cleverness in the world.

A small baby has no ego of wealth, name, fame, beauty and awareness of sexual feelings as these are not yet developed. As the child grows up, the parents and the society of the people around the child corrupt, and bring the notions of lies, cleverness and the importance of money and material things. The innocence of a child is thus lost during the process of growing up. This is the story of Gautama Buddha, the enlightened sage.

Gautama Buddha upon seeing an old man with backbone bent with age and dragging his feet, realized that the world is full of suffering and disease; and he wanted to find a way out of the agony of old age, sickness and death.

He renounced all the comforts of his palace life, his loving wife Yashodhara and son Rahula. After many years of severe penance and a celibate life of renunciation, Buddha finally became enlightened and he understood that the purpose of human life is to attain enlightenment, and go back to the eternal Spirit from where the mankind has emerged.

After enlightenment he visited his home to meet his wife and son, and later they also joined his ascetic community and became his disciples. Buddha had seen the joys and sorrows of both the marital life, as well as the bliss of ascetic life. He regained his lost innocence to become pure and innocent like a child, and thus enter the Kingdom of heaven.

Buddha's practice of total abstinence from sex was a natural outcome of his deep spiritual practice. Patanjali's yoga sutra says, "When a yogi is firmly established in 'Brahmacharya' or total abstinence from sex; then vigour is gained."

Bhagavad Gita says that a yogi attains purity of body, mind and intellect, by living a life of celibacy or Brahmacharya. Long-term celibacy is followed by monks and nuns for spiritual gains. The householders and others have the choice to voluntarily follow short-term or long-term celibacy to rejuvenate the body, mind and soul. It should be a natural outcome of one's free will for physical and spiritual benefits.

Adi Shankaracharya in Bhaja Govindam text says, "To enjoy sensual pleasures, one readily indulges in sexual and carnal acts; but alas later on come bodily diseases. Although in this mortal world, death is the ultimate outcome, yet one does not leave his or her lustful conduct."

Thus constantly uniting the Self-soul with the Cosmic Soul; the yogi wipes away all the sins, and easily enjoys the bliss of contact with Super-consciousness (Brahman). (28)

A person of unified Consciousness perceives the same Cosmic Spirit abiding in all beings as in one's own Self-soul. (29)

Once a lady asked a renunciate monk, "Most of the people I have met in life are selfish and unhappy in life. Normally people are not as cheerful and helpful as you are. What is the secret of your happiness?"

The monk smiled and replied, "When you make peace with yourself, you are at peace with the rest of the world. If you can recognize the Self-soul in yourself, then you can recognize the same soul in everyone. Thus one is kind and well disposed to everyone. If your thoughts are under your control, then you become strong and firm."

One who perceives My Universal Spirit dwelling and sustaining all, (the entire Creation of beings); such a person never loses sight of Me (My God-consciousness), nor do I ever get separated from him or her. (30)

A unified yogi who worships Me as one Universal Spirit abiding in all beings, while always living in the present moment of time, follows My path in every way, whatever may be his mode of living. (31)

An enlightened man is not governed by the rules of the society and he is free to live his life as per the calling of his inner voice. It is not necessary for him to mingle with the crowds if he prefers seclusion and wants to be just by himself. In meditation and in life one has to live in the present moment of time. When you live in the past, you live in a grave because you are not allowing the fresh air to reach you. It is as if you are living with dried up petals of old flowers and you are afraid of new buds and new flowers to blossom.

It is the situation of millions and majority of the people who live with memories of good old days; as it seems comfortable and familiar and it does not pose a danger to life. These people cling to dried up artificial flowers with memories and nostalgia of good old days; of the times when they were young. Time and tide waits for none and life goes past, whatever may be one's mode of living.

The present makes one capable of receiving the future with courage. The present moment is what a man has in his hands. Why worry to store-up possessions and wealth for the future, and who knows how your inheritance will be utilized later, and who will enjoy your wealth?

A passage from Bible says, "Take care, and be on your guard against all covetousness, for one's life does not consist in the abundance of his possessions." And Jesus Christ told them a parable saying, "The land of a rich man produced plentifully, and he thought, 'What shall I do now, for I have nowhere to store my crops?' And he said, 'I will do this: I will tear down my barns and build larger ones, and there I will store all my grains and my goods. And I will say to my soul, Soul, you have ample goods laid up for many years; relax, eat, drink and be merry.' But God said unto him, you fool, this night your soul shall be required of thee: then whose shall those things be, which thou hast provided?–So is he that lays up treasure for himself, and is not rich toward God."

O Arjuna! That yogi is deemed as the highest, who considers the joy and sorrow of everyone, by the same standard as he applies to himself. (32)

Bible (Job) says of God, "Who shows no partiality to princes or regards the rich above the poor, for they all are the work of His hands?"

All living beings seek happiness and joy in life. How can a person be happy if he seeks happiness only for himself or herself alone, while the surrounding world is full of suffering? Human beings are tied up with each other by the same breath and the same Spirit of God. No man is an island unto himself. One can be happy only if one wishes the welfare and happiness of all living beings in the world.

The Sanskrit mantra which is chanted for the welfare of all beings is, ***"Om Sarve Bhavantu Sukhinah; Sarve Santu Niramayaah; Sarve Bhadranni Pashyantu; Maa Kashchid-Duhkha-Bhaag-Bhavet.—Om! Shanti! Shanti! Shanti!"—*** Translated into English it means, ***"May we all be happy; May we all be free from diseases; May we all see what is auspicious; May none suffer."***

Bible says, "Judge not, so that you are not judged. For with the judgment you pronounce you will be judged, and with the measure you use, it will be measured back to you. Why do you see the speck that is in your brother's eye, but do not notice the log that in your own eye? Or how can you say to your brother, 'Let me take the speck out of your eye,' when there is a log in your own eye? You hypocrite, first take the log out of your own eye, and then you will see clearly, to take the speck out of your brother's eye."

Arjuna said :

O Madhusudana Sri Krishna! Due to inherent restless nature of mind, I am not able to understand how constant equanimity of mind can be maintained on this 'yoga path,' as spoken by you. (33)

O Sri Krishna! The mind verily is restless, turbulent, powerful and obstinate. I consider the mind as difficult to control as the mighty wind. (34)

Sri Krishna said:

O mighty-armed Arjuna! Undoubtedly the mind is very hard to control, due to its inherent restless nature. But

certainly, the mind can be brought under control by constant practice and non-attachment (dispassion). (35)

The above verse says that by constant practice (Abhyasa); the mastery over mind can be attained gradually over a period of time. It means self-training in which one is conscious of one's thoughts, action and speech. There are no instant results, like making an instant coffee or tea.

It is a gradual upward climb to the top of the mountain through perseverance and patience. Habits which control human behaviour are gradually formed over a period of years from the formative years in childhood and in youth. In a similar manner, mind control and practice of meditation have to done regularly over a period of time with perseverance and regularity.

All achievements take place by constant and regular practice over a period of time, be it in the field of medicine, engineering, aeronautics, or any other discipline, and the same logic applies to spirituality as well. Knowing is mere information, while practising gives direct experience. Self-realization is direct experiencing of spiritual knowledge, through the eight fold ***'Yoga path**.'*

By ***'Abhyasa'*** or constant practice, one becomes firmly rooted in one's being and capable of withstanding the turmoil and challenges of the world. When the tree has become firmly rooted, then let the winds come, and let the rains lash out; the tree is capable of withstanding all turbulence. But when a tree is a small and a tender sapling like a child then you have to provide fencing around it to protect it, nourish it and water the sapling. If a sapling is not protected, then even a stray cattle or a dog can easily destroy it.

The mind can be similarly controlled with the practice of ***'Vairagya'*** or detachment from the external objects of distraction. One must be detached and independent and free from vain occupations of the world during the time of Yoga practice. The thoughts of your wife, children and material possessions, should not exert a pull over you, and distract you away from your one-pointed meditation practice. All entanglements must be put aside.

Mind is restless and turbulent by nature and will find many excuses to postpone the spiritual practice. The above verse says that constant practice on a regular schedule is the method to tame and control the mind. Rome was not built in a day.

A holy man was travelling from one town to another town, with a few of his followers. During the mid-day sun, they happened to pass by the side of a village pond. They stopped there under a tree, and the holy man, told one of his disciples, "I am thirsty, and get me some water from that pond, over there."

The disciple went to the lake and noticed that right at that moment, a bullock cart had crossed the shallow waters of the pond. As a result, the water had become very muddy and dirty. The disciple thought, "How can I give this muddy water to the holy man to drink!" So he came back and told the holy man, "The water in the pond is very muddy right now. I do not think it is fit for drinking at this moment." After about half an hour, the holy man again asked the same disciple to go back to the pond and get some water.

This time he found that a few village ladies were washing clothes in the pond, and the water was still dirty and he came back, and accordingly informed the holy man. After one hour, the disciple again went back to the pond. This time he found that the pond water was absolutely clean and pure from all impurities. The mud had settled down, and the water was fit for drinking. He collected some water in a pot, and brought it to the holy man.

The holy man looked at the water, and told the disciple, "See, after the mud in the water had settled down on its own, the water became free from the impurities, and has become fit for drinking. Similarly, our mind is also like that! When it is disturbed, give it time to settle down, and then engage in the practice of meditation. The key to control and calm the mind is regular practice of meditation, and non-attachment with the worldly impurities."

It is indeed difficult to achieve the goal of this 'Yoga path' by a person whose mind is not under control. But success

can be obtained by a person with self-control, who makes earnest efforts in the right direction. (36)

Arjuna said :

O Sri Krishna! What is the end results of efforts by an embodied soul, who though possessed with faith and devotion, has not been able to subdue his passions due to lack of self-control. What happens if he diverts from this Yoga path of meditation, and fails to achieve the final goal of Self-realization? (37)

O Sri Krishna! Having strayed away from the path of Self-realization due to delusion, does one not forego the enjoyments of this world as well as of the hereafter (the regions of the next world), like a scattered cloud which disperses, without rain ? (38)

Arjuna here asks his spiritual mentor Sri Krishna a very valid question. A cloud that had the possibility to shower rains dispersed, as it was carried away by the strong winds. The cloud was thus deprived of its potential to deliver rains for the bounty of crops and food grains. Similarly what happens to a person who strays away from the path of 'Yoga meditation' due to the turbulent winds of lusts and desires, and does not achieve his goal of Self-realization?

It is a pitiable situation as the person gave up all enjoyments and material comforts of this world; and he still fell short of the final goal of Self-realization. Was it that he was neither on this side nor that side? He got sucked by the temporary joys of this world and lost his spiritual gains. Have his massive efforts and deprivation of the joys of this world come to a naught or zero? Sri Krishna here replies to Arjuna to clear his doubts.

O Sri Krishna! You should clear this doubt of mine, for there is none other than Yourself, who can remove this doubt of mine. (39)

Sri Krishna said :

O Partha Arjuna! The efforts put in by an earnest seeker on this path of Self-realization are never lost either in this world or in the next. The performer of righteous deeds who makes earnest efforts on this 'Yoga path' never comes to any harm, and there is never any loss of effort for him or her. (40)

Failing to achieve the final goal of enlightenment, due to deviation from this 'Yoga path' of meditation and spiritual practices; one accumulates the meritorious rewards of the virtuous karma; and dwells in the higher realms of heaven, for a countless number of years. Thereafter, one again takes rebirth in a pious and prosperous family. It is very hard to obtain such a rebirth, in the family of the wise and virtuous. (41–42)

O Arjuna! Once again in the new birth, one regains the hidden inherited virtues of the previous life. And he or she again strives harder than ever before, to achieve perfection on this 'Yoga path' with renewed efforts. (43)

By the momentum of one's previous attainments, one is carried forward in spite of oneself on this path of Self-realization. Even a new aspiring seeker, who makes earnest and just preliminary efforts on this yoga path, is far superior to a person, who merely performs Vedic ritualistic practices. (44)

The striving yogi, who makes consistent efforts with perseverance, gets gradually purified from all sins; and being perfected through many births, he finally attains oneness with the All- pervading Spirit of God (Nirvana).

(45)

The Yogi thus united in oneness with the Divine Spirit is superior to the ascetics (who perform severe penances); is superior to Jnana yogis (men of knowledge); and even

superior to the Karma yogis (performers of selfless-actions). Therefore O Arjuna! You become a Yogi. (46)

And among all the Yogis, one who with utmost faith worships Me by uniting his innermost Self-soul with My universal Spirit of God (Krishna-consciousness); is considered as the highest among all Yogis. This is My firm conviction. (47)

CHAPTER 7

THE YOGA OF KNOWLEDGE AND SELF-REALIZATION JNANA VIJNANA YOGA

Sri Krishna said :

O Partha Arjuna! Listen to me with full faith and total attention. By taking refuge in My Spirit and practising this 'Yoga path,' you will undoubtedly understand My teaching in full. (1)

Sri Krishna tells Arjuna to listen attentively to the spiritual teachings in full faith and with an open mind to absorb the knowledge. If a person's mind is full of preconceived notions and dogmas, then he is not ready to listen attentively and assimilate new teachings.

A child goes to school to learn new things, and the mind of a child has space to grow and absorb new ideas. As one starts growing up and aging, one's mind and intellect gets fixed with preconceived ideas, and then it becomes increasingly difficult to learn new topics and accept fresh concepts. If a glass of water is already full, and you still keep on pouring water in the full glass, then water will keep on spilling out. It is the same with spiritual knowledge if one is not ready to listen attentively with full faith.

An Indian Swami and his American disciple were walking through Connaught Place in Delhi to go to the Metro Station Terminal. The streets were filled with people. Cars were honking their horns, taxi cabs were squealing around corners, sirens were wailing and the sound of the road was almost deafening. Suddenly, the Indian Swami said, "I hear the lovely sound of birds chirping."

The American man was surprised and said, "What? You must be crazy. You could not possibly hear birds chirping in all this noise!"– The Indian Swami said, "No, I am sure of it. I hear lovely sound of birds chirping."–The American disciple insisted, "That is crazy. But how do you say that."

The Indian Swami again listened carefully for a moment, and then walked to a big cement planter by the side of pavement, filled with shrubs. He looked under the branches and sure enough, he found the birds chirping. His friend was utterly amazed.

The American said, "That is incredible. You must have super human ears!"–The Indian Swami replied, "No! My ears are no different from yours. It all depends on what you are listening to."–"But that cannot be!" said the American, "I could never hear the sound of birds chirping in this noise."

"Yes, that is true," said the Indian Swami, "It all depends on what is really important to you. Here, let me show you."

He reached into his pocket, took out a few coins, and discreetly dropped them on the pavement. Then, with the noise of the crowded street still blaring in their ears, they noticed that every head of the crowd turned and looked to see if the money on the pavement had fallen from their pockets.

"See what I mean?" said the Indian Swami, "It all depends on what is important to you and what you want to listen to."

I shall declare to you the complete knowledge along with Self-realization; after knowing which nothing more remains to be known. (2)

Among thousands of human beings, scarcely one strives for Self-realization and perfection; and of those who strive hard and finally succeed; scarcely one realizes My Supreme Spirit of God in true essence. (3)

The eightfold division of My Primordial Prakriti is Earth, Water, Fire, Air, Space, mind, intellect and egoism. (4)

O mighty-armed Arjuna! This constitutes My lower Prakriti, but distinct from this is My higher Prakriti in the

form of soul-consciousness, which sustains and upholds the entire world. (5)

Know that the entire creation takes place by the union of this twofold Prakriti. The beginning, sustenance and ending of the entire Universe takes place due to My infinite Universal Spirit. (6)

O Dhananjaya Arjuna! There is nothing whatsoever higher than My Cosmic Spirit. The entire creation is held together by My Cosmic consciousness like a garland of different gems threaded together on a string. (7)

O Son of Kunti Arjuna! My all-pervading Spirit is the sapidity in water; the radiance of the Sun and the Moon. I am the sacred syllable AUM in all the Vedas; the sound in ether (space), and the virility in men. (8)

The splendour of My glory is the sweet fragrance of earth; the heat in fire; the life-force prana in all living beings; and the penance in ascetics. (9)

O Partha Arjuna! Know that My all-pervading Consciousness is the reproductive seed in all creatures; the intelligence of the wise and the splendour of the glorious. (10)

O Best of Bharata Arjuna! Understand that My consciousness is the vigour and strength of the strong; the sexual desire in all living beings for propagation of the race, but not contrary to the tenets of Dharma. (11)

Different qualities of nature; Sattva (purity and goodness), Rajas (passionate activity), Tamas (slothful inertia) evolve and arise from My manifestation of Prakriti consciousness; yet I am not in them, they are in Me. (12)

The world deluded by these threefold disposition of Prakriti, does not know My all-pervading and imperishable

consciousness, which is beyond these attributes of Prakriti. (13)

Indeed, My Divine illusion or Maya, made up of three Gunas of Prakriti, is very difficult to cross-over; but those who take refuge in My Divine Spirit, they go beyond the bondage of Maya. (14)

Translation of the above verse is, "***Daivi***: —divine: —***hi***: —verily:— ***esha***:—this:—***gunamayi***:—made up of three Gunas:—***Mam***.. ***maya***...***duratyaya***:—My Maya is very difficult to cross-over:— ***Mam***:—in Me:—***eva***:—only:—***ye***:—those:—***prapadyante***:—take refuge:—***Maya***:—illusion:—***etam***:—this:—***taranti***:—cross-over:— ***te***:—they."—

The ***Maya*** made up of the three Gunas of Prakriti veils the true knowledge; and a person thus remains entangled in the illusions of this world, considering them as real.

What is '***Maya***'? The Sanskrit word '***Maya***' means that which does not exist perennially in real terms. That which appears to be real, but in fact is an illusion, a dream. When a person looks at the sea from a distance, the sea and the sky appears to meet in the distant horizon, but this is just an illusion. Actually there is no meeting point between the sea and the sky. *Maya* is a subtle force that creates an illusion that the phenomenal world that we see is real. It is said to be neither true nor untrue.

The Universal Spirit (Brahman) is the only truth for eternity, ***Maya*** or illusion is a relative phenomenon which is constantly changing with time. The Spirit of God is the only eternal Reality, rest all will come and go. This illusion of *Maya* is extremely difficult to cross over in this world, except by surrender to the Divine Spirit of God. These illusions are so strong that one's entire life goes past and a person does not even come to know the real purpose of one's life.

Adi Shankaracharya says, "During childhood, one is attached to toys and play; during youth to the lusts of the body; in old age to anxieties; but alas no one is attached to the Spirit of God. —Day and night, evening and morning, winter and spring keep coming and going again and again; time goes past and span of life ebbs away, even then one does not leave multitude of hopes and desires. O man and woman! Seek the eternal Spirit of God! Govinda Krishna!"

The moment a person attains merger with the Spirit of God, the outside world loses its attraction, as everything is just an illusion. Your friends and relatives of today may become your enemies tomorrow; one can lose all wealth and become poor, one who is healthy can become sick, the joys of life can turn into sorrow.

Maya and the world is constantly changing and is illusory. Sri Krishna here is talking from the highest standpoint of a perfect yogi. Those who take refuge in the Spirit of Krishna as Cosmic consciousness, cross over the turmoil and the illusions of this world. How do you explain '*Maya*' which is illusory, by means of a story?

Few children were playing on the sand on the sea side beach. They made separate houses on the sand for themselves on the sand, each complete with master bedroom to sleep with their spouses, drawing-dining, kitchen and other bed-rooms for their kids, who will be born later when they will get married. Each child defended his or her own sand house, saying this is mine and that is yours.

Each child will not allow the other children to interfere with what he or she was making on the sand. Every child took pride in his or her house, saying that my house is better than yours. While building their houses on the sand, they were enviously glancing at other houses, so as to make their house bigger than others. They developed attachment and pride with their own sand house, and will not allow the other children to touch their house.

Then suddenly one child kicked over someone else's sand house and completely destroyed it. The girl who was the owner of this sand house flew into a rage. This girl pulled the other boy's hair and struck a blow on his face with her fists and shouted, "How dare you destroy my house? Come along all children and help me punish this rascal of a boy who has demolished my house! I will give him the punishment he will never forget!"

Other children also joined the fight and helped this girl to kick the naughty boy. After beating the small boy–they all went back to their respective sand houses, each saying, "This house is mine, and no one dare touch my house. Keep away! My house is the best."

Then evening shadows slowly crept over the sand houses. It was getting dark, and the children thought that their mother and father will get worried, if they do not go back home at nightfall. As the shadows lengthened, no one cared about their sand houses any more.

One child stomped on his sand house with his feet, and another pulled down her sand house with her hands. The high tide was approaching, and all the sand houses were finally swept away by the sea water. The children turned away, and said good bye to 'each other,' and went to their parent's house.

This is what is called ***'Maya'*** or illusion. Everything looked real, even the sand houses; yet it was an illusion, and nothing is permanent. The property, cars, sons, daughters, grandchildren, bank balances, and everything looked so real at that particular point of time.

The beautiful looks of a model girl with enhancement of plastic surgery, and the tall handsome macho young man with a broad chest and abdomen of five packs, everything looks so real at that moment of time. But when you see the withered looks of the same people after a gap of forty years, nobody can believe that it is the same flamboyant people of yester years whom they had met. It is all *Maya*.

And finally when the soul departs at death, the body becomes lifeless and starts to give foul smell; and all the beauty is gone in a flash. It was like a sand house which was kicked in the evening of life; as dark shadows crept in. This is called illusion, when one gets identified with the physical body as real, with no awareness of the soul. The soul is the Lord and master of the body and nobody is aware of that. And this illusion has ever been like this for generations.

The foolish evil-doers, the lowest among mankind lacking wisdom; deprived of discrimination due to the illusion of Maya and following their evil nature; do not seek refuge in My Divine consciousness. (15)

O Bharata Arjuna! Four types of people worship My Divine consciousness; those in distress; those seeking knowledge; those seeking wealth and the men of wisdom. (16)

Out of these, the men of wisdom who are ever united with My Divine consciousness in singular devotion and meditation are the best; and they are extremely dear to Me, and I am supremely dear to them. (17)

On wisdom, Bible says, "Praise be to the name of the God forever and ever; wisdom and power are His. He changes times and seasons; he sets up kings and deposes them. He gives wisdom to the wise and knowledge to the discerning. He reveals deep and hidden things; he knows what lies in the darkness, and light dwells with him."

Noble indeed are all these people; but the wise men who have attained Oneness with My Supreme Spirit as the highest goal in life; and ever steadfast, are very dear to Me. (18)

At the end of many births, such a great soul takes refuge in Me, uniting his Self-soul with My God consciousness, realizing that the Spirit of Sri Krishna (Vasudeva) is all that pervades the entire Universe. Such an enlightened soul is very rare to find. (19)

One has to possess all the qualities and traits of the 'Enlightened' saint, as stated in the scriptures, to qualify for Nirvana. What are these characteristics as stated in Bhagavad Gita? Enlightenment means one who has the qualities of non-violence, truthfulness, honesty, leading a life of celibacy with no desire for sensual pleasures, non-possession, non-attachment, fearlessness, simplicity, asceticism, non-anger, forgiveness, compassion for all beings, non-greed, free from all desires, free from the pairs of opposites, treating everyone with an equal vision and being always in union with the Spirit of God.

One who has attained this highest state in 'Yoga path' and has no doubts and conflicts in his mind and has the qualities of a firm resolve, free from jealousy, and one who observes silence and leads a life of seclusion.

And how many of the striving saints in today's world possess all these qualities to be called 'Enlightened.' —The above Gita verse says that such an enlightened soul is very rare to find.

But people, whose wisdom has been carried away by this or that desire; they following their inborn nature, worship other deities and perform various rituals. (20)

Whatever form of god or deity a devotee wishes to worship with reverence, I make that faith of his steady in that very form. (21)

Endowed with that faith, the devotee engages in worship of that form of deity; and from that deity obtains the fulfilment of his or her desires. But the fulfilments of these desires are verily bestowed by My infinite Spirit of God only. (22)

Limited are the rewards of worship which are obtained by these people of small intellect. The devotees of other deities go unto them, and those who worship My Krishna —consciousness, come to My Universal Spirit of God. (23)

People due to ignorance think of My Krishna-consciousness which is unmanifest (invisible), as having a finite visual human form. They do not know My Supreme infinite Spirit which is unsurpassed and changeless. (24)

This verse implies that those who worship only human form of God as a stone idol or a picture of god, lack true knowledge. Hindu religion worships idols but to think that infinite Spirit of god can be contained within a stone idol is also ignorance.

The idol of a deity is just a symbol to turn the mind towards the Spirit of God. The picture of your wife in your purse is just a symbol of your wife, and not the wife in flesh and blood. Whereas in the Christian and Muslim religion, people worship the invisible and unmanifest Spirit of God, and not as an idol of Jesus Christ or Allah. Both manifest and unmanifest aspects of God have to be understood, to have a clear understanding of the above verse.

This aspect is explained in Isha Upanishad which says, "They fall into darkness who worships the unmanifest (unseen) or the Absolute Spirit. But they fall into greater darkness, who worship the manifest (with form) only...For it is other than the manifest and the unmanifest. Thus we have heard from the seers. Absolute (unmanifest) and relative (manifest)...those who know these two together, through the relative leaves death behind, and through the Absolute gains immortality."

The meaning of this verse points out that one cannot take a rigid stand that one particular form of worship is the only right way. The world is the manifest form of God, and God is the unmanifest form of the world. The manifest shows the way to the unmanifest. Both the manifest and the unmanifest aspects have to be accepted, and followed together to reach the ultimate goal.

My infinite Spirit is not revealed to all, due to the illusion of 'Yoga Maya.' The deluded world does not understand that My Krishna-consciousness is unborn and imperishable. (25)

O Arjuna! I know all beings of the past, the present, and those who are yet to be born in the future. But no one knows My infinite Spirit of God. (26)

O Bharata Arjuna! All beings are deluded from birth itself, due to the duality of the likes and dislikes and the conflict of the pairs of opposites. (27)

Those with virtuous deeds, whose sins have come to an end; freed from the conflicts of the pairs of opposites; they worship and meditate upon My Supreme Spirit with a firm resolve. (28)

Those who take shelter in My Cosmic Spirit of God consciousness (Brahman) and strive hard to attain deliverance from the decay of old age and death; they come to know the true nature of Absolute Spirit, Karma and Self-soul in its entirety. (29)

Sri Adi Shankaracharya in Bhaja Govindam gives bouquet of verses which are addressed to the humanity to always remember the main purpose of life for which one is born. One has to seek union with the Spirit of God.

Bhaja Govindam verse says, "The body has become worn out with age. The head has turned grey. The mouth has become toothless. The old man or woman moves around with the help of a walking stick, but even then one does not leave the numerous desires (in the form of lust, anger and greed)."—Spiritual progress has to be attained while living in the human body. The time for an individual comes to an end with death. It is then just the account of one's karma during the earthly life, and nothing more can be added or subtracted to it.

Those who understand the governing principles of Adhibhuta, Adhidaiva and Adhiyajna, and being of unified intellect and heart; they realize My Spirit of God even at the time of death. (30)

CHAPTER 8

THE YOGA OF ETERNAL SPIRIT
AKSHARA BRAHMA YOGA

Arjuna said:

O Sri Krishna! O best of the Supreme Purusha!–What is Brahman?–What is Adhyatma?–What is Karma?–What is the nature of Adhibhuta?–And what is Adhidaiva? (1)

O Madhusudana Sri Krishna! How and who dwells in this body as Adhiyajna? And how Your Supreme Spirit is to be realized by those with steadfast mind, at the time of death? (2)

Sri Krishna said :

The imperishable Supreme Spirit is called 'Brahman.' The dwelling of the Spirit as the embodied individual soul (Jivatma) is called 'Adhyatma.' The creative force or the offering which causes the origin of beings is called karma. (3)

O Arjuna! Adhibhuta is the perishable physical body (comprising of earth, water, fire, air, and space—(five elements of nature); Adhidaiva is the all pervading Universal Spirit (Purusha); and I alone am the Spirit within the body as Adhiyajna sacrifice (as the inner witness of all actions). (4)

And whoever, at the time of death, while leaving the physical body goes forth remembering Me alone as the Divine Spirit; he or she attains to My being. There is no doubt about this fact. (5)

O son of Kunti Arjuna! Whatever last thoughts occupy the mind of a dying person while leaving the physical body just before death, to that alone he or she attains, being ever absorbed in the last thoughts thereof. (6)

The last thoughts of a dying person, is given the utmost importance in all religions of the world. In Hindu religion or in Christianity, a priest is called to perform prayers and guide the soul to the higher regions by remembrance of God, if it gets known that a person is going to breathe one's last breath. Even for a criminal who is going to be hanged till death, the last wish of that person is asked to be fulfilled, before death.

There have been cases of Indian Yogis in the past who knew that their time of death was near, and they made prior preparations of their departure from the earth. They chose to die consciously remembering the name of the Lord so that it will be the last thought in which their mind will remain absorbed after death.

The above verse of Bhagavad Gita says that whatever last thoughts occupy the mind of a dying person, to that alone he or she attains. It is like a person who is just drifting off to sleep at night with some thoughts in his mind, and he wakes up in the morning with the same last thoughts. If a man has to catch a flight early in the early morning and he sleeps with that thought in his mind, then he automatically wakes up in the morning with the same thought that he has to catch a flight in the morning.

Sri Krishna tells Arjuna that you engage in this battle, while constantly remembering My Krishna-consciousness of God. Who knows when the messenger of death will arrive to claim the soul? A story with a moral, best explains the importance of the last thoughts just before death.

A religious man lived near a temple. In the opposite house lived a prostitute. Noticing that a large number of men were visiting her house daily for bodily pleasures; the monk summoned the prostitute, and warned her of the bad consequences of her actions. She lamented over her lot in life, as she could not find another work for survival.

Each time she gave her body to a man; she would pray to God for forgiveness, and to put an end to her base profession.

The religious man used to brood inwardly in his mind over the sensual enjoyments which he was missing, but outwardly he used to pretend that he is a very pious man. The religious man then started recording her sins by putting a stone pebble, each time a man went to her house for bodily pleasures. The heap of stones grew large in front of his main door, and the religious man again summoned the prostitute and showed her the pyramid of stones, as the proof of her sins. He told her that she will have to pay for her sins by dwelling in hell for an indefinite period of time.

The heart-broken prostitute wept and prayed to God fervently to forgive her sins and end her life. With these last thoughts of forgiveness and deliverance from her sins, it so happened, that she died. By a strange hand of destiny and as a coincidence, the religious man also died the same very night with the last thoughts of how the neighbourly prostitute was enjoying, and doing sins with her body.

The dead body of the religious man was carried in a huge procession, and the crowd paid their last marks of respect to the departed soul with lavish praises that he had led a very pious life. On the other hand, there was no one to even lift the dead body of the prostitute, and her body was given over to the vultures to eat.

In the Yama loka of the dead, the soul of the prostitute was escorted to heaven, while the soul of the religious man was consigned to hell. The religious man sought an audience with God to know the cause for this injustice. He bitterly cried out, "Is this Your justice, O Lord? I spent my whole life in devotion to God and prayers, and now I am being carried off to hell, and the soul of the prostitute, who lived all her life in sin, has been taken to heaven! What kind of justice is this?"

The spirit of God replied, "Inviolable justice alone prevails with God as per the karma of an individual, and there is no question of any favouritism for anyone. Although living in a polluted body, the prostitute's mind was always fixed on the divine thoughts of God to deliver her from all the sins, she had committed. Whereas your mind as a religious man was always wandering on the unholy concerns of others, due to the deep rooted craving of unfulfilled sexual desires in your perverted mind."

The Spirit of God further added, "Unholy concerns of others ought to have been none of your business. Your dead body was fittingly cremated with all religious ceremonies as per your hypocrisy and show as a religious man; and the dead body of the prostitute was treated like a rotten flesh. The laws of the earth are different from the laws of heaven. Here there is no favouritism with God, and the laws are just and fair for all, irrespective of their status on the earth. Your soul and the soul of the prostitute have thus been accordingly assigned to their befitting regions."

The moral of the story is to be aware of your thoughts at all times and constantly remember God. The teaching of Bhagavad Gita says in verse 9:29 that I am the same to all beings and there is none hateful nor dear to Me, but those who worship Me, I am in them and they are in Me.—Verse 16:21 says, "Lust, anger and greed are the three gates to hell, which ruin and destroy the Self-soul. Therefore, one ought to give up these three vices."

A similar story is narrated in Bible as follows, "The poor man Lazarus, died and was carried by the angels to Abraham's side. The rich man also died and was buried, and in Hades, being in torment, he lifted up his eyes and saw Abraham far off and Lazarus at his side. And he called out, 'Father Abraham, have mercy on me, and send Lazarus to dip the end of his finger in water and cool my tongue, for I am in anguish in this flame.' But Abraham said, 'Child, remember that you in your lifetime, you received your good things, and Lazarus in a like manner bad things; but now he is comforted here, and you are in anguish. And besides all this, between us and you a great chasm has been fixed, in order that no one can go from here to you, and none may cross from there to us."

Therefore, constantly remembering My Divine Consciousness at all times engage in war, (as your duty). With your mind and intellect dedicated to My Spirit, you will surely come to My Being only,–without any doubt. (7)

Life is short and uncertain. One has to be constantly aware that this life is a bridge to cross over to the next world. A person should keep constant remembrance of God-consciousness, and perform the assigned worldly tasks at the same time.

Bhaja Govindam text by Adi Shankaracharya says, "The existence of water drops moving on a lotus leaf is very uncertain and fleeting. Similarly human life is also very uncertain and fleeting. Understand that the whole world is consumed by disease and conceit and enveloped by sorrow.–As long as there dwells breath in your body, till then your family members will enquire of your welfare. Once the life breath departs at death and the body decays, even your own loving wife will fear the putrefied body. O deluded people! Seek the Spirit of Krishna-consciousness, the source of bliss!"

O Partha Arjuna!–By constant and steadfast meditation practice on this 'yoga path'; the wanderings of the mind on irrelevant thoughts can be controlled. Thus meditating, the mind should be focussed on the Divine, resplendent and Supreme Purusha. (8)

My Supreme Spirit of God, is to be meditated upon as the sustainer of the entire Creation, ancient from the beginning of the Universe, the Ruler, all-knowing, subtler and even smaller than an atom, self effulgent like the Sun and beyond all darkness, whose form is inconceivable, and beyond any human perception.—Whoever at the time of death leaves the body with an unshaken mind, fixed in devotion to God and united with My Spirit by the power of 'Yoga meditation,' having placed the entire prana force in the middle of the eyebrows,–such a person attains My Supreme Consciousness. (9–10)

I shall declare to you that Supreme state, which the knower's of the Vedas describe as imperishable. Desiring to enter that exalted state, the self-controlled ascetics freed from all passions and attachments, lead a pure life of celibacy (free from any sexual defilement in thoughts, words and deed). (11)

How does leading a life of celibacy voluntarily, free from sexual indulgence in thought, words and deed help a spiritual aspirant to reach higher states of mind? Brahmacharya means '***Brahman***': Spirit of God and '***charya***': conduct,' meaning one whose conduct is pure like the Spirit of God. A pure mind has no scheming thoughts of sensual enjoyments and distractions.

It is important that the celibacy should be taken up voluntarily to observe the spiritual discipline. A forced celibacy will lead to sexual perversions. Patanjali's Yoga sutra says that by following celibacy one develops a dislike for any bodily touch by others. A short story in the form of a parable explains this point.

Young spiritual aspirants in an ashram were celibates and very ardent in their disciplined life of meditation and devotion to God. Over the years with single-minded practice of Yoga meditation, they attained an exalted status of mind and intellect, and were held in high esteem by the people who visited the ashram.

Visitors thronged to the ashram to receive their advice and blessings. Seeing this ruling king got worried, and asked these celibates to meet him at his palace. But these celibates refused to go there, and told the messenger to tell the king to meet them in the ashram if the king was so interested in meeting them.

After consultation with his group of ministers, the king arranged marriages of these young celibates with beautiful young girls. From there on, the king did not have to send for them. They would come to the king every now and then of their own accord, without being called.

They would say to the king, "Your majesty, we have come to seek your blessings for the rice-taking ceremonies of our babies, and for building a small house, and so on for other favours."—Being house holders now, they always had the need of money and other material things, which were never ending.

Controlling all the gates of the body (two eyes, two ears, two nostrils, one mouth, genital organs, excretory organ

anus); with the mind confined within the heart (with no external thoughts); fixing the prana energy in the head (in the middle of the eye-brows); thus engage in the practice of Yoga meditation. (12)

Chanting the sound of indestructible single syllable 'AUM'; while meditating on My infinite Spirit, one who thus departs from the body, attains My Divine Being. (13)

O Partha Arjuna! My Divine Spirit is easily attainable by that steadfast yogi, who without any other worldly thoughts, constantly remembers Me at all times, and meditates on My Spirit. (14)

The great souls, who have reached the highest goal of Self-realization through 'Yoga-sadhana,' are no more subject to rebirth, as life on earth is transitory and the abode of pain and suffering. (15)

Adi Shankara says in this context, "Repeated birth and death; and again lying in the womb of a woman for birth. This world is a suffering and very difficult to cross-over. O Murari Sri Krishna! Save me through Your infinite grace!"

O Son of Kunti Arjuna! All the worlds (different planes of existence) including the Brahma-loka (heavenly regions) are subject to rebirth again and again; but those who attain union with My Divine Consciousness, are freed from the cycles of birth and death. (16)

The day of Brahma the Creator, lasts a thousand Yugas, and his night is of equal duration of thousand Yugas. Those who understand this are the real knower of time-scale measurements of the Universe. (17)

At the beginning of Brahma's Cosmic day, the entire Creation of beings emerges from the unknown invisible unmanifest state; and at the onset of Brahma's Cosmic night, the entire manifest Creation dissolves back into unmanifest void again. (18)

O Partha Arjuna! The multitudes of beings are born again and again, and die again and again during the Cosmic day cycle of Brahma. The beings dissolve during the Cosmic night cycle, to re-emerge again in Brahma's Cosmic day. (19)

Beyond this unmanifest Spirit, there is yet another Absolute unmanifest eternal Spirit, which is not affected by the cycles of Cosmic dissolution. (20)

That Absolute eternal Spirit is called the Imperishable, and is said to be the Ultimate goal. Having attained to this Supreme Abode, there is no further return on this earth (rebirth). (21)

O Partha Arjuna! That eternal Supreme Spirit of God (Purusha) in which all beings dwell, and which pervades the entire Universe, is attainable by single-minded and exclusive meditation and unswerving devotion. (22)

O Best of Bharata Arjuna! Now I shall declare to you the time in which yogis depart from the body at death never to be born again, and also the time in which they depart to return again for rebirth in this world. (23)

One path is Fire, light, day-time, the bright fortnight of moon (waxing moon) and the six months of the northern path of the Sun, dying during this combination of timings, the knower of the Supreme Spirit goes to the abode of Absolute Spirit (Brahman), never to be reborn again on this earth. (24)

Smoke, night-time, the dark fortnight of moon (waning moon), the six months of the Sun's southern passage; the yogi departing from the body during this conjecture of timings, follows the lunar path and is reborn again on this earth. (25)

The light and the darkness; these are the two eternal paths followed by the beings of this world. Path of light

leads to liberation while the path of darkness leads to rebirth in this mortal world. (26)

O Partha Arjuna! Knowing these two paths, a yogi is never deluded. Therefore at all times, remain united with the light of My Divine Spirit through Yoga meditation. (27)

The yogi who with constant practice of 'Yoga meditation' realizes My Supreme Spirit; he transcends and goes beyond the fruits of good deeds obtained by the study of Scriptures, performance of sacrifices, penances and charitable acts. (28)

Sri Krishna exhorts Arjuna to constantly remember the Spirit of God at all times and thus engage in battle. Nobody knows when the bells of death will toll.

Bible also similarly echoes the same teaching and says, "Remember your creator in the days of your youth, before the days of trouble come and the years approach when you will say, that I find no pleasure in them—before the Sun and the light and the Moon and the stars grow dark, and the clouds return after the rain; when the keepers of the house tremble, and the strong men stoop, when the doors to the street are closed and the sound of grinding fades; when men rise up at the sound of birds, but all their songs grow faint; when men are afraid of heights and of dangers in the streets; when the almond tree blossoms and the grasshopper drags himself along and desire is no longer stirred. Then man goes to his eternal home and mourners go about the streets."

"Remember God–before the silver cord is severed, or the golden bowl is broken; before the pitcher is shattered at the spring, or the wheel broken at the well, and the dust returns to the ground it came from, and the spirit returns to God who gave it."

CHAPTER 9

THE YOGA OF ROYAL SCIENCE AND ROYAL SECRET RAJA–VIDYA RAJ–GUHYA YOGA

Sri Krishna said :

To you, who is free from fault-finding and envy, I shall declare this most profound knowledge together with wisdom; after Self-realization of which you will be freed from the evils of worldly existence. (1)

This knowledge is a profound science for direct Self-realization, in accordance with righteous-deeds (Dharma). This eternal 'Yoga science' is a supreme purifier, and very easy to practise. (2)

O Parantapa Arjuna! Those who lack faith in the teaching of this eternal Dharma do not attain union with My eternal Consciousness, but return back to this mortal world of birth and death. (3)

A man had to crossover a swollen and turbulent river, to go across to the other side. His master Dwarka came over and wrote a name on a leaf and tied the leaf in a cloth; and fastened it to the man's back, and said, "Your worries are over now. Do not be afraid, it is now for the grace of God to take you across the turbulent waters of the river. Your faith will take you across the waters of this river. But the minute you lose your faith, you will be drowned."

The man had faith in his master Dwarka and he immediately jumped into the water, and started to swim across the flooded waters of the river without any difficulty. It seemed so easy, just floating and being pushed along with the water currents. But he had an overwhelming urge, to know what his master had written on the leaf tied to his back.

He removed the leaf, and read what was written, "O Lord Krishna! Help this man to cross the turbulent river." The man thought, "Is that all? And who is this Lord Krishna to save me?" The moment this doubt came to his mind, he was hit by a strong wave of water and was drowned.

The entire Universe is pervaded by My unmanifest and unseen Spirit. All beings are sustained by the Spirit of My life energy, but still I do not abide in them. (4)

Behold the mystery of My wondrous Yoga Prakriti! While I bring forth the entire Creation, and sustain all beings therein; yet I do not dwell in them. (5)

Just as the mighty wind moving everywhere, always exists in the Space (Akasha); by the same example know that all beings and the entire Creation exists in My all pervading Spirit of God. (6)

Swami Ramakrishna Paramhansa in his lifetime used to say to his followers, "What is God-consciousness or 'Brahman' like? It cannot be defined in words. It cannot be perceived with the human senses. Defining 'Brahman' or God-consciousness is much more difficult after experiencing God-consciousness, as one simply becomes silent, and it is unthinkable and beyond words."

The four basic elements of earth, water, fire and air have their own characteristics. The gross elements like earth, water and air can be weighed and their quality can be assessed. The quality and purity of air and the pollution in air can be scientifically measured. The temperature of fire can also be measured.

The fifth element Akasha or space undergoes no modifications and remains changeless. The element of Akasha is insentient while the consciousness is sentient. The above verse gives the analogy of the wind which although moving everywhere always exists in Akasha. Similarly all beings and the entire creation exist in the all-pervading Spirit of God at all times.

O son of Kunti-Arjuna! At the end of a Kalpa cycle, the dissolution of the Universe takes place and the entire Creation merges in My Prakriti Spirit. At the beginning of the next Kalpa cycle, My Cosmic Spirit again regenerates the entire creation afresh. (7)

The regime of Prakriti by its inherent Nature, generates multitude of beings in spite of themselves (in accordance with their past karmas); and they are helplessly driven into existence and extinction, again and again. (8)

The world is created by Prakriti to facilitate the reaping of our karma. Getting attached to Maya and attempting to possess it, we perform various deeds which result in good and bad karma. In the process, human beings are forced to take birth again and again, in order to fulfil their desires from the previous births.

O Dhananjaya Arjuna! My Supreme Spirit remains untouched and unaffected by all these acts (of Creation and Dissolution); nor do these acts create any bondage for Me. (9)

O son of Kunti Arjuna! Prakriti Nature under the control of My Supreme Spirit generates all moving and unmoving beings and things; and thus the world moves round and round. (10)

The deluded are unaware of My Supreme Spirit of God as the great Lord of the entire Universe. The ignorant consider Me, as dwelling in the human Form. (11)

The above verse brings out the truth that God is everywhere both within and without. The worship of an idol in a temple is just a symbol to turn the mind towards God. The mystic saint Kabira said that if the infinite Spirit of God can be contained within a stone idol, then I will worship a mountain as the mountain is made of infinite number of stones. The above verse says that only fools consider God dwelling in a human form, as the Spirit of God is omnipresent, omnipotent and omniscient.

People with evil and devilish nature have futile hopes, deceitful actions, irrational and senseless minds with deluded knowledge. (12)

O Partha Arjuna! Contrary to these evil people, there are pious people with divine nature. The divine people know My imperishable Spirit as the very source and the sustainer of all living beings. They worship My infinite Spirit, with a single-minded exclusive devotion. (13)

People of divine disposition always glorify My Spirit of God, and chant My holy names. They strive on the spiritual path with determination and firm vows. Ever united with My Divine Spirit, they bow down to Me in reverence. (14)

Yet others worship My Spirit by following the path of knowledge (study of Holy Scriptures); some worship Me as One Spirit of God controlling the entire Universe; whereas some perceive My Spirit as having different manifestations and forms according to their faith. (15)

Bhagavad Gita says that there is only one Supreme Spirit of God which governs and controls the entire Universe of Stars, the Sun, the Moon, numerous galaxies in space, planet earth and all beings inhabiting this earth. Different incarnations of God took human manifestations from time to time in different ages and yugas, and imparted their teachings; but there is one underlying unity as one Spirit of God.

In essence Vishnu-consciousness, Krishna-consciousness, Christ-consciousness, Buddha-consciousness, Allah and all the different faiths have emerged from that One Spirit of God. This verse says that God fulfils the desires of human beings according to their different faiths, but those who worship Krishna-consciousness, reach the Spirit of God directly, and not through a via media.

My Spirit is the Vedic rituals, I am the sacrificial Yajna to the ancestors, I am the food and the medicinal herbs, the sacred Mantra hymns, and My Spirit is the sacred fire and

also the act of offering clarified butter as oblation into the fire. (16)

Agni or fire is considered sacred in all the religions as it sustains all life and is manifest in many forms. In the manifest seen form, fire is used as a cooking medium. In the unseen form it is Agni or fire as body heat, which keeps the living bodies alive. Sri Krishna says in chapter 15 that abiding in the bodies of all living beings as the Vaishvanara fire, and associated with the incoming and the outgoing breath, I digest four kinds of food.

Isha Upanishad pays tribute to Agni the god of fire by saying, "O Agni, show us the right path, lead us to eternal freedom. Thou knows all, may we not be diverted from our goal. You know all our deeds, and deliver us from evil. For with all devotion we bow to you in prayer, again and again."

My Spirit is the Father of this world, the Mother, the Grandsire; the sustainer and ruler of the entire Universe. I am the one to be known and the purifier. Know Me as the sacred sound AUM and the Rik, Saman and the Yajur Vedas. (17)

The sound of Pranava 'AUM' in the Rik, Sama and Yajur Vedas are all sacred. The primal Spirit of God is the sustainer and nurturer of the world.

Sound is one of the basic elements, and a means to focus the mind during meditation. In the beginning was the sound of 'Word' and the creation started from there. The Upanishads say that the Word was 'AUM.' As all leaves are held together by the stem of a plant, similarly all speech is held together by the Word 'AUM.' Christians use a similar Word 'Amen.'

It is the symbol of manifest God in waking, dreaming and deep sleep state. The fourth state is known as 'Turiya' state, which is the final state of merging with the super consciousness. The first letter 'A' of the sound 'AUM' is the waking state of consciousness. The second letter 'U' of the sound is the dreaming state of consciousness; and the third letter 'M' is the deep sleep state of consciousness.

That is why deep sleep is invigorating and refreshing to the body, mind and soul as during this time the individual soul is in deep touch with the super-conscious state to rejuvenate. The fourth state is the total silence after the sound of AUM, and is called the 'Turiya' state which is non-dual and the ultimate merging with the Absolute Spirit.

If one meditates on the Supreme Being with the syllable Aum, then one becomes one with the light; and is led to the world of Brahman (the Absolute Being). The word AUM according to Hindu philosophy is the primordial sound from which the whole universe was created. AUM is the original Word of Power, and is recited as a mantra. A mantra is a series of verbal sounds having inherent sound power that can produce a particular physical or psychological effect, as the human body is also a form of miniature universe.

In the yoga tradition, AUM is the most sacred and a holy word, the supreme mantra. Aum is a Sanskrit word which means controller of life force (prana) and life giver. Aum is called the Shabda Brahman or the energy of God as Sound Vibration. According to yoga theory, the universe has emanated from this primal energy.

Mandukya Upanishad explicitly explains the full significance of the word 'AUM' and the different states of consciousness. The Upanishad states that the word AUM establishes a direct link between our individual consciousness and the cosmic Divinity.

By chanting and meditating on the sound 'AUM'; the energy level is raised higher and higher when one keeps awareness and significance of the sacred Word 'AUM.' It is regarded as a mystic syllable representing the essence of the Vedas and the Universe. It is indeed a syllable of the everlasting Spirit of God.

The Rig-Veda the most ancient scripture of the world says, "First was the absolute Spirit of Brahman, and then there was 'Waak,' the sound as the vibrating energy which became the universe. —'AUM' is the root of all sounds. Every other sound is contained in this sound, and one has to finally go beyond all sounds."

Someone asked Swami Ramakrishna Paramhansa, "What will you gain by merely hearing this sound of AUM repeatedly?" He replied, "You hear the roar of the ocean from a distance. By following the roar you can reach the ocean. As long as there is roar, there must also be the ocean. By following the trail of AUM you can finally attain the Spirit of God (Brahman)."

Bhaktivedanta Swami Prabhupada said, "If you are a serious student of Vedic mantras, then you will chant 'AUM' because Vedic mantras begin with 'AUM,' which is Omkara. Many people are fond of chanting Omkara and that is the same as Krishna-consciousness. If we simply remember, 'This Omkara is Krishna'; then we become perfect, because the goal is to merge in Krishna-consciousness. So you can merge with Krishna-conscious while chanting the Word AUM."

Ramana Maharshi said, "The purport of prescribing meditation on the Pranava sound is that Pranava is Omkara; the advaita-mantra which is the essence of all mantras. In order to get at its true significance, one should meditate on the 'Pranava' sound. The fruition of this process is samadhi which yields Moksha or liberation, leading to the state of unsurpassable bliss."

Late Swami Dayananda Saraswati of Rishikesh said on the sound of Pranava, "AUM is the highest Name of God, and comprises many other names of God. It should be borne in mind that AUM is the name of God exclusively...and not of other objects or materials."

My Spirit is the Supreme goal to be achieved, the nourisher, the Lord, the witnesser of all actions, the refuge and the shelter, the well-wisher and friend of all. My infinite Spirit is the Origin, the Dissolution, the resting place, the store-house of all knowledge, and the imperishable seed.

(18)

O Arjuna! I radiate the heat of the Sun by which all creatures and beings survive; I hold and send forth rains. I am immortality and also death. My Spirit is manifest (seen) as well as unmanifest (unseen). (19)

Some pray to reach the heavenly regions in the next life by doing sacrificial rituals and studying the three Vedas and the Soma. Having cleansed their sins by performance of virtuous deeds, they go to celestial regions to enjoy the happiness of paradise. (20)

Having enjoyed the celestial regions of the heavens for a certain period of time ; and upon exhaustion of their accumulated merits of good deeds, they once again return back to this mortal world of birth and death. These men and women due to their worldly desires, thus move between the heaven and earth in accordance with the laws of the three Vedas. (21)

To those people, who at all times worship My Krishna-consciousness ever united with My Spirit, thinking of none other; to them I provide protection and attend to their needs. (22)

"***Ananyah***:—none other:—***chintayantah***:—thinking:—***mam***:—me:—***ye***:—who:—***janah***:—people:—***paryupasate***:—worship:—***tesham***:—to them:—***nitya...bhiyuktanam***:—ever united with My Cosmic consciousness;...***yoga***:—yoga of needs and requirements:—***kshemam***:—protection and safety:—***vahami***:—provide:—***aham***:—I"

The above verse of Gita makes a firm promise to the humanity that those who worship the Spirit of Krishna-consciousness thinking of none other, to them He provides ***yoga-kshemam- vahami*** and attends to their needs and provides protection from all pitfalls of life. Here the investment is not in the form of money or wealth, but singular devotion by the human beings.

Life Insurance Corporation of India has adopted this verse of Bhagavad Gita, as their motto. The story of insurance is probably as old as the story of mankind. The same instinct that prompts modern businessmen today to secure themselves against any loss and disaster existed in the primitive men also. They too sought compensation for the evil consequences of fire, flood and loss of life, and were willing to invest their money, in order to achieve some form of security. The Motto of Life Insurance Corporation of India is '***Yoga-kshemam-vahami-aham.***'

This story describes the '***Kshemam'*** or protection provided by God. —- Deep in his sleep, one night a man had a dream, which seemed as real as his own life. He dreamt that he was walking barefoot along with God, on the wet sandy beach. As he looked up at the sky, he saw the scenes of his life flash by. Down below there were two sets of footprints on the sand; one set his own footprints; and the other set of God.

Later as the flashes of his life continued, he looked back again at those footprints in the sand and noticed something which he found quite disturbing. During the most difficult periods of his life, he saw only one set of footprints.

This deeply troubled the man and he asked God, "You said that if I followed you, then you will always walk with me through all the circumstances of my life, whether in joy or sorrow, honour and insult, sickness and health, riches or poverty. But while looking back, I saw that during my most painful and difficult times, there was only one set of footprints. O God! Why did you leave me, when I needed you the most?"

God replied, "My child! I love you more than you can ever imagine; and I never left you alone when you were in deep trouble and crisis. It was during those difficult times when you were suffering the most, and could not cope up with life, that I was carrying you on my shoulders, and that is why you saw only My set of foot prints on the sand."

O Son of Kunti Arjuna! Even those devotees who though endowed with faith, worship other deities and goddesses; they in fact worship My Divine consciousness only, but by the wrong method. (23)

For My Spirit is the enjoyer and the receiver of all Yajna sacrifices, and the one Lord of the entire creation. The

ignorant do not know My true infinite Spirit, and hence they fall again and again (return to the suffering in this mortal world of birth and death). (24)

Worshippers of the astral deities (Devas) go to their spirits (upon death); those who worship ancestors go to their spirits; spirit worshippers go to the realm of those dead spirits. But know that, those who worship My Krishna-consciousness come to Me only. (25)

The choice is with individuals according their mental disposition whether they want to worship different gods or goddesses as deities; their ancestors; the spirits of the dead; or the true Spirit of God. In the ancient era, materialism had not taken firm roots as in the modern world today. It was then possible to find a living and an enlightened Guru to guide and steer one's spiritual path. In the modern era it is almost impossible to find an enlightened saint who can serve as a role model and a guide. There are numerous fake Gurus who may claim to be enlightened and one can easily be misled to mistake the fake person as the real Guru.

The fake Guru will look more authentic than the real Guru, as he will wear the ochre robes and pretend to be real. The safest path to follow is to have faith in the time tested scriptures to act as one's guide and spiritual teacher. The scriptures will act as a guide as to what is right and wrong; and the scriptures do not ask for anyone's wealth, possessions and women. Sikh religion follows the 'Guru Granth Sahib' as their Guru, and they do not permit any living Gurus, so that fake cults do not emerge.

Whoever with devotion, offers to My Spirit of God, a leaf, a flower, a fruit or water; I accept that loving offering of the pure in heart. (26)

O Son of Kunti Arjuna! Whatever deeds and actions you perform; whatever you eat; whatever Yajna sacrifices you perform; whatever charities you give; whatever penances you undertake; do it as an offering to My Supreme Spirit of God. (27)

It means God in our waking, God in our speaking, God in our cooking, God in our eating, God in our recreation, God in our digesting, God in our working, God in our resting, God in our charity and God in our sleeping. Bible says the same thing, "Whatever you eat or drink, or whatever you do, do all to the glory of God."

In this way you will be freed from the bondage of actions, yielding good and bad results. Thus freed and renouncing the fruits of actions by the yoga of renunciation, you shall certainly attain to My Spirit. (28)

My Spirit of God is unbiased and dwells equally in all beings. To Me there is none hateful nor affectionate. But those who meditate and worship Me wholeheartedly; they are in Me, and I am in their heart. (29)

Translation of this verse from Sanskrit to English is: ":—***Samah***:—the same:—***aham***:—I:—***sarva...bhuteshu***:—to all beings:—***na***:—not:—***me***:—to Me:—***dveshyah***:—hateful:—***asti***:—is:—***na***:—not:—***priyah***:—dear or affectionate:—***ye***:—who:—***bhajanti***:—worship:—***tu***:—but:—***mam***:—Me:—***bhaktya***:—with devotion:—***mayi***:—in Me:—***te***:—they:—***teshu***:—in them:—***cha***:—and:—***api***:—also:—***aham***:—I."

In worldly affairs there is corruption, bribery, favouritism, hypocrisy and nepotism. Worldly dealings do not apply in the kingdom of God. In the domain of God, the only thing that matters is one's sincerity of heart and whole-hearted worship to get remission from one's trespasses and sins.

Bible says, "Then Peter began to speak. I now realize that it is true that God treats everyone on the same basis. Whoever worships him and does what is right is acceptable to Him, no matter what race he belongs to.—All the saints spoke about him, saying that everyone who believes in him will have his sins forgiven through the power of his name."

Even if a person has committed biggest of heinous and vicious crimes, but finally becomes virtuous with a firm resolve to worship My Spirit of God wholeheartedly with an

undeviating devotion, such a person must be considered as righteous, as he or she has rightly resolved. (30)

Very soon such a person becomes a righteous soul and attains lasting peace. O Kaunteya Arjuna! Know for sure, that My ardent devotee never perishes. (31)

O Partha Arjuna! Even those who are of inferior birth,– Women, Vaishyas (businessmen and trading class) and Sudras (servant class and labourers); even they by taking refuge in My Spirit of God, attain the highest goal. (32)

Then what to talk of the devoted royal saints and learned Brahmin class people (well-versed in Holy Scriptures), who having come into this transitory and sorrowful world, ardently worship My Supreme Spirit to attain salvation. (33)

Fix your mind on My Spirit of God with utmost devotion, sacrifice and bow down to Me, having united your Soul with My Spirit as the Supreme goal, you shall surely attain My Supreme abode. (34)

CHAPTER 10

THE YOGA OF DIVINE MANIFESTATIONS
VIBHUTI YOGA

Sri Krishna said :

O mighty-armed Arjuna! Once again listen to My Supreme words of wisdom. You are dear to Me, and desiring your welfare and good, I shall declare this teaching to you. (1)

Neither the multitude of deities nor the great sages know My origin. I am the source of all the deities; the great sages; and everything else in this Creation. (2)

Understand that My Supreme Spirit is unborn and without beginning, and rules over the entire Universe. One, who thus understands, overcomes all delusions in this mortal world, and is freed from all sins. (3)

Intelligence, wisdom, non-delusion, forgiveness, truth, control of the senses, calmness of the heart, pleasure and pain, birth and death, fear and fearlessness.... non-violence, equanimity, contentment, austerity, charity, fame and dishonour; all these different qualities in beings arise from My Spirit only. (4–5)

The Primeval seven great Rishis and the four ancient Manus were born out of My Being, in My image. And from them have come forth all the creatures in this world. (6)

One who thus understands My wondrous glories and manifestations in true essence, is firmly united with My Spirit in this 'Yoga path.' (7)

My Spirit is the origin of everything and from Me everything evolves. The wise know this and worship My Spirit with their innermost heart. (8)

With their mind and life-force prana ever fixed and united in meditation with My Spirit; rejoicing with each other in singing My Divine Glories, these pious people are thus ever content in life. (9)

To those who are ever devout and worship My Krishna-consciousness with utmost love; to them I give the Yoga of discrimination by which they attain My being. (10)

With My divine grace and compassion for the ever devout; and the dwelling of My Spirit in their hearts; I destroy the darkness of ignorance by the luminous light of wisdom. (11)

Arjuna said :

You are the manifestation of the Absolute Supreme Spirit of God (Brahman), the Supreme Abode, the Supreme Purifier, the Eternal Divine cosmic Soul (Purusha), the first Primeval Spirit of God, the Unborn and the Omnipresent Spirit. (12)

All the Sages (Rishis) have thus acclaimed You, and also the Dev Rishi Narada; so also Asita, Devala and Sage Vyasa; and now You yourself say this to me. (13)

O Keshava Sri Krishna! What Thou declare to me is absolute truth...O Blessed Lord. Neither the Devas (demigods) nor the demons know the secret of Your Divine manifestations. (14)

Verily Thou alone know Yourself by Yourself, O Purushottama, O Lord of all beings; O source of all beings; O God of gods; O Ruler of the Universe. (15)

O God! Describe Your glories and manifestations fully without reserve. And in what manner Your Supreme Spirit exists and pervades the entire world and the Universe? (16)

O Supreme Yogi...Sri Krishna! By what regular practice of meditation may I realize Your Supreme Spirit? O Blessed lord, in what various manifestations and aspects thou art to be meditated upon by me? (17)

O Janardhana Sri Krishna! Describe to me in full detail Your Divine manifestations and attributes. I want to hear more of Your nectar-like sweet words. (18)

Sri Krishna said :

Very well Arjuna! I shall now describe to you a few of My prominent glories, but My glories and manifestations are endless and infinite. (19)

O Gudakesha Arjuna! I am the Self-soul seated in the hearts of all creatures. I am the beginning, the middle and also end of all beings. (20)

We all live our life like a story. We have a beginning, middle and an end. And everyone's life has a different story, of success and failures, and struggles in the world. Some of us have empowering stories that transform and change our life.

Most of us go through our life completely unaware; as if driven by the unconscious mind, with certain habit patterns and thoughts that have been programmed into our brain and body at an early age. But if we start living on the spiritual path with awareness, then it is possible to alter the story of our life for a happy and purposeful ending. The divine spark of Self-soul is within all human beings, and it is up to the individual to explore its infinite potential.

I am the Lord Vishnu among the shining Adityas gods; among the radiant luminaries, I am the effulgent Sun; among the winds I am the Marichi; and among the constellations, I am the Moon. (21)

The Spirit of Lord Vishnu is all-pervading, and expands into everything. He is the maintainer and Creator of the Universe. He presides over Prakriti and its various Gunas by which all beings function.

He is also called Narayana, which means the shelter, the resting place or the ultimate goal of all living entities. The Spirit of Lord Vishnu also means one who lives in the hearts of all beings. In this sense, Lord Vishnu is also called Hari, or one who removes the darkness of illusion. Due to this illusion and ignorance all living beings consider themselves, as separate from the Lord to create duality.

References to the glories of Lord Vishnu are found in ancient books such as the Rig Veda. Many of them are in relation to His form as Vamana avatar; the Dwarf incarnation who begged for only three steps of land from King Bali, and with those three steps, he covered the whole of the Universe.

Lord Vishnu is often portrayed as resting on the huge serpent Sesha Naga. We see the thousand heads of Sesha Serpent all turned inwards, representing a tranquil mind and looking towards the Absolute Truth of Lord Vishnu. Thus Lord Vishnu is also seen in the Yogic sleep called Yoga-nidra. The Yoga-nidra (Yoga or the root yuj means to connect or join) is a cosmic sleep, wherein the Lord is focused on the infinite Reality of His own creation.

The verse says I am the radiant Sun among the luminaries. —Light and heat of the sun is the most concrete and visible manifestation of the glories of God. Vedas enumerate the glories of the Sun as all-seeing, which nourishes all life by its radiant heat. No life can exist on earth without the heat of the Sun, as otherwise earth will become a frozen planet.

Sun is conceived in the Vedas as a bird traversing the space, a gem in the sky, as a variegated stone set in the midst of heaven. Sun shines equally on all, whether good or bad, a saint or a sinner, plant life or animal kingdom. He dispels the darkness, measures the days and prolongs life. The Sun drives away sickness, diseases and evil.

Among the Vedas I am the Sama Veda; I am the Vasava (Indra) among the deities. Among the senses I am the mind, and in living beings I am Consciousness. (22)

The functioning of the five senses is possible due to the presence of mind. If the mind wanders away, the senses cannot cognize the sense objects, and we say that the person is absent-minded. Mind is the recorder of all the sensations, and it is an attribute of the Lord.

The difference between the living and the dead is due to the presence of soul-consciousness. The consciousness gets purer and cleaner from impurities, as the level of consciousness rises to higher levels. The spiritual path is like the process of cleaning the dirty water from all impurities, like a filtration process.

Among the Rudras I am the deity of Shiva; I am Kubera among the Yakshas and Rakshasas; I am fire-god (Agni... Pavaka) among the Vasus; and of the mountains I am Meru. (23)

O Partha Arjuna! Among the priests, know Me to be the chief-Brihaspati; Of the warrior-chiefs I am Skanda; and among the bodies of waters, know Me to be the Oceans. (24)

Among the Maharishis (great Rishis) I am Bhrigu; among the holy words I am the single syllable word 'AUM'; among Yajna sacrifices I am silent meditation of japa Yajna (chanting of holy names); and among the immovable objects I am the Himalaya Mountains. (25)

Mighty Himalayan ranges are a testimony of the majestic glory of God. The above verse says that the glory of the Spirit of God is reflected in the mighty Himalayan ranges among the immovable objects of the world. In Hinduism, the Himalayas have been personified as the god Himavat, father of Ganga and Parvati. Several places in the Himalayas are of deep religious significance in Buddhism, Hinduism, Jainism and Sikhism.

The Himalayas is home to nine of the ten highest peaks on Earth, including the highest peak above the sea level, Mount Everest. Many Himalayan peaks are sacred in both Buddhism and Hinduism. According to the scientific theory of plate tectonics; its formation is a result of a continental collision along the convergent boundaries between the Indo-Australian Plate and the Eurasian Plate.

Today, the Indian plate continues to be driven horizontally below the Tibetan Plateau, which forces the plateau to continue to move upwards. The Indian plate is still moving at 67 mm per year, and over the next 10 million years it will travel about 1,500 km into Asia. About 20 mm per year of the India-Asia convergence is absorbed by thrusting along the Himalayan southern front. This leads to the Himalayas rising by about 5 mm per year, making them geologically active.

The movement of the Indian plate into the Asian plate also makes this region seismically active, leading to earthquakes from time to time. The glories of God are infinite and geologists can only do the measurements, but they cannot prevent the natural occurrences of earthquakes and geological happenings.

Among the trees I am Ashvattha tree; and among the celestial sages I am Narada Muni; among the Gandharvas (celestial musicians) I am Chitraratha; and among the Siddhas I am Kapila Muni. (26)

Among horses, know Me to be the celestial horse... Ucchaisravas; among elephants I am the grace of Airavata elephant; and among men I am the glory of an Emperor.

(27)

Among weapons I am thunderbolt (lightning); among cows I am Kamadhenu (celestial milch cow that fulfils all desires). I am Kandarpa of the progenitors; and among serpents I am Vasuki. (28)

Of the Naga serpents I am Ananta; of the water-deities I am Varuna (the god of the oceans); I am Aryama of the

departed ancestors; I am Yama (god of death) among the controllers of the Universe. (29)

Among the Daityas (demons) I am Prahlada (born of demon but devoted to God); Of measures I am time (kala); among animals I am the majesty of a lion; and among the birds I am the grace of Garuda bird (vehicle of lord Vishnu). (30)

Among the purifiers I am the wind; of the wielder of weapons I am Lord Rama; among the fishes I am shark; among the rivers I am river Ganga (Jahnavi). (31)

Sri Krishna as the Spirit of Lord Vishnu says that among wielders of weapons He is Sri Rama who won the war against the evil forces of Ravana; the abductor of his wife Sita. Sri Rama was the seventh avatar of Lord Vishnu.

Sri Rama is also the protagonist of the Hindu epic Ramayana, which narrates His glories and greatness. Sri Rama is one of the many popular figures and deities in Hinduism, and Vaishnava religious scriptures in South and Southeast Asia. Both Sri Krishna and Sri Rama are complete avatars of Lord Vishnu, although they took incarnations in different generations and periods of time.

Born as the eldest son of Kausalya and Dasharatha, the King of Ayodhya, Sri Rama is considered as Maryada Purushottama, literally the Perfect Man or the Lord of self-control and virtue. His wife Sita is considered by Hindus to be an avatar of Lakshmi and the embodiment of perfect womanhood.

Rama's life and journey is one of adherence to Dharma despite the many hardships and obstacles in his life. For the sake of his father's honour, Rama abandons his claim to Ayodhya's throne to serve an exile of fourteen years in the forest. His wife Sita and brother Lakshmana decide to join him, and all of them spent the fourteen years in exile together. While in exile, Sita is kidnapped by Ravana, the evil monarch of Lanka.

Rama fights a colossal war against the army of Ravana. In a war of powerful weaponry and magical beings, Sri Rama slays Ravana in the battle and liberates his wife Sita. Having completed his exile, Sri Rama returns back to be crowned as the King of Ayodhya. This is celebrated throughout India as the festival of lights known as, 'Deepavali.' Sri Rama then became the King and ruled the kingdom. The period of His rule is known as Ram Rajya or as the time of prosperity and peace for the people in his kingdom.

The legend of Sri Rama is deeply influential and popular in the societies of the Indian and across South-East-Asian continent. The epic scripture of Ramayana was written by saint Valmiki to describe the lifetime of Sri Rama. There is a total reverence for chanting the Holy Names and glories of Sri Rama and Sri Krishna for their unending compassion, courage and devotion to uphold righteousness and Dharma.

The Divine incarnations of Lord Vishnu in the human form as Sri Rama and Sri Krishna are venerated by the Hindus, and chanted in the form of a Maha Mantra as, " Hare Rama, Hare Rama; Rama-Rama Hare Hare; Hare Krishna, Hare Krishna; Krishna-Krishna Hare Hare."

Sri Krishna says that among all the Rivers of the world; I am the Ganga River descending from the heavens, in the form of melting snow from the lofty Himalayas. The Ganges or the Ganga River is a sacred river to Hindus, along every fragment of its length. All along its course of flow, Hindus take bath in its waters, paying homage to their ancestors and to their gods by cupping its water in their hands, lifting it in reverence, and letting it fall back into the River.

They offer flowers and rose petals and float shallow clay dishes filled with oil and lit with wicks (diyas) on the Ganga waters. On the journey back home from the Ganga River, they carry small quantities of Ganga water with them, for use in religious rituals. When a loved one dies, Hindus bring the ashes of the deceased person to the Ganga River, to be immersed in its waters.

The Ganga River is the embodiment of sacred waters in Hindu mythology. There is nothing more stirring for a Hindu than to take a dip in the Ganga River, which is considered to remit sins, especially at one of the famous tirthas such as Gangotri, Haridwar, Prayag, or Varanasi. The symbolic and religious importance of the Ganga River is a matter of faith.

India's first Prime Minister Late Jawaharlal Nehru, after Independence of India on 15 August 1947, asked for a handful of his ashes to be immersed into the Ganga waters, and some on top of the Himalayas after his death.

He wrote in his Will, "The Ganga is the river of India, beloved of her people, around which are intertwined her racial memories, her hopes and fears, her songs of triumph, her victories and her defeats. She has been a symbol of India's age-long culture and civilization, ever-changing, ever-flowing, and yet ever the same Ganga."

Kumbh Mela is the most sacred of all the pilgrimages. Millions of men and women attend this auspicious festival to take a dip in the Ganga River to attain the merit associated with the ritual of a holy bath on these special days. The sadhus are seen clad in saffron sheets with ashes and mud dabbed on their skin as per the ancient customs of renunciation. Some of the so-called Naga-sanyasis do not wear any clothes and remain naked as a mark of renunciation.

The Ganges River, also known as the Ganga, is one of the world's major rivers, running for more than 2,550 kilometres from the Himalayas to its final discharge in the Bay of Bengal. Nature provided the purest form of water by melting of snow in the glaciers of the Himalayas, but mankind apart from veneration of the river water, has also misused the Ganga waters, for their own convenience and selfish interests.

Ganga is now one of the most polluted rivers; and the primary source of pollution of the river comes from sewage, from animal carcasses, human corpses, soap and other pollutants from bathers. Indeed, scientists measured the harmful bacteria present in the Ganga waters, at thousands of times more than what is permissible.

The level of oxygen in the water was also found to be unhealthy. But due to faith and the divine dispensation people still drink its water and yet survive for a healthy living. Cleaning of the Ganga River has been taken up by the Government-sponsored Ganga Action Plan (GAP), from time to time, but the desired results have not been satisfactorily achieved.

The Ganga River starting from its source and origin as the Bhagirathi River, Gangotri Glacier at Gomukh; travels through many cities in India in the Gangetic plains, before its final discharge in the Bay of Bengal.

The pollution by the mankind, and ever increasing over-population living near the banks of the river, has foiled all attempts to clean the pollution of the river waters. Several western-style sewage treatment plants were built along the river, but they were no match for the massive increase in population along the banks of the River.

O Arjuna! Of all created things, I am the beginning, middle and the end. Of all branches of knowledge, I am the science of Self-realization. I am logical reasoning of those who debate. (32)

Of the letters I am the first letter 'A'; —Of the pairing of words, I am the connective element (dvandva);—I am never ending Time; and I am the omnipresent support for the entire Universe facing everywhere. (33)

And I am the all-devouring death of the born and the origin of all beings yet to be born; and of the feminine qualities of Prakriti, I am fame, prosperity, speech, memory, intelligence, firmness and forgiveness. (34)

Of the hymns in Sama Veda I am Brihat-Saman; among the sacred verses I am Gayatri mantra. Among the months I am the Margashirsha; and of the seasons I am the flowery spring season. (35)

Of the deceitful I am gambling; I am splendour of the powerful; I am victory and I am effort; I am goodness of the righteous. (36)

Of the Vrishnis I am Vasudeva (Sri Krishna); among the Pandavas I am Dhananjaya (Arjuna); among the sages I am Vyasa; and among the wise seers I am Usana saint. (37)

Of justice I am the rod of punishment; I am statesmanship of the victorious; I am silence among the secrets; and I am wisdom of the knowledgeable. (38)

O Arjuna! I am the seed of all life. There is no creature either moving or unmoving, that can exist without My Spirit of Consciousness. (39)

O Parantapa Arjuna! There is no end to the glories of My infinite consciousness. What has been declared by Me, is just a mere indication of My infinite glories. (40)

Whatever being is of a brilliant mind, prosperous and full of vitality; know that it is a manifestation of a tiny spark of My splendour. (41)

O Arjuna! What is the need for such a detailed knowledge? Understand that My infinite Spirit pervades and supports the entire Universe by just a tiny fraction of My Being. (42)

CHAPTER 11

THE VISION OF THE COSMIC FORM
VISVARUPA DARSHANA YOGA

Arjuna said:

On my humble supplication, You have declared the most profound and secret science of Self-knowledge. My confusion and delusion has now been dispelled. (1)

O Lotus eyed Sri Krishna! I have heard from You the detailed description of the beginning and the end of all living beings; and also of Your inexhaustible and immortal glories. (2)

O Supreme Lord! You have declared Yourself as the embodied incarnation of the Supreme God. I greatly desire to see Your Divine Sovereign form. (3)

O Sri Krishna! Lord of the Yoga! If You think that it is possible for You to reveal Your Imperishable Cosmic form, then kindly show Your Universal form to me. (4)

Arjuna here says that O Supreme Purusha! You have declared yourself as the embodied incarnation of God and therefore, "I greatly desire to see your Divine Sovereign form."

Similarly in Bible Jesus says, "Unless you people see miraculous signs and wonders, you will never believe."—It is a strange irony, that worldly human beings do not believe when real God appears before them in human form; but they are ready to believe and touch the feet of imposters and fake Gurus in the world.

Sri Krishna said:

O Partha Arjuna! Behold My manifold and Divine forms in different colours and shapes, by hundreds and thousands. (5)

O Bharata Arjuna! Behold existing in Me the Adityas, the Vasus, the Rudras, the twin Aswins and the Maruts. Behold the many wonders that have never been seen before. (6)

O Gudakesha Arjuna! Today behold within My Cosmic body, the entire Universe of the moving and the unmoving, and whatever else you want to see, all integral within My body. (7)

But it will not be possible for you to see My Cosmic divine form with your human eyes. Behold My Yoga power and My grace, I give you the Divine sight to see everything. (8)

Sanjaya said to King Dhritarashtra:

O King! Having thus spoken, the great Lord of the Universe Sri Krishna (Hari) revealed to Arjuna His supremely glorious Cosmic form of God. (9)

Arjuna saw the wondrous sight of the Cosmic form of God, with many mouths and eyes, decked with innumerable celestial ornaments, wielding many uplifted divine weapons. (10)

Wearing Divine garlands and robes, anointed with celestial fragrances, all wonderful, resplendent, and boundless of infinite form facing the Universe everywhere. (11)

The splendour of that cosmic form of God was so dazzling, as if all of a sudden a thousand Suns had suddenly blazed forth in the sky. (12)

Then Pandava Arjuna, saw within the cosmic form of God, the entire Universe drawn together into one place. (13)

Dhananjaya Arjuna with his body tingling in complete amazement, bowed down his head in obeisance to the great Lord, and with folded hands thus spoke to Sri Krishna in adoration: (14)

Arjuna said:

O Incarnation of Cosmic God! I see within Your celestial Body all the angel-gods as well as multitudes of different beings....I see Brahma the Creator seated on the lotus plant and all the divine sages and the celestial serpents.

(15)

O Lord of the universe, O Cosmic God! I see You with infinite arms, bellies, mouths and eyes, boundless on all sides....I see neither Thy beginning nor the middle nor the end. (16)

I see You with a crown, mace and discus (form of Lord Vishnu); a mass of radiance blazing all around, dazzling like a flaming fire, and like the Sun of immeasurable intensity and very hard to look at. (17)

Lord Vishnu has ten avatars, nine of which have already taken place, and the last avatar of Sri Kalki is yet to appear in the Kali Yuga. Lord Vishnu, the Hindu God of preservation of Universe, is said to descend in the human form of an avatar to restore the cosmic order. The Sanskrit word ***Dashavatara*** is derived from ***dasha***, meaning 'ten' and ***avatar*** meaning 'incarnations.'

The list of the incarnations of Lord Vishnu is; ***Sri Matsya avatar*** or in the form of fish, from Satya yuga; – ***Sri Kurma avatar*** in the form of tortoise, from the Satya Yuga;–***Sri Varaha avatar*** in the form of boar, from the Satya Yuga;–***Sri Narasimha avatar***, the half-man and half-lion form, from Satya Yuga;–

Sri Vamana avatar in the form of a dwarf, from the Treta Yuga;–***Sri Parashurama avatar*** as a warrior with the axe from Treta Yuga; –***Sri Rama avatar*** as the prince of Ayodhya from the Treta Yuga;– ***Sri Krishna avatar*** as the son of Vasudeva from the Dwapara Yuga;–***Sri Gautama Buddha*** avatar as the founder of Buddhism;– and ***Kalki avatar*** which is yet to appear in the Kali Yuga.

Thou are the imperishable Supreme Spirit of God as the ultimate goal for Self-realization by human beings. The entire Universe dwells in Thy Supreme Spirit. Your Supreme Spirit is indestructible, eternal and protector of the Dharma. Thou indeed are the One and the only Supreme Purusha. (18)

I see You without beginning, middle and end of infinite power. You have infinite arms and flaming fire is coming out of Your mouth, the Sun and the Moon are Thy eyes. The radiance of Your infinite energy is heating the entire Universe. (19)

The space between the heaven and the earth and all the quarters of the Universe are filled with Thy Spirit. O God of all shining deities; the blazing radiance of Your universal form is fearful for human beings to look at, and the three worlds are trembling and stricken with fear. (20)

The multitudes of shining deities are entering Your infinite Universal form. With folded hands in obeisance and veneration, they are singing hymns of praise in Your glory and greatness. The Rishis and realized saints are saying 'May it all be well with the world.' (21)

The shining deities of Rudras, Adityas, Vasus, Sadhyas, Vishvedevas, Asvins, Maruts, and Ushmapas, host of Gandharvas, Yakshas, Asuras and Siddhas...are all looking at You in astonishment and wonder. (22)

O Lord Krishna!...I as well as the whole world is alarmed and terrified upon seeing Your unimaginable Cosmic form

with numerous mouths and eyes, many arms, thighs and feet, with myriad stomachs and huge tusks....O incarnation of Lord Vishnu! Seeing You in this form touching the sky, effulgent with many colours and mouths wide open with large fiery eyes, I am frightened and I find no peace and solace. (23–24)

Arjuna says to Lord Sri Krishna in the above verse: —I see your cosmic form touching the sky with glory: ***'nabhah***...***sparasham***... ***diptam***...***aneka***...***varnam'***:—touching the sky with glory, effulgent with many colours.

The Motto of the Indian Air Force has been taken from this verse of eleventh chapter of the Gita, during the discourse given by Lord Krishna to Arjuna on the battlefield of Mahabharata War at Kurukshetra.

The Lord is showing His Supreme Divine form to Arjuna and this great form is reaching the heights of the sky with glory, evoking fear and loss of self-control in the mind of Arjuna. The aircraft of the Indian Air Force, Navy and Army Helicopters, similarly touch the skies with glory, to show their mighty powers to the adversaries.

O God of all gods! I have lost my balance of mind and sense of bearing, after seeing your mouths wide open with huge tusks emitting blazing flames which looks as if it will destroy the world. Have mercy on me and be gracious to all! O Abode of the Universe. (25)

I see all the sons of Dhritarashtra with multitude of kings, Bhishma, Drona and Sutaputra (Karna), and many of our warriors, entering in Your huge mouth with massive teeth, which is frightening to look at. Some are hanging in the gaps of Thy teeth with their heads crushed to powder.

(26–27)

As the many streams of rivers rush towards the Ocean, similarly do these heroes in the world of men enter Your flaming mouths. (28)

As the moths and winged insects rush with great speed into a blazing fire for destruction, so do creatures and people enter Your mouths. (29)

O incarnation of Lord Vishnu! Swallowing all the creatures and beings of the world from all sides with the flaming fire of Your mouth, thou are licking them all around. Thy fiery rays of light are filling the entire Universe with radiance. (30)

Tell me who You are of such a fierce incomprehensive form? Salutations to thee! O Supreme God! Be merciful unto this world. I desire to know Thyself as I cannot comprehend Thy working, O Primal God. (31)

Sri Krishna said:

I am the mighty devouring 'Time' (Kala), into which the entire Creation dissolves in due course of time. Even without you these warriors arrayed in the battle shall cease to exist. (32)

O Arjuna! Therefore you arise and conquer your enemies to attain glory. You will thus enjoy unrivalled kingdom. These warriors already stand killed by My wheel of time 'Kala,' and you just be an outward instrument for their destruction. (33)

Kill Drona, Bhishma, Jayadratha, Karna and other brave warriors who already stand killed by My powers. Be not distressed and fight the battle, and you will surely win.

(34)

Sanjaya said to King Dhritarashtra:

Having heard these words of Keshava Sri Krishna; Arjuna the crown wearer, prostrated with folded hands while

still trembling with fear (after seeing the Cosmic form of God), and thus spoke to Sri Krishna in a choked voice. (35)

Arjuna said:

O Hrishikesha Sri Krishna! Very rightly the world delights and rejoices in singing Thy glories and Thy holy names. The evil forces of demons flee in terror in all directions. The multitude of perfected sages bow down to You in obeisance. (36)

And why should they not bow down and pay homage to Thy infinite Spirit, the Lord of all gods? Thou are the Abode of the Universe, the Primal cause even of Brahma (the Creator), and thou are the imperishable Spirit, the being and the non-being, which is Supreme. (37)

You are the Primal God, the Ancient Purusha and the Supreme refuge of the Universe. You are the knower and the One to be known and the Supreme Abode. By Your Spirit alone this entire Universe is pervaded. O infinite Being! (38)

You are Vayu (the wind god), Yama (the god of death), Agni (the god of fire), Varuna (the god of the oceans), the Moon, Brahma (the Lord of Creation) and the grandsire of all beings (being the First in Creation). Salutations and veneration to thy infinite Spirit, a thousand times. (39)

The spirit of Lord Vishnu as Krishna-consciousness is glorified as the first in the Creation, as the originator of all beings. The same all-pervading Spirit is in the Fire, Wind, Oceans, Moon and Yama (the god of death).

The deity of ***'Varuna'*** is a Hindu god of the oceans; as well as the god of the law of the underwater world. The origin of the deity ***'Varuna'*** is stated in ancient Vedic Scriptures, as the keeper of the souls of the drowned.

O God! O God of infinite boundless Power and strength! You pervade the entire Universe and You are everything. Salutations and deep obeisance to You from everywhere in all directions. (40)

Not knowing that Thou are the incarnation of Lord Vishnu, I have unknowingly and carelessly addressed You as, "O Krishna! O Yadava! O my friend," due to my boundless love and familiarity with you and considering You as a mere human being....

O Achyuta Sri Krishna! I implore Thy forgiveness for not having given You the proper marks of respect, while in jest at play, resting, sitting or while eating together or in the company of others. (41–42)

You are the Father of the moving and the unmoving world; worthy of adoration and veneration by the world. You are the greatest Master and Guru (teacher), and there is none who can excel You in the three worlds. —O Lord! All power and glory belongs to You, and who can be greater than You? (43)

O Adorable Spirit of God! Bowing down and prostrating myself in obeisance, I implore Your forgiveness. Grant me pardon O Lord, as a father to a son, a friend to his dear friend, as a lover to a beloved. (44)

I rejoice upon having seen Your wondrous cosmic form which was hitherto never seen before by any human being; yet my heart is perturbed with fear due to Thy formidable and incomprehensive form. O Lord! One God of this entire Universe! Have mercy on me, and I pray to You to appear in Your earlier sublime human form. (45)

Human mind is comfortable within the confines of a known environment, and within the boundaries of one's family circle. The Universe is so vast that it frightens a person out of one's wits to know such vastness, with the limited capability of a human mind.

There are millions of stars, galaxies in the Universe, out of which Sun, Moon and the Earth are just a small part.

The planet earth looks so small in comparison to the millions of galaxies in the Universe. Arjuna is so frightened upon seeing the vastness of the Universe which Sri Krishna shows to him, that it was an out of the world experience.

Arjuna upon seeing the Cosmic Form of Sri Krishna which encompasses the entire Universe loses the orientation and composure of his mind. Totality and such vastness are frightening to the human beings, as it is not a familiar domain for the human mind. A person individually is not as much as even a drop of water in the vast ocean. Yet human consciousness being a part of the Divine consciousness has infinite capabilities and powers to solve complex problems.

O Thousand-armed God of the Universe! O incarnation of Lord Vishnu!—I desire to see Your earlier sublime manifestation of four-armed Lord Vishnu, with a crown on the head, a mace and a discus in hand. (46)

Lord Vishnu is also seen standing on the whirl of a lotus flower with four hands, which represent the four directions and indicates His absolute power in the four corners of the Universe. Each hand holds an item; a disc, a lotus flower, a conch shell and a mace.

When a conch shell is blown, it is said to produce a sound related to the original vibration of the Creation of the Universe. The Lord also blows His conch to call everyone to turn to the higher reality of life rather than remaining in the darkness of material existence. This calling is the inner voice which nudges all beings to seek the Absolute Truth.

The disc or chakra signifies the universal mind or awareness. It gets rid of all ignorance and shows the higher path of awareness. The disc is called Sudarshana Chakra, the limitless power and light. It indicates the revolving nature of the Universe (Maya), around an unmoving and changeless centre, as the Self-soul.

The mace represents the cosmic intellect or knowledge. It is called Kaumodaki, meaning that which captivates the mind. It is also associated with time, which destroys all and is thus related to the revolving wheel of time or Kala. The lotus flower in His hand shows the changing nature of the Universe. It also indicates that the real purpose of human existence is to live like a lotus flower, untouched by the dirt of the world.

Sri Krishna said:

O Arjuna! By My own Yoga power and grace, I revealed to you My infinite, resplendent, effulgent, primeval, Universal Cosmic form; which has never been shown to anyone before. (47)

O Arjuna! Not by the study of the sacred Vedas, or by sacrifice or charity, or by rituals or severe penances, can I be seen in this Cosmic form by anyone in this world of human beings. (48)

Do not be distressed or bewildered upon seeing this massive form of Mine encompassing the entire Universe. Free from fear and with a cheerful mind, again see My previous embodied incarnation (Four-armed form of Lord Vishnu with a conch, discus, mace and a lotus flower). (49)

Arjuna as a human being was bewildered to see the massive Cosmic Form of Sri Krishna, but the entire Creation is the glory of the God.—***Bible*** (***Matthew***) says, "Jesus looked at them and said: With man this is impossible, but with God all things are possible."

Sanjaya said to King Dhritarashtra:

Vasudeva Sri Krishna having thus spoken to Arjuna, once again resumed His previous gentle and pleasing human incarnation. And mighty Sri Krishna once again reassured

and consoled Arjuna, who was terrified after seeing the Cosmic form. (50)

Arjuna said:

O Janardana Sri Krishna! Seeing You now in Your former gentle human form, my mind is once again composed and my balance of mind is restored. (51)

Sri Krishna Said:

Indeed, it is very hard and difficult to perceive and comprehend the entire Universe in My human form as you have seen. Even the multitudes of shining demigods (Devas) are very eager to see My Universal form. (52)

This Divine Universal form as seen by you, cannot be seen either by the knower of the Veda scriptures, or by austerities, or by charities or by any sacrificial Yajna. (53)

O Parantapa Arjuna! Only by single-hearted devotion and by full absorption in meditation, one can perceive and realize the essence of My Divine Spirit of Cosmic consciousness in reality. (54)

O Pandava Arjuna! One who dedicates all work to Me, who looks upon Me as the Supreme Lord, who is devoted to Me, free from all worldly attachment, without hatred for any being, such a person is fit to attain Oneness with My infinite Spirit. (55)

CHAPTER 12

THE YOGA OF DEVOTION
BHAKTI YOGA

Arjuna said:

Those devotees who are ever steadfast and worship You in the embodied human manifestation with attributes; and those who worship You as unseen in unmanifest form as the imperishable Spirit of God; of these two who is better versed in 'Yoga path' for Self-realization. (1)

Sanskrit to English translation reads as: "***Evam***:—thus in manifest form:—***satata-yuktah***:—ever steadfast:—***ye***:—those:—***bhaktah***:—devotees:—***tvam***:—You (thee):—***paryupasate***:—worship:—***ye***:—those:—***cha***: and:—***api***:—also:—***aksharam***:—the imperishable:—***avyaktam***:—the unmanifest:—***tesham***:—of these:—***ke***:—which:—***Yoga vittamah***:—better versed in Yoga path."

In this chapter of Bhakti Yoga, Arjuna is asking whether God is to be worshipped in the visual manifest form as Lord Vishnu, Sri Krishna, Sri Rama, and others; or else if God is to be worshipped in the unmanifest form without any physical form, as the all pervading Spirit. God (Brahman) is both with and without attributes. Is God to be visualized with a form or without form? This is the basic question. Arjuna here asks a pointed question, and asks which of these paths is better for Self-realization. Sri Krishna replies to these questions as follows:

Sri Krishna Said:

Those who worship Me with their mind fixed on Me with their innermost soul, with utmost faith and devotion—them I consider to be the best in Yoga path. (2)

But those who worship and meditate upon My Supreme Spirit as Imperishable, Indefinable, the Unmanifest, the Omnipresent, the Unthinkable, the Unchangeable, the Unmoving, the Eternal Spirit; having controlled all their senses, even-minded everywhere, rejoicing in the welfare of all beings; they also attain My Supreme Being. (3–4)

Different religions are divided on this issue and there is a very rigid stand on this aspect by different sects. All religions agree that there is only one Supreme God or Reality, which governs the entire Universe. But then why are there so many religions and so many different faiths?

Every religion and faith firmly believes that only their faith is right and all others will go into the fire of hell. Why is the entire human race divided in their beliefs and faith when everybody accepts that there is only one governing principle and there is only One God? Why the divide in faith and beliefs between Hindus, Muslims, Christians and other religions, when all Scriptures state the same truth and the same tenets.

When India got Independence on 15 August 1947, the erstwhile British India was divided into India and Pakistan, and it resulted in a massive massacre of Hindus and Muslims among themselves, due to discrimination of faith and religion.

Pakistan became a predominant Muslim state, and India became a predominant Hindu state. India is a secular country where all the minority communities live in harmony with the Hindu population. What was the cause of division of British India in the first place? Why is Kashmir still a bone of contention between India and Pakistan?

Bhagavad Gita says that those who with total faith and devotion worship the spirit of God with their innermost soul are dear to God. This is the basic underlying criteria, irrespective of different castes, creeds or dogmas adopted by the human beings.

Different religions should not create rigid barriers and water tight compartments to separate the humanity. Both the aspects of God with form and God without form have to be accepted as both complement each other. God does not divide humanity on the basis of religion, but it is human beings who are responsible for that. Mankind has created different sects and have erected walls around them.

Take the case of water as a liquid which is with a form, but when the same water is boiled and it evaporates into the air, it becomes formless. The water from the oceans evaporates due to the heat of the sun and forms clouds. These clouds of vapour rise up in the air to higher altitudes and due to moisture again condense into rain water as a visible form.

The water from the rivers again flows back into the sea. The water cycle thus is both with form and without form. The spirit of God manifests as incarnation of God in different ages and Yugas as messengers of God; and once again merges back into the Cosmic Spirit.

Greater is their difficulty whose minds are set upon the Absolute unmanifest (without visual form); for the goal of the unmanifest is very hard to attain for the embodied human beings. (5)

Unmanifest or Nirguna Brahman or Absolute Spirit is without form, abstract and without any attributes. Whereas manifest or Saguna Brahman is with form and has attributes, as in idols (Murti) of gods in temples. Idols in temples or pictures of deities are not God themselves, but with faith they help the devotees to turn their thoughts and mind on the chosen deity and tune up their minds in prayer to the chosen form of God. It is like tuning to a particular chosen frequency on the radio.

Both the aspects of with form and without form are of the same God. Even if one is a follower of one particular faith or worship, still you cannot deny the other. The fire and its heating characteristic cannot be separated from each other. The Sun and its rays of light are one and the same.

Sri Krishna manifested as an incarnation of God in the human form five thousand years ago to deliver the message of Bhagavad Gita to the humanity. And Sri Krishna is present even today in the unmanifest form as Krishna-consciousness.

Both these aspects are true. One can reach the ultimate goal, by both manifest as well as the unmanifest paths. But the path of absolute unmanifest Spirit is arduous and difficult to reach for the worldly human beings. Human beings believe more easily what they see with their own eyes.

Late Swami Sivananda of Divine Life Society Rishikesh stated that human beings are closely identified and attached with the physical human body; therefore it is easy for a common man to meditate on God in a manifest visual form. But difficulty arises when gullible, ignorant men and women start worshipping the Gurus and Swamis as real Gods.

In Muslim religion and in Quran, worshipping of God in any physical manifest form such as idols or pictures is strictly prohibited. A Muslim, is therefore required to offer his prayers (namaz) at the stipulated times to the Absolute unmanifest Spirit of God. Prophet Muhammad declared that he was a messenger of God, and Quran forbids worship of idols or any other visual form of God in pictures, in any mosque or at any other place.

Islam religion is based on five basic pillars as a foundation. These five pillars of faith are Shahada (That there is only one God); Salat (prayers); Zakat (Giving of Alms); Sawm (Fasting during Ramadan) and Hajj (pilgrimage to Mecca).

These five practices are essential to Sunni Islam; Shi'a Muslims subscribe to eight ritual practices which substantially overlap with the five Pillars. Christian religion also offers prayers to the almighty unmanifest Spirit of God as the Divine Father, and forbids idol worship. —Bhagavad Gita says that God can be worshipped as both in manifest forms, as well as in the unmanifest Absolute Spirit.

For those who perform all actions in a spirit of self-surrender to My Supreme Consciousness; and worship My Supreme Spirit with a single-minded devotion;—O Partha-Arjuna, for them whose hearts are thus fixed on Me to the exclusion of all else; I very soon become the saviour from the suffering of 'birth and death' in this mortal world. (6–7)

Fix your mind on Me alone, with your thoughts absorbed in My Consciousness of God, exclusively. You will thus dwell in My Spirit of God only, hereafter. There is no doubt in this. (8)

O Dhananjaya Arjuna! If you are not able to steadily focus your mind On My Divine consciousness; then by perseverance reach My Spirit of God by regular practice of yoga meditation (Abhyasa-yoga). (9)

But if you are not able to practice 'Yoga meditation' regularly; then dedicate all your work and actions to My Spirit of God. Even by performing all actions for My sake you will attain perfection. (10)

This verse gives the method for seeking oneness with the spirit of God by dedicating all actions to God whether good or bad. Then a human being is no more a doer of actions but only a medium through which the spirit of God is functioning.

When a person's individual doership merges with the infinite spirit, then a person neither takes praise nor blame for the results of one's work and efforts. It is death of the individual 'ego' of 'I' and 'Mine,' and results in peace of mind, and then one is not concerned and worried about the results of one's actions.

Jesus says, "Knock and the door shall be opened unto you. Ask and it shall be given. Seek and you shall find."—Man has to put efforts in the right direction and dedicate all actions to God, and then the door opens. Sri Krishna says that actions performed with awareness are better than those actions which are performed in ignorance.

And if you are not able to do even this; then take refuge in Me with total dependence on My Spirit of God alone. Abandon the fruits and results of all actions with mind and senses controlled. (11)

Sri Krishna is a Master guide and a dear friend to Arjuna. God is near and far away. God is near when the work is worship, and all actions are dedicated to God. God is far away when you think that God is sitting somewhere in heaven on a golden throne of diamonds, to pass judgements on your good and bad actions.

When you consider the Spirit of God dwelling in your heart, then there is no duality between you and the Spirit of God, and there is oneness. If you consider God as far away in heaven, then you create a duality and separateness.

Knowledge is better than mere ritual practice of religion. Meditation on the 'Spirit of God' is better than mere knowledge; better than meditation is the renunciation of the fruits of actions; as peace of mind immediately follows, thereafter. (12)

In spirituality one has to carve out one's own path, and not bother about what other people will think and say. May be they will think that you are crazy, a mad person or childish. When one has no expectations and attachment with others, then the opinion and thinking of others is of no consequence and does not matter at all.

Bhaja Govindam text says, "The yogi who wears clothes made of discarded pieces of rags left on the roadside; and walks the spiritual path which is beyond virtue and sin; one whose mind is ever in union with the infinite spirit of God, he then lives as a child or a madman."

One who has no ill-will towards any being, who is friendly and kind to all, who is free from the feeling of ownership and possessions, balanced in suffering and happiness and one who forgives others— (13)

The verse says in Sanskrit ***'Kshami'***; which means one who forgives others. If a person does not forgive others for the mental and emotional hurt caused to him; then one causes further hurt and harm to oneself by keeping that grudge and ill-will towards that person in his heart. A story best explains this point.

Two friends went for a walk on the sea shore. While walking on the beach they had a heated argument, and one friend slapped the other on the face. One who got slapped was red-faced with indignation and deeply hurt by the action of his friend. He did not say anything to his friend, but wrote the following words on the sand, "Today my best friend slapped me on my face."

After that, they continued walking for some distance on the beach, and then decided to take a bath in the sea water. The one, who was slapped, entered the deeper side of the sea water and a large wave of water hit him on the face. He started drowning, but in the nick of time, his friend who was a good swimmer rushed to his rescue and saved his life.

After he came out of the water and had recovered from the experience of the drowning trauma, he wrote on a nearby stone rock the following words, "Today, my best friend saved my life."

The friend who had slapped, and saved the life of his friend asked, "When I slapped, you wrote on the sand. And now when I saved your life, you have written on the stone rock, why?"

The friend replied, "When someone hurts us, it should be like writing on the sand; where the winds of forgiveness will quickly erase it away. But when someone does a life-saving virtuous act of kindness and goodness; then one must engrave the remembrance of the act on a stone, where the winds and the passage of time will not erase it."

One who is ever content, steady in meditation, self-controlled with a firm determination, with mind and intellect fixed on My Spirit of God;–such a devotee is dear to Me. (14)

One who does not afflict and cause disturbance to the world, and who is similarly not afflicted by the world;

one who is free from the feeling of joy, envy, fear and anxiety—such a devotee is dear to Me. (15)

This verse with Sanskrit translation reads as: "***Yasmat***:—from whom:—***na***:—not:—***udvijate***:—is agitated:—***lokah***:—the world:—***lokat***:—from the world:—***na***:—not:—***udvijate***:—is agitated:—***cha***:—and:—***yah***:—who:—***harsha...amarsha... bhaya...udvegaih***:—by joy, envy, fear and anxiety:—***muktah***:—free from:—***yah***:—who:—***sah***:—he or she:—***cha***:—and:—***me***:—to Me:—***priya***:—dear."

One should not cause disturbance and hurt the feelings of others around him; and similarly one should be mentally strong not to be upset by the behaviour and anger of others. The world has different kinds of people, who have their own frustrations, anger, jealousy and hatred; and one should not meddle with the affairs of others unnecessarily. One should not step on other people's toes, and should not allow others to do that to oneself either. Read the story below.

Once I took a taxi to go to the Airport. My taxi was on the right lane, when all of a sudden out of nowhere; a black car raced and speeded out of a petrol pump at a racing speed. My taxi driver slammed the brakes, and we narrowly missed the collision with other speeding car by a fraction of an inch. It was a close call and a narrow escape. I was jolted out of my seat.

The driver of the black car accusingly waved his arms, and yelled at my taxi driver for careless driving; and for not looking around for other cars in the vicinity. My taxi driver just smiled and waved back to the other driver with a friendly smile.

I asked my driver, "Why did you not react to the reckless driving of the other driver, and instead you gave him a friendly smile, as if nothing has happened? The other driver almost crashed into our taxi, and it could have been a serious accident."

My driver explained that many people are like a garbage truck. They run around full of garbage, full of frustration and disappointments. When their garbage piles up and the stink rises, then they need a place to dump their garbage, and sometimes they will dump it on you.

Do not react to such people as they will dump their anger on you. It is best to just smile, and wave to them from a distance and move on. Why take their garbage and anger, and further spread it in your workplace, and at home and among your friends?

One who has no wants, pure in body and mind, efficient in work, impartial and unconcerned, untroubled and who has given-up all selfish undertakings;—thus devoted to My Spirit of Krishna-consciousness, he or she is dear to Me. (16)

All worldly activities have a selfish tinge with an effect of karmic bondage. A rich politician or a businessman may undertake charitable projects to build schools, colleges and hospitals to get name, fame, wealth, power and fulfil his desire to be well known by people around him.

But none of the worldly activities are everlasting or eternal. What was the experience of King Solomon who had all the wealth and resources at his command to achieve and accomplish anything he wanted? Finally it all turned out to be fleeting, like a wind arising and just passing away.

One who neither rejoices nor hates nor grieves nor desires, renouncing good and bad; full of devotion to My Spirit of God; —such a devotee is dear to Me. (17)

One who is same to a friend and an enemy; and also in honour and dishonour; same in cold and heat; in pleasure and sorrow and free from all worldly attachment. (18)

One who is same in praise and blame, given to silent contemplation, content in all circumstances, without a fixed destination as a home; full of faith and devotion,– such a soul is dear to Me. (19)

Those who follow and practice the teachings of this immortal Scripture and Dharma as declared, with total faith and devotion, considering this as the Supreme Goal in life; –they are exceedingly dear to Me. (20)

CHAPTER 13

THE YOGA OF DISCRIMINATION OF BODY AND SOUL

YOGA OF KSHETRA AND KSHETRAJNA

Arjuna said:

O Keshava Sri Krishna! I desire to learn what is Prakriti (inherent nature principle), what is Purusha (cosmic soul principle); the Kshetra (body as field), Kshetrajna (Self-soul as the knower of the body field); and what constitutes real Spiritual knowledge which ought to be known.

Arjuna here asks these questions as an earnest seeker. Sri Krishna answers these questions as follows:

Sri Krishna said:

O Kaunteya Arjuna! This body is called the field (Kshetra), where both good and bad actions are sown and reaped; and the Self-soul Atman in the body is a witness of all the actions and is the knower of the field (Kshetrajna). (1)

The human body is like soil or a field in which the seed of karma is sown and one reaps the results as good or bad. The fruit can be in the form of a good tree or as poisonous weeds. The Self-soul is a witnessor of all actions and one's consciousness tells a person whether the action is good or bad.

O Bharata Arjuna! And know Me to be the 'conscious soul principle' (Kshetrajna) in all living bodies (Kshetras). This knowledge of matter and Spirit (Kshetra and Kshetrajna), is deemed by Me as the basis of true Spiritual knowledge.

(2)

Hear from me in brief as to what Kshetra (field) is, and what are its properties and modifications; from whence it arises, and what is the conscious soul principle, and what are the powers associated with it. (3)

The knowledge of Kshetra and Kshetrajna has been illustrated by the realized sages in many different ways, in various Vedic hymns, and also in conclusive and well-reasoned Brahma-sutras passages. (4)

The aggregate body field with its modifications has been briefly described as comprising of five cosmic elements (space, air, fire, water, earth), egoism, intellect, as also the unmanifest (nature); the ten senses (eyes, ears, skin, tongue and nose—as senses of knowledge; and hands, feet, mouth, anus, and genital organs...as organs of action), the mind and five sense-objects (taste, sight, touch, sound and smell). (5)

Attraction and aversion; pleasure and pain; the aggregate, consciousness and fortitude—thus Kshetra (body) has been briefly described with its modifications. (6)

Humility, lack of hypocrisy (modesty), non-violence, forgiveness, simplicity and uprightness, respect for the learned teachers, purity (of body and mind), steadfastness, self-control of senses;– (7)

Dispassion towards objects of enjoyment in the world, absence of egoism, realization of inherent suffering associated with birth, death, old age, disease and pain;... (8)

Non-attachment, non-identification and clinging with son, wife, home, etc (near and dear ones and the like); and also keeping equanimity and sameness in desirable as well as unfortunate happenings in life— (9)

The above verse implies that in order to attach with God-consciousness, one has to detach from all earthly clinging of relationships and objects which are dear to a person. It does not mean that a person is indifferent to one's relatives and friends, but it means that a Self-realized saint has no preferential treatment for one's relatives and dear ones, but treats everyone equally, as just the same.

Other scriptures also say the same truth. —Adi Shankaracharya says in Bhaja Govindam, "Thus enquire! Who am I? Who are you? From where did I come from? Who is my mother? Who is my father? This world is made up of dreams and leaving aside the world of experiences, thus engage in enquiry."

Bible says, "Someone said to Him, behold, Your mother and Your brothers are standing outside seeking to speak to You. But Jesus answered and said, 'Who is My mother and who are My brothers?' And stretching out His hand toward His disciples, He said, 'Behold My mother and My brothers!'...Pointing to his disciples, he said, 'Here are my mother and my brothers.'—He that loves his father or mother more than me is not worthy of me."

In the above Bible passage, Jesus Christ implied that all those who follow the spiritual teaching are like his mother, father, brothers and sisters; and not those who are merely his biological mother, brothers and sisters.

Total devotion and one-pointed faith in following this 'Yoga path' of union with the Divine Spirit of God; staying in peaceful solitary places, away from the distraction and company of the men and women. (10)

Constantly striving towards knowledge and Self-realization, and seeing God as the object of true knowledge; this is declared to be true spiritual wisdom, and what is opposed to this is ignorance. (11)

The above verse explains that each day of one's life, which is spent to get closer to the Spirit of God; is a day usefully spent in wisdom. All other activities to enhance your family interests, earn more money and in sensual pursuits, is a day spent without any spiritual gains.

A very rich young man went to see a holy man to seek his advice about what he should do with his useless life with no purpose. The holy man led him over to the window and asked him, "What do you see through the window glass?" The rich man replied, "I can see men and women moving around on the street, and a blind man begging for alms."

After that, the holy man showed him a large mirror and said to him, "Look in this mirror and tell me what you see now." The rich man said, "I can see reflection of my body and face in the mirror." The holy man said, "And you cannot see others through this mirror. But the window glass and the mirror are both made of the same basic material of glass. The glass in the mirror has a coating of a fine layer of silver. Thus you can only see your own reflection, and cannot see people on the other side. You should compare yourself with these two types of glasses."

The holy man then said, "You have a coating of ignorance on your eyes, like the silver coating on the glass. You can only see yourself, your selfish interests and your accumulated wealth; and not the poor people on the streets."

The holy man further said, "Your worth in this world will count only when you have the courage to tear away the silver coating from your eyes. Then you will be able to see people on the other side and have love and compassion for your fellow men and women, who are poor. If you are sufficiently rich, then do charity to mitigate the suffering of those who lack resources and money."

I shall describe to you that which ought to be known, by knowing which one attains immortality. The Supreme Spirit is ancient and without a beginning. It cannot be described as 'Sat' or 'Asat.' (12)

The Supreme Spirit pervades and envelops everything in the world; with hands, feet, eyes, heads, and mouths everywhere and all around. (13)

Enabling all the senses to function, yet beyond the senses; absolute and unattached, yet supporting and sustaining the entire creation; free from the modes of Prakriti, yet experiencing them. (14)

The body senses of ears, eyes, nose, mouth and sense of touch cannot function by themselves as an independent identity, until and unless there is Self-soul behind them to cognize and perceive their functions. These body senses may be functionally well individually, but when the soul behind these senses leaves at death, then these senses become useless. Consciousness enables the senses to perform their respective functions.

The healthy body organs of a dead person at death can be donated to a living diseased person for implant. An electrical appliance like a refrigerator or a television may be functionally well by itself, but if there is a power cut and there is no electric supply to energise these appliances, then these cannot function.

Similarly it is the Jivatma or the Self-soul which is absolute and enables the body to function. A channel of television transmission station enables all television receivers to receive the broadcast. Similarly it is the Self-soul consciousness which enables all the body senses to function.

The Omnipresent Spirit of God is outside as well as within all beings; and constitutes the moving (animate) and unmoving (inanimate) creation. It cannot be known directly due to its subtlety. The Supreme Spirit is far away and yet very near. (15)

The Supreme Spirit is far away and yet very near. It is prima-facie contradictory as an object can either be near or far away, and it cannot be both. The above verse is in the form of a metaphor, to explain the hidden and unseen aspect of the Spirit of God.

Isha Upanishads also explains the same phenomenon, and says in succinct verses, “The Self-soul is motionless, yet it is faster than the mind. The senses cannot reach it. It is beyond the grasp of the senses. Remaining still, it is beyond all activity. Yet in Self-soul rests the breath and all life.....The Atman (Self-soul) moves, yet moves not. It is far, yet it is near. It is within all this, and yet without all this.”—This beautiful verse of Isha Upanishad also explains Self-soul riddle in the same way as the above Gita verse.

A Hindu saint went to the Ganga River to take a bath with his disciples. There was another group of family members on the river bank who were shouting at each other in anger. He turned to his disciples and asked, “Why are these people shouting at each other so loudly while fighting with each other?” The disciples thought for a while and then one of them said, “Because when we lose our calm, we shout in anger.”

The saint further queried, “But, why should you shout when the other person is just next to you? One can as well tell the other person what one has to say in a soft voice.” The disciples, who were accompanying him, gave a few more answers, but none satisfied the saint.

Finally the saint explained, “When two people get angry with each other, the distance between their hearts becomes very far. To cover that distance they must shout loudly at each other so that the other person can hear what he has to say. The angrier they get, the louder they will have to shout. Their hearts then get farther and farther from each other, and the distance gets longer and longer.”

The saint further said, “What happens when two people are in love? They do not shout at each other but talk softly, because their hearts are very near. The distance between them is very small. When they love each other whole-heartedly, then what happens? They do not have to speak, but only whisper.”

When they love so much that they are just like one soul in two bodies, then they need not even whisper; they just look at each other, and that is enough. Then there is no need to say anything. This is what happens when two persons are deeply in love with each other.

He looked at his disciples and said, "So when you argue, do not let your hearts get distant and get far from each other. Do not say words that will distance you from each other, or else there will come a day when the distance is so great that you will not be able to return to each other."

The above verse says that the Spirit of God is very far away and yet very near; and there is no distance at all if God resides in your heart. The distance is very far if you go through the path of your argumentative and doubting mind. There is no distance at all if you follow the path of deep love and devotion with God in your heart. The all pervading and omnipresent Spirit of God is both outside and within your heart.

The All-pervading (invisible) Spirit is undivided and exists everywhere (like all-pervading akasha or space), but apparently seems divided in living beings. It is to be Self-realized as the substratum supporter of all beings (as the Spirit of Lord Vishnu). It sustains and dissolves all beings, and then re-generates them afresh. (16)

The Supreme Spirit of God is seated in the hearts of all beings and is the Light of all lights (beyond the darkness of Maya). The Supreme Spirit is knowledge itself, the object of knowledge and the goal to be achieved. (17)

The nature of body field (Kshetra), the knowledge and that which has to be known (the absolute Spirit) have thus been briefly described. My devotees thus understanding and practising enter into My Being. (18)

Know that Prakriti (Nature) and Purusha (Soul) are both without beginning; and understand that all modifications and Gunas (qualities) are born of Prakriti. (19)

Prakriti is said to be the cause for the creation of the body and the senses. The embodied Purusha Spirit (Soul) is said to be the cause for perception of pleasure and pain. (20)

The Conscious Spirit Purusha seated in Prakriti experiences the Prakriti-born qualities. The attachment to the qualities of the Gunas becomes the cause for the soul to take birth in either good or evil wombs. (21)

Prakriti has two main functions–one is to veil and conceal the real Universal Spirit (Brahman). The other function is to project the material world as real, and thus create a duality. In this way the wisdom of the indwelling soul in the living beings is veiled, and the physical body which is mortal is considered as real. The body is unreal in absolute terms as it is constantly changing and will die one day; but apparently it looks real.

The Supreme Spirit dwelling in the body is said to be the Witnessor (of all activities of the body and mind); one who permits all activities; the Sustainer (of life-force); the experiencer (of pleasure and pain); the great Lord, and the Supreme Self. (22)

One who thus knows the Conscious Spirit Purusha and the Primordial Nature Prakriti, together with their attributes (Gunas); he or she while living in the present moment of time, is not subjected to the agony of rebirth and death. (23)

Here and now this moment, is the only moment in life. There is no other moment of time in reality. The clock ticks for the present moment only, and not for the past or the future. The past is finished, however much you may like to alter the past, nothing can be done. You cannot alter the life and the decisions you took in the past.

The future is yet to arrive and nobody knows what will happen. If the work and actions in the present moment are right, then one is moving in the right direction for the future. If a person lives now for this moment totally, then the next moment will also be now, and the next to that also will be now. Do not worry about the future.

Bliss and joy is always in the present moment; and from moment to moment, and it can extend to eternity. Bliss is man's intrinsic nature embedded in the Self-soul. Searching for happiness and bliss in the outside objects of the world, is a sure to way to miss it. How can the joy from outside world flow into your Self-soul?

One has to generate joy within one's Self-soul through meditation and then radiate the aura of bliss to the surrounding world. Whatever joy and bliss you have been seeking from the outside world throughout the ages in many births, is within your own soul. The key of the house was in your pocket, and you were searching for it in the outside world in vain.

Why become a beggar in the outside world, when you can be the emperor within your Self-soul? The outside world can only give you what they have, which is misery and their jealousy. The outside world does not even want to see you in bliss, so you have to keep your bliss within you.

The outside world is a jealous world and how can you be happy when everyone else around you is so unhappy? The Kingdom of God is not an object outside, but within you. It is behind your eyes, and not in front of your eyes.

A man once had a dream that he had an interview with an enlightened Yogi in heaven. —"Come in," the enlightened Yogi said, "So, you want to have an audience with Me?"

"If you have the time, Sir," the man said. —The Yogi smiled and said, "My time is eternity. I have enough time to attend to everything. What questions do you have in your mind, to ask me?"—I wanted to ask you Sir, "What surprises you most about the mankind?"

The Yogi thought for a few moments, and then answered, "That mankind gets bored of being children and are in a big rush to grow up and start earning, get married; and when they grow older; they long to be children once again for those carefree and happy days."

"That men and women lose their health to amass more and more wealth and possessions; and then lose their money to the doctors and the medicines to restore their health."

"That in the process of worrying about their future, they forget the present moment of time; and thus they neither live in the present moment of time nor the future."

"That they live as if they will never die; and they die as if they had never lived."

The enlightened yogi placed my hands in his hand, and we were silent for a while. Then I asked, "As a wise enlightened Yogi, what message you will like to give to the humanity?"

To learn and know that human life is most precious, and each available minute should be used on the spiritual journey of enlightenment.

To learn that it is not good to compare yourself with others. All will be judged individually on their own merit; and not as a group or as a family.

To learn that a rich person is not the one who has the most wealth, but one who is satisfied with what he or she has; and one who has bare minimum needs for survival and lives a simple life.

To learn that it only takes a few seconds to open wounds in people we love, and it takes years to heal them.

To learn to forgive others and not harm ourselves, by remembering the insults and praises of others.

To learn that money can buy all material wants, but not happiness and bliss.

To learn that two people, can look at the same thing and be in the same circumstances; and yet see things from totally different perspectives.

To learn to dedicate and surrender all actions to God; and thus free yourself from the bondage of actions.

To learn to perform your assigned and obligatory duties skilfully and wholeheartedly;and not worry about the results and fruits of your actions.

And, with that the interview of the man with the enlightened Yogi came to an end, and the man woke up from his blissful sleep, a wiser man.

Through meditation, some realize the Self-soul in oneself, by the self. Others realize through the Yoga of knowledge; and yet others by the path of selfless work (Karma Yoga). (24)

Yet others, though not having spiritual knowledge, worship as they have heard from others. They also cross-over death by their devotion and practice, as heard from others. (25)

O Bharata Arjuna! Whichever beings are born, the moving (animate) and the unmoving (inanimate), know them to be created by the union of Kshetra (body field) and the Kshetrajna Spirit. (26)

They truly see who behold the Supreme Spirit of God dwelling equally in all creatures and realize that the imperishable soul does not die when the body perishes. (27)

Because one who is consciously aware of the same Spirit of God dwelling everywhere; does not harm one's Self-soul by one's own self, and therefore attains the highest good. (28)

The same Spirit of God resides equally in all living beings, and when the Spirit finally departs from the body, the body becomes lifeless and dead. Life is a gift of God, and human beings misuse this gift, to follow useless and selfish pursuits for their personal motives and sensual gratifications. How many people thank God that they are alive today, to fulfil their destiny and purpose of life?

Today before you think of saying any unkind or rude words; think of someone who cannot speak;

Before you complain about the taste in your food; think of someone who has nothing to eat;

Before you complain about your husband or wife; think of someone who has no companion, and is lonely in sickness and in life;

Today before you complain about your life; think of someone who died in childhood, and did not see the joys of youth;

Before you complain about your children; think of someone who wants to have children, but they are barren;

Before you argue about your dirty house; and that someone did not clean or sweep; think of those people who are living on the streets and have no house;

Before you complain about the long distance, you have to drive your car to reach home; think of someone who has to walk the same distance on foot, because he does not have money for the bus ticket.

And when you are tired and complain about your job; think of the unemployed and the disabled; and those who wished they had your job;

But before you think of pointing a finger, or condemning another; remember that none of us are without sins; and we all are answerable to our Creator;

And when depressing thoughts seem to get you down; put a smile on your face, and thank God you are alive and still moving around in the world;

Life is a gift; live it, and be grateful to God for all the bounties and the mercies that you enjoy and take for granted.

One truly sees when he realizes that all actions are done by Prakriti alone, and that the Self-soul Atman is a non-doer. (29)

When one realizes that the whole diverse existence of beings and creatures, dwell in One Supreme Spirit

of God only; and perceives that the entire Creation spreads from that One source only; then one attains to God-Consciousness. (30)

O son of Kunti Arjuna! The imperishable Supreme soul has no beginning (uncreated), and is pure without attributes of Gunas (Qualities). While dwelling in the living bodies, it neither performs actions nor is tainted by actions. (31)

As the all-pervading space (Akasha) is not tainted by the other elements of nature, because of its subtlety; similarly the Self-soul while pervading the whole body is not tainted. (32)

O Bharata Arjuna! As the one Sun illumines the whole world; similarly the embodied soul (Atman) illumines the whole body of living beings (Kshetra field). (33)

Those who perceive with the eye of wisdom, this difference between the body (Kshetra) and soul (Kshetrajna); and the deliverance of beings from the evolutes of Prakriti, they go to the Supreme Spirit. (34)

CHAPTER 14

YOGA OF DIVISION OF THREE GUNAS
GUNATRAYA VIBHAGA YOGA

Sri Krishna Said:

I shall explain to you that Supreme wisdom, the best among all knowledge, by knowing which all the sages of the past attained perfection and liberation from the suffering of this world. (1)

Those who by regular and constant practice of this knowledge and wisdom, attain Oneness of union with My Spirit of God; they do not take birth at the start of a new Cosmic cycle of Creation, nor do they suffer the agony at the time of dissolution of the Cosmic cycle. (2)

O Bharata Arjuna! The great Prakriti is My womb, the birth of all beings (animate and inanimate) takes place by the impregnation of the seed of consciousness in that womb. (3)

A seed is sown in the soil. The soil is the mother earth or the womb of all plant life. The seed contains the entire DNA of that particular plant and acts as the conscious principle. The union of the mother earth as womb and the seed as conscious principle gives rise to birth and sprouting of the plant. As the type and quality of the seed and the soil, so is the quality of a plant either healthy, or the one which will wither away. The same analogy applies to human beings.

O Kaunteya Arjuna! Whatever beings are born, the great Prakriti is their Mother womb, and My Spirit of consciousness is the seed giving Father. (4)

O mighty-armed Arjuna! The three Gunas; Sattva, Rajas and Tamas are the attributes of Prakriti. These attributes

of Prakriti tie down the imperishable embodied soul to the body. (5)

Wicked people with predominant attributes of Rajas and Tamas Gunas are also needed in the world. Once it happened that tenants of an estate building refused to give rent to the landlord. The landlord then sent Lalu Prasad, a known ruffian and a scoundrel in the area. He was such a terror in the locality that the tenants used to tremble in his presence. Lalu Prasad just went to meet the tenants, and his reputation was such that he did not have to say a word, and thereafter, the rent was paid on time.

There is a need for everything in the world; the good, the bad and the ugly. A mixture of all the qualities of Sattva, Rajas and Tamas are needed to keep the world moving. If everybody in the world is tall and an epitome of beauty, then the word beautiful will lose its meaning. God has provided a mix of everything; different kinds of vegetables; different types of fruits; different kinds of animals; numerous varieties of fishes; and different types of men and women.

Human beings have varying degrees of Sattva, Rajas and Tamas qualities; which keep on varying from time to time, during the course of one's life. A man has more of Sattva quality, when he prays and meditates in the morning; and a predominance of Rajas quality over the other qualities, when he goes to work and has to accomplish the task assigned to him by all means; and a mixture of Rajas and Tamas Guna, when he sleeps with his wife at night.

Of these three attributes of Gunas–Sattva being pure goodness, is of the nature of luminous light, and is free from impurities. It binds one by attachment to happiness and by attachment to knowledge. (6)

O Kaunteya Arjuna! Know that Rajas is of the nature of passion and greed, producing craving for pleasure and worldly attachment. It creates bondage for the embodied soul by attachment to action to fulfil desires. (7)

What is the nature of passions and craving for pleasure and attachment? —Ashok arrived in New Delhi at eight o'clock in the morning. He thought, "I will only be here in Delhi for a few hours only, before I catch my next flight, so it is not worthwhile to telephone my old friends, and arrange to meet them." He then decided to go for a walk alone in the park opposite to the hotel where he was staying. He sat down on a bench in the park and was lost in memories of his past life.

An old man finding no other vacant bench, joined him on the bench and said, "You seem to be lost in memories of the past life; but past life is gone forever, and there is no point in recalling those memories."

Ashok replied, "Now that we got talking, I was remembering my college days when I used to sit here on this bench with my ex-girl friend twenty years back, and she used to sing lovely songs." The old man said, "Enjoy your past memories, but do not forget that memories are like salt in the food, the right amount brings out the flavour, but too much salt will ruin the dish. If you live with past memories at all times, then you will have no present moments to remember later on, and life is living in the present moment of time."

O Bharata Arjuna! Know Tamas (lethargic dullness) to be born of ignorance thus deluding the embodied beings to believe that they are just the physical body only. It binds the individual soul through heedlessness, laziness and excessive sleep. (8)

O Bharata Arjuna! Sattva binds one to happiness; and Rajas to ceaseless action; while Tamas by covering the wisdom binds one to heedlessness and sloth. (9)

O Bharata Arjuna! Between the three Gunas of Prakriti Sattva, Rajas and Tamas; sometimes Sattva predominates over the other two, and at other times, Rajas and Tamas similarly predominate and assert over the others. (10)

When the light of wisdom and discernment shines forth through the mind and the gateways of the body, then Sattva quality is predominant. (11)

O Bharata Arjuna! When Rajas (passion) becomes dominant, then greed, restlessness, undertaking of new activities and craving for sensual enjoyments arise. (12)

O Arjuna! When Tamas becomes predominant then carelessness, delusion, idleness, stupor and indiscrimination takes place. (13)

If a person dies at a time when Sattva quality is predominant over other qualities; then one goes to the pure and higher regions attained by men of noble deeds.

(14)

Meeting with death at a time when Rajas quality is predominant, one is reborn among those attached to action. And dying while in predominance of Tamas quality (ignorant dullness), one is reborn in inferior wombs of the deluded. (15)

The fruits of Sattvika actions (righteous deeds) are peace and harmony; the fruits of Rajasika actions are pain and suffering; and the fruits of Tamasika actions are ignorance and foolishness. (16)

Sattva quality gives rise to wisdom and knowledge; Rajas gives rise to passion and greed; and from Tamas arises ignorance, stupor and error. (17)

Those who are established in Sattva quality rise to heavenly regions; those with Rajasika disposition remain in the middle; and those abiding in Tamasika quality sink further lower down. (18)

When one gets the awareness and understanding that all actions proceed from the qualities of these three Gunas of Prakriti; and realizes that My Supreme Spirit of God is

above the functioning of these three Gunas of Prakriti; then one attains union with My Being. (19)

These three Gunas of Prakriti are the cause of repeated birth and death of the embodied human beings. One who goes beyond the influence of these three Gunas of Prakriti is freed from birth, death, decay, suffering and attains immortality. (20)

Arjuna said:

O Lord! What are the signs and marks of a person, who has gone beyond the influence of these three Gunas? How does he conduct himself? And how does one rise above these modes of Gunas? (21)

The marks and signs of an enlightened soul, who has attained the state beyond the three Gunas of Prakriti, are stated in the following verses:

Sri Krishna said:

O Pandava Arjuna! One who is without hatred for these Gunas of Prakriti in the form of pure goodness, activity and delusion when these are present; nor longs for them when they are absent. (22)

One who remains unperturbed like a mute witness and is not affected and shaken by the different modes of Gunas. Knowing that Gunas operate in this manner, he remains firmly rooted in God Consciousness, and never falls off from that state. (23)

One who is established in Self-soul consciousness and remains balanced in suffering and joys, and who regards as same, a lump of earth, a stone and gold alike, as if of equal worth. Endowed with a firm mind, he remains the same to the dear ones and those disliked. He keeps his

equilibrium in pleasant and unpleasant circumstances and remains balanced in praise and criticism. (24)

One is said to have risen above the three Gunas, when one is same to a friend and an enemy; is same in both honour and dishonour; and has renounced all further undertakings. (25)

Having thus crossed-over and gone beyond the influence of these Gunas; one who serves Me and worships My Krishna-consciousness with unswerving devotion, such a person is fit to attain oneness with My Spirit of God (Brahman). (26)

For My Spirit of God is absolute bliss, Immortal (beyond death), indestructible, eternal, and righteous Dharma. (27)

CHAPTER 15

THE YOGA OF THE SUPREME SPIRIT PURUSHOTTAMA YOGA

Sri Krishna said:

The ancient sages compared the Creation with an indestructible ashvattha tree, with its roots above (life-sustaining prana in the Spirit of God); and branches below (in the mortal world). Its leaves are the Vedas, and one who thus understands the worldly Creation, is the knower of the Vedas. (1)

Here Sri Krishna is talking in the form of a parable, as it contains the deep hidden mystery of Creation in the form of a tree. One needs intuitive wisdom and deep reflection to understand such verses.

In Bible, the disciples came to Jesus and said, "Why do You speak in parables?" Jesus answered and said to them, "Because it has been given to you to know the mysteries of the kingdom of heaven, but to them it has not been given. Therefore I speak to them in parables, because seeing they do not see, and hearing they do not hear, nor do they understand."

The branches of this tree are spread below and above nourished by the Gunas (in the form of watery sap of the modes of Prakriti). Its buds are like the sense-objects. Its roots are spread below in the mortal world of human beings, resulting in actions and bondage. (2)

This tree of Creation is not seen in the world as such, in this form; neither its origin, nor existence, nor its end. To break the bondage with this world, the roots of this tree have to be cut with the sharp axe of non-attachment with the world. (3)

Here the Creation of the world is compared with a non-existing ashvattha tree as an example. Its roots above seek nourishment of the Self-soul from the eternal Spirit, and the roots below in the world of men and women cause action, which create bondage. Its branches spread above and below, take nourishment from the three Gunas of Prakriti.

If the roots of this tree which extend in the soil below, are cut with a sharp axe of non-attachment; then this tree of samsara will wither away and die. There will thus be no further branches, and no further action and karma; and no further birth and death in the world. This sharp axe for going beyond this world of suffering is the weapon of non-attachment.

The attachment and bondage is born of the mind due to ignorance and delusion. The attachment can be in very subtle forms, such as emotional bonding to wife, husband, children, grandchildren; and material things like house, car, property and wealth.

A child can be attached to a doll for that matter, and does not want to give it away. One can be attached to one's old dilapidated car and does not want to give it away. Attachment can be even to one's job and the field of one's activities, which one performed as a profession throughout one's life. One may not be able to give it up even after retirement or in old age.

These chains of bondage can be very subtle, which become an obstacle and a hurdle in the spiritual path. When work is performed in the spirit of dedication and for the glory of God, then the entire Karma is dissolved; as any quantity of salt put into the sea is dissolved, and the sea still remains just the same.

What are these bondages and how do they settle down in the heart to seek fulfilment? How to overcome these attachments and cut its roots? Read the story below to understand the very subtle forms of bondages.

A farmer ploughed his land with a hoe and a shovel, day after day, year after year. The work was hard, but the harvest was plentiful. And yet, one day he could not help but ask himself, "Why am I working so hard? Such a life is meaningless and boring! What is the purpose of my life? Where is my life heading?"

Shortly afterwards, a monk came to his house to ask for alms and some food. The monk looked carefree and happy, which deeply impressed the farmer and he had a feeling of envy for such a life. Being a monk and living an unencumbered life seemed impressive and admirable to the farmer. He thought to himself why not become a monk and have a carefree life? The farmer made up his mind to give up the farming work and become a monk.

He joined the monastery as a novice monk, but he was troubled by the feeling of how empty his hands were. He was so used to holding a hoe and shovel in his hands to work in his fields. That was his daily routine all his life. Now without the hoe and a shovel to work in his farmland, he felt very uneasy and lost.

From the monastery he went back to his nearby house, and picked up his hoe and shovel, and tried to think hard, as to what to do with these gardening tools. It was a fine hoe and a shovel to dig the earth and clear the shrubs. The shaft was smooth and shiny from daily use. It would be heart breaking to simply throw it away.

"OK, then," he thought, "I will wrap it up and put it away in the store-room of the house." He found a secure place in the house to hide it. Now everything was settled. With his mind at ease, the farmer left his house and went back to the monastery.

The farmer wholeheartedly followed all the rules and regulations of the monastery, and did everything to be a true monk and follow the disciplined life for true spiritual elevation. However, he could not resist the temptation to work with his hoe and shovel, whenever he came across the green paddy fields in the monastery. That was what he had done his whole life in the past. Every now and then whenever he found time, he would rush back to his house nearby, just to feel the hoe and the shovel, and then return back to the monastery.

Time quickly flew past. After seven or eight years, he felt that something was missing in his life and that, he had not achieved peace of mind and the spiritual progress for which he had joined the monastery, and he thought, "Why have I not been able to fulfil my dream of becoming a carefree and a happy monk even after living a celibate life of no sexual defilements, and rigorous discipline of the monastery? There is something which is holding me back from my spiritual attainments. It is now time to fix the problem!"

He rushed back to his home, picked up the hoe and the shovel, and threw it into the nearby lake. —Splash, there it went! —"I have won! I have succeeded in getting rid of my attachment to the hoe and shovel!"—- He could not resist being overwhelmed, and shouted in joy that he has won. Just at that moment, a King, who was leading his victorious army happened to pass by. He overheard the shouts of joy of the monk that he has won, and went to ask him, "What did you win? Why are you so happy and joyful?"

The monk replied, "I have conquered the attachment and the bondage of my heart, which was troubling me ever since I took up the spiritual journey. I have let go the entire burden of my heart."

The king saw that the monk was really happy and carefree from all the worldly burdens and delusions. The king thought to himself, "I have won the war. It was a splendid victory over my enemy. But am I really happy in life now? I have conquered the lands and territories of others, which did not belong to me. But it is not a real victory."

Then and there, the king realized that although he had won the war against his enemy, but in fact he was not the real winner. He had now even more misery and burden on his mind of how to preserve the new territories and the lands that he had won. The king understood that in order to become a real winner, one has to be a master of oneself, and conquer one's desires, greed for power and attachments of the heart.

Then that goal leading to union with the Spirit of God should be sought, going where one does not again return to this mortal world of suffering. One should seek refuge in that Primeval ancient Purusha Spirit (Lord Narayana),

from where this entire Creation has emerged from the beginning itself. (4)

Free from pride and delusion; having cut-asunder the bonds of attachment with the world and ever dwelling in union with the Supreme Spirit; free from all worldly desires and having gone beyond the duality of the pairs of opposites known as happiness and suffering; the undeluded attain the eternal goal of God-realization. (5)

Existence is undivided, but the human mind due to ignorance divides everything into polar opposites. The day and night are extensions of each other and so is birth and death. Man and woman are not opposites, but complement each other.

Man is born from the womb of a woman, and how can they be opposite to each other. Woman too cannot conceive without the seed from the man. It is like planting a seed into the earth, the seed remains in the warmth of the soil and then sprouts.

This verse says that to attain union with the Spirit of God, one has to cut and break all bondages of attachment with wife, son, daughter, husband, and near and dear ones; and material possessions of house, cars and bank balance. In the first place a person at birth came empty handed into the world, and then how come he or she in the journey of life has got so entangled in the chains of bondage, that he is not able to free himself from this bondage?

To be proud means you are thinking of yourself as separate from the existence as someone special. To feel higher than others means deep down you are suffering from an inferiority complex. In your arrogance and pride you want to show to the world that you have more wealth, power, name and fame. It inflates your ego that you have more possessions and a well to do family, and are superior to others.

Word spread across the countryside about a wise holy man who lived in a small house on top of the mountain as a hermit. A couple from the village decided to make the long and difficult journey to visit him. When the couple arrived at the house, they saw an old man inside, who greeted them at the door. "We want to pay our homage to the wise holy man," they said to the old man.

The old man smiled and led them inside. As they walked through the house, the couple from the village looked eagerly and carefully around the house, anticipating their encounter with the holy man. Before they knew it, the couple had been led to the back door and escorted outside the house.

The couple stopped and turned to the old man and said, "But we want to meet and prostrate with respect unto the feet of the wise holy man! We have come from a long distance just to meet him."– "But you have already met him," said the old man.

When you meet someone in life, if he appears to be plain and insignificant; you cannot make out whether he is wise or foolish from the outer appearance. Society and people put a tag and value on the individuals, and the real wise men are thus ignored as they do not crave for publicity or praise from others. Due to this the fake and clever men and women with a coterie of followers around them, fool the gullible and simple public, and the wise and holy men are not even recognized.

That which neither the Sun, nor the Moon, nor the fire can illumine, that is My Supreme Abode. The Self-realized sages, after having reached My eternal Abode, do not again return back to this mortal world of suffering. (6)

A small portion of My eternal Spirit having become the (Jiva) Soul in this world sustains all beings of the world. The Self-soul attracts to itself the five senses with the mind as the sixth, while abiding in Prakriti. (7)

The soul takes on the manifestation of a new body at birth (with previous accumulated vasanas and impressions); and when the soul departs from the body at death, it carries forward the new accumulated karma and goes (the stored impressions of this life-time are taken forward);

just as the wind carries away the odour and scents from their dwelling places. (8)

Vasanas are subtle impressions, which the individual soul carries forward, when the soul separates itself from the physical body upon death. This new term 'Vasanas' is a store-house of impressions and tendencies, accumulated in the present life which is carried forward to the next life. It is very subtle like the space or 'akasha.'

These, latent stored impressions start to function when the soul enters a new body. It is like a seed which has the potential to take up the shape of a huge tree, and the impressions are stored within seed. It is similar to the DNA of the human body. These vasanas are essentially the tendencies and impurities inherited from the previous births, which must be cleansed to attain union with the Spirit of God.

These tendencies and impurities are created by desires and worldly attachments which separates the individual soul from the Spirit of God. That is why Sri Krishna repeatedly says that a yogi ought to be free from all desires and the evil of attachment with the world, so as to attain Nirvana or '***Moksha.***'

The embodied soul while presiding over the mind and also the senses of hearing, sight, touch, taste, and smell; experiences the sense-objects of the world. (9)

The ignorant do not perceive the indwelling soul (Jivatma) joined with the three Gunas of Prakriti; while it stays in the body to experience sense-objects and when this Self-soul departs from the body at death. But those with an inner eye of wisdom perceive the indwelling soul. (10)

The verse translated from Sanskrit reads as **"*Utkramantam*:**—departing from the body:—***sthitam***:—staying in the body:—***va***:—or:—***api***:—also:—***bhunjanam***:—enjoying or experiencing:—***va***:—or:—***gunanvitam***:—joined with the Gunas:—***vimudhah***:—the deluded or the ignorant:—***na....anupashyanti***:—do not see:—***pashyanti***:—perceive or see:—***jnana...chakshusah***:—those with an eye of wisdom."

The yogi striving for perfection on this 'Yoga path' having purified the mind through meditation practice; perceives the Spirit of God in one's own Self-soul. Although striving hard, the unrefined and the unintelligent with impure minds; do not perceive the Self-soul in their own beings. (11)

The light and radiance of the Sun which illumines and sustains the whole world, the reflected light of the Moon, the heat in the fire; know that radiance and energy to be My glory of God. (12)

Permeating the whole earth and all beings, I sustain all life by My life-force prana energy. My infinite energy of God nourishes all plant life and herbs by the watery sap energy of the Moon. (13)

Dwelling in the bodies of all living beings as universal life-force (body heat as Vaishvanara), and associated with the incoming and outgoing breaths (Prana and Apana); I digest four kinds of food (by masticating, sucking, licking and swallowing). (14)

My Spirit of God dwells in the hearts of all living beings; from Me is all knowledge and memory, as well as the loss of this faculty. The knowledge of God-realization is the subject matter of all Vedic Scriptures; I am indeed the author, as well as the knower of all the Vedas. (15)

The perishable and the imperishable; these are the two Purushas in the world. Of these, the physical bodies of all beings are perishable, while the Jivatma Purusha (Self-Soul) is known as the imperishable (Kutastha). (16)

But distinct and above this is the Highest Being called the indestructible Supreme Spirit of God (Supreme Purusha); the One Lord who pervades and sustains the entire Cosmos and the three worlds. (17)

My infinite Spirit of God is beyond the perishable matter of the world, as well as above the imperishable Self-soul Spirit. Therefore I am known in the Vedas and in the world as Purushottama (Supreme Being), the Highest Purusha. (18)

O Bharata Arjuna! That wise person is free from delusion who knows Me as the Highest Purusha, he knows all; and worships Me wholeheartedly. (19)

O Arjuna! Thus, this most secret and profound knowledge has been declared by Me (for the benefit of mankind). By understanding this teaching one becomes wise, and all his duties are accomplished. (20)

CHAPTER 16

DISTINCTION BETWEEN THE DIVINE AND EVIL DAIVASURA SAMPAD VIBHAGA YOGA

WHAT ARE THE DIVINE QUALITIES?:

Sri Krishna said:

Fearlessness, purity of heart, constant and regular practice of 'Yoga meditation' for Self-realization, charity, control of body, mind, and senses, sacrifice (Yajna), study of sacred Scriptures (svadhyayah), austerity and simplicity:— (1)

Non-violence (in thoughts, words and deeds), truthfulness, absence of anger, sense of non-doership and giving up the fruits of action, peacefulness of mind, absence of malicious gossip, compassion towards all beings, absence of greed, non-covetousness, gentleness, modesty and absence of fickleness:– (2)

Vigour, forgiveness, firmness, purity, absence of hatred and pride; O Bharata Arjuna! All these qualities belong to a person with a divine disposition. (3)

The above verses of Gita list out the various divine qualities. The same truth is breathed out by different scriptures in different ways.—Bible states the observance of ten commandments as follows;—that thou shall respect your parents;—do not commit murder or do not kill ;–do not commit adultery or sexual transgression;–do not steal;–do not accuse anyone falsely or tell a lie;–do not covet others possessions (wealth, house, land, or wife);—do not make images or idols;—do not use name of the God for evil purposes;—observe Sabbath;—Worship no other God but me.—Jesus proclaimed himself as the son of God, to deliver the message of God to the humanity.

WHAT ARE THE EVIL TRAITS AND QUALITIES ?

O Partha Arjuna! A person with evil disposition has the qualities of hypocrisy, arrogance, pride, anger, harshness, cruelty and ignorance. (4)

The divine qualities are deemed for liberation from the worldly bondage; whereas the evil traits create further bondage and suffering. Grieve not O Partha Arjuna! You are born with a divine nature. (5)

O Partha Arjuna! There are two types of people in the world; those with divine qualities and those with evil qualities. The divine qualities have been described at length. Now, hear from Me, the evil traits and qualities.

(6)

People with evil and conceited nature do not know what actions to perform and what actions to refrain from? They have neither purity, nor righteous conduct nor truthfulness. (7)

The evil and conceited people say that the world is without any truth and a moral basis, and without any higher governing Spirit of God. They say that, "The world is born of mutual union of man and woman to satisfy lust. What else is there in the world?" (8)

Without any knowledge and holding fast to their misconceived and false beliefs, these misguided and ignorant souls perform cruel deeds, and rise up as enemies of the world for its destruction. (9)

What are the false and misconceived deeds and beliefs? In this context Bible Proverbs say, "There are six things that the Lord hates, seven that are an abomination to him: haughty eyes, a lying tongue, and hands that shed innocent blood, a heart that devises wicked plans, feet that make haste to run to evil, a false witness who breathes out lies, and one who sows discord among brothers."

Filled with innumerable insatiable desires; full of hypocrisy, pride and arrogance; holding harmful and evil beliefs with a deluded intellect; these people work with evil motives, for their own selfish interest and enjoyment. (10)

Human life has an uncertain existence like the water drops on a slippery lotus leaf and nobody can predict what will happen tomorrow. A story emphasizes this point.

Once there was a man, who was a miser and lived a very frugal life to save every penny. He wanted to amass wealth to enjoy life later on. All of a sudden by unfair and clever manipulations, he succeeded in making ten million dollars. He had no family and was all by himself. Finally he decided that from now on for a year, he will live a luxurious life of comforts and luxury. After that he will decide where to invest the rest of his money, to make his wealth grow.

By the strange hand of destiny, the angel of death came to take away his soul that very night. The man begged and pleaded and used a thousand arguments that he has not enjoyed his wealth and life so far, and that he be allowed to live for at least one more year. The angel of death did not listen to his pleas and was adamant.

The man then said to the angel of death, "All right, give me just three days to live, and I will give you half of my wealth."—The angel of death said nothing doing, your time is up. The man further pleaded, "OK!–Give me just one day, I beg of you, and you can take my entire wealth thereafter, which is earned through so much effort and life-time savings. The angel of death again told him that his time was up, and he has come to take away his soul.

However he was able to get a small concession from the angel of death….just a few moments in which to write down his last goodbye note to the world.

He wrote in his death note, "Whoever happens to read this note, take advice from a dying man. If you have just enough money to live on in life, do not waste your life in accumulating wealth. Live life to its fullest potential and sing the glories of the Lord, and have a purposeful life. In this way you will not have any regrets when you have to quit this temporary abode on earth suddenly, without any notice. My fortune of ten million dollars could not buy me a single hour of life!"

These evil people are beset with immense worries and innumerable desires which end only in death. They consider sexual enjoyment and gratification of lust as their highest purpose in life; sure in the false belief that life is just that, and nothing else. (11)

Having hundreds of expectations and hopes, given over to lust and anger, they strive to amass wealth by unfair means for gratification of sensual desires. (12)

As one sows, so one reaps. The proof of a pudding lies in its eating. Bible teaching is in consonance with Bhagavad Gita teaching, and exhorts mankind to remember that gratification of desires, and amassing of wealth is meaningless.

Bible says, "Light is sweet, and it pleases the eyes to see the Sun. However many years a man may live let him enjoy them all. But let him remember the days of darkness, for there will be many. Everything to come then is meaningless. Be happy, young man, while you are young, and let your heart give you joy in the days of your youth. Follow the ways of your heart and whatever your eyes see, but know that for all these things, God will bring you to judgment. So then, banish anxiety from your heart and cast off the troubles of your body, for youth and vigour are meaningless."

These evil people say, "Today, I have gained this wealth for enjoyment; this desire also I shall fulfil; this is mine, and abundant wealth shall also be mine in future to fulfil my fancy desires." (13)

Adi Shankaracharya says, "O Man! Give up the desire to possess more and more wealth. Instead strive for wisdom with a mind free of desires. Be content with whatever you get as a result of your work.

—Remember that all your dependents are attached to you as long as you have wealth and the ability to earn. Later on when your body becomes old and infirm, no one at home cares to speak even a word with you!"

These evil people say, "This enemy has been killed by me, and I shall kill others also who dare to oppose me. I am the ruler of the people, and the world is for my enjoyment. I am successful, powerful and happy." (14)

These people of evil disposition, deluded by ignorance say that, "I am rich and have a large influential family. Who else is equal to me? I will perform sacrifices, give alms and enjoy the pleasures of the world." (15)

Addicted to the enjoyment of sensual pleasures and lust, their minds confused and bewildered by many fancy thoughts; these men and women of evil disposition further fall down into the lower realms of painful and foul hell. (16)

A lawyer died, and arrived at the junction of the gates of heaven and hell. Yamraj, the presiding deity of death said, "What good deeds did you do on the earth to merit your entrance in Heaven?"

The lawyer said, "Let me plead my case Sir; a month ago I gave a ten rupee currency note to a poor beggar."– Yamraj checked his records and said, "That is correct, but that is not really enough to get you a place in Heaven. What else?"—The lawyer said, "Wait! Wait Sir! There is more! Three years ago I had given twenty rupees to a poor girl on the roadside."—The record of his deeds was checked and it was found to be correct.

Yamraj asked his fellow assistant and enquired, "Well, what do you suggest we do with this fellow? —-The assistant of Yamraj said, "Let us give him his thirty rupees back, and tell him to go to Hell."

Intoxicated by wealth and honour, self-glorifying and haughty, stubborn and filled with pride; these men and

women perform Yajna sacrifice, as a mere outward show of hypocrisy, disregarding the Scriptural injunctions.(17)

Given over to egoism, brute force, arrogance, lust and anger; these malicious people, despise the consciousness of Self-soul dwelling in their own bodies, as well as within other beings. (18)

These degraded evil-doers worst among mankind in the world, are born again and again, in the impure and demoniac (Asuras) wombs. (19)

O Kaunteya Arjuna! Not striving to reach My Divine Spirit; these ignorant and deluded souls remain in the cycle of degraded (unclean) demoniac wombs birth after birth, and further fall down in the realm of evolution. (20)

Bible (Job 8:13 to 8:19) says, "Godless men are like those reeds; their hope is gone, once God is forgotten. They trust a thread—a spider's web. If they lean on a web, will it hold them up?—If they grab for a thread, will it help them stand? —Evil men sprout like weeds in the Sun, like weeds that spread all through the garden.—Their roots wrap round the stones and hold fast to every rock.—But then pull them up —no one will ever know they were there.—Yes that is all the joy evil men have; others now move and take their places."

Triple is the gate of hell–lust, anger and greed; which destroy and ruin the Self-soul. Therefore one should abandon these three evils. (21)

The above verse says that the three gates of lust, anger and greed are very difficult to conquer for human beings, and the gate to heaven opens only after one has gone beyond the temptations of these vices. The whole world is full of temptations, but when a person takes refuge in the Spirit of Krishna-consciousness then the Lord gives the wisdom of discrimination and keeps the temptations away.

Why do famous temples of Khajuraho, Puri and Konark in India, depict explicit images of naked couples in poses of sexual intercourse (maithuna)? Erotica on the walls of these famous world heritage temples arouses curiosity and even puzzles the mind. The brazenness and ethereal beauty of these temples will ever continue to amaze the common masses.

There is a deep secret behind this. All these exquisite carvings are on the outer walls of the temple and not inside the sanctum-sanctorum (garbha-griha) of the temple, which is like the soul of a temple, where the main deity is enshrined. The real reason behind these sensuous carvings in close embrace and interlocked in lovemaking has remained shrouded in mystery to the curious onlookers. The human body is also in likeness of a temple where the embodied-soul dwells as unseen. The dualities of male and female energies are on the outer surface of a body like the outer walls of a temple.

To reach the inner portals of one's soul, one has to cross the barrier of all these dualities. The state of a man and woman in embrace is a union of two basic principles of life–Purusha and Prakriti. One has to leave behind all lust and clean one's mind before entering the central shrine of the temple so as to attain oneness with cosmic consciousness of God.

The bliss of deep meditation is also similar to sex experience. The same state of no-mind, no-time, non- identification with the body; and blissful glimpse of super consciousness of God can be attained in a state of deep meditation within. In meditation there is no time-limit, and no loss of energy. Meditation is Sattvika bliss from the beginning to the end. The Bible Psalm says, "Be still and know that I am God." It is the stillness of the mind, with no-thoughts and just emptiness for God-consciousness to fill the space.

It is a union of one's soul with infinite consciousness of the Universe. The other person is not needed and one can joyously meditate while alone in one's room or at any other place, for any duration of time. Dependence on the other person is slavery, and the other can even manipulate and exploit you for selfish reasons.

Deep meditation is experienced in aloneness, where there is no distraction of husband, wife, beloved or other worldly attachments. It is a state of no-desires and total bliss which the Upanishads say, "Tat Twam Asi–(That thou art)."—Bhagavad Gita says in chapter 6 that a yogi should meditate living alone in solitude, without any desires, and without the burden of possessions.

O Kaunteya Arjuna! Freed from these three gates to hell (lust, anger and greed); a person performs actions which are conducive for one's liberation and attains the supreme good. (22)

The whole world is moving like a wheel due to the greed of acquiring material wealth and enjoying sensual pleasures. Wealth gotten by unfair means and indulgence in pleasures also brings associated problems and misery in its wake.

There was an enlightened laughing saint who lived in a cave and used to sing the glories of God. He was always blissful with a cheerful mind; whether there was a storm, rains, cold or hot weather. Before dying the Master left his last testament and Will, on a piece of paper in his own handwriting.

His followers and devotees were astounded and surprised because in his last testament he had stated that beneath a nearby stone boulder, he had buried all the gold and money that he had hoarded during his life time.

The eager disciples hurriedly got on with the task of digging under the large rock boulder. Deep underneath the rock, they discovered a ragged piece of cloth bundle. Opening the knotted bundle with shaking hands and suspense, they discovered only a lump of dried shit.

There was another scribbled note in the cloth bundle which stated, "If you understood me and my teaching so little that you actually believed that I ever valued or hoarded wealth in my lifetime, then you are truly heirs to my shit."—The note was signed by the "The laughing enlightened Master."

But one who ignores the holy Scriptural teachings, and acts on the impulse of desires; neither attains perfection, nor happiness in this world, nor the Supreme goal of life. (23)

Therefore, let this scripture be your sole authoritative guide to determine what actions should be performed, and what actions should be avoided. Having known what is stated in the scriptures; one should then act and perform one's work in the world. (24)

The teaching of Bhagavad Gita is considered as the final authority on all spiritual matters and for this reason, before giving any testimony in Indian courts, one has to take oath by placing one's hand on Gita book, and testify that what he or she is going to tell is 'Truth' only and nothing else.

Similarly in Sikh religion, 'Sri Guru Granth Sahib' is the final authority and 'Guru' for the Sikhs. Sri Guru Granth Sahib is the central religious text of Sikhism, considered by the Sikhs to be the final, Sovereign Guru after the lineage of 10 Sikh Gurus. It is essentially derived from the teachings of different incarnations of Lord Vishnu and the Vedas, and it echoes the teachings of Bhagavad Gita.

The tenth Sikh Guru, Sri Gobind Singh affirmed the sacred text of 'Sri Guru Granth Sahib' as his successor and the final Guru, as after him there was no further lineage of Gurus. Sikhism believes that there were many messengers of God from age to age like Sri Krishna, Sri Rama and others. The three duties of Sikhs are Naam Japna (mindful of God's name at all times), Kirat Karni (earning honest living) and Vand Chakna (sharing one's earning with others).

CHAPTER 17

THE YOGA OF THREE FOLD FAITH
SRADDHATRAYA VIBHAGA YOGA

Arjuna said:

O Sri Krishna! What is the position and standing of those, who worship with full faith and devotion; but do not follow the rituals and instructions of the Scriptures? Is this faith (Sraddha), of the nature of Sattva, Rajasika or Tamasika? (1)

Sri Krishna Said:

Hear from Me, the description and characteristics of three kinds of faith (Sraddha) of the embodied souls; — Sattvika (pure goodness); Rajasika (of passionate nature) and Tamasika (ignorance). (2)

O Bharata Arjuna! The faith of every person is according to his own nature and mental disposition. Human beings are verily that, what their faith is. (3)

People of Sattvika faith, worship the Devas (the shining spirits of gods); people of Rajasika faith worship the demigods and guardian spirits of wealth; and those of Tamasika faith, worship the spirits of the dead and ghosts. (4)

Know that, people of evil and destructive resolves; impelled by the force of lust and attachment; perform severe penances, as an outward show of hypocrisy to the world. These ignorant fools torture their body organs as a penance, which is not enjoined in the scriptures; and

thereby they also torture My Spirit of God dwelling in their bodies. (5–6)

In accordance with the inherent disposition of each person; three different types of food; sacrifices; austerities and charity, are dear to these people. Hear their distinction as follows. (7)

THREE TYPES OF FOOD:

The food which promotes life-force energy, longevity, purity, strength, good health, joy and a cheerful mind; which is savoury, wholesome, substantial, agreeable, and nourishing to the body; is liked by people of Sattvika nature. (8)

The food which is bitter, sour, saline, over-hot, pungent with chillies, dry and burning is liked by people with Rajasika disposition. Such food produces pain, grief and disease. (9)

The food which is stale, tasteless, stinking, rotten, putrid, polluted and impure is liked by people of Tamasika disposition. (10)

THREE TYPES OF YAJNAS–(SACRIFICES):

That sacrificial Yajna is called 'Sattvika,' which is performed in accordance with the Scriptures; desiring no fruits of action or rewards; in the belief that such a Yajna ought to be performed as a part of one's duties and gratefulness to God. (11)

O Best of Bharata Arjuna! That Yajna sacrifice is called 'Rajasika,' which is performed as an outward show of hypocrisy to the world, with an eye to get rewards and recognition in society and for self-glorification. (12)

That sacrifice is declared to be 'Tamasika,' which is contrary to the Scriptural tenets, in which no food is distributed, which is devoid of mantra chants, gifts, and lacks faith. (13)

THREE TYPES OF AUSTERITIES–(TAPAS):

Worship of the gods, holy renunciates, respect for one's teachers, elders and wise men, purity, straightforwardness, abstinence from sex (Brahmacharya) and non-violence... these are called the austerities of the body. (14)

Speech which causes no excitement or annoyance to others; which is truthful, pleasant and beneficial; chanting of divine holy names and mantras and regular study of holy Scriptures. These are said to be the 'austerities' of Speech. (15)

Cheerfulness of mind, kindness to others, keeping silence, self-control, purity of thoughts; these constitute the austerities (tapas) of the mind. (16)

One day a student asked an enlightened Master, "What is the most important teaching of Bhagavad Gita?"—The Master replied, "Refrain from all selfish deeds and perform 'wholesome' deeds."

The student thought to himself and said, "Sir, even a child knows that."—The Master replied, "Yes! A child may know it, but not even an eighty year old man can do it!"

There are many things we take for granted, and think that we know everything. The 'wholesome' deeds implied here are the qualities of; always speaking the truth; without lust, anger and greed; non-covetousness; not hurting anyone; honesty; self-control; cleanliness; study of Scriptures, performance of selfless actions, and many more.—A child may know it, but how many people can do it?

This threefold austerity (of body, speech and mind), practised in full faith and devotion, desiring no rewards in return, is called as 'Sattvika.' (17)

The austerity (tapa) which is practised with the object of gaining respect, honour and reverence of people, with an outward show of hypocrisy is transitory and non-lasting. This austerity is of the nature of 'Rajasika.' (18)

The austerity which is practised, with a perverted and foolish obstinacy, with self-torture of the body or with the intention to harm others, is of the nature of 'Tamasika.' (19)

THREE TYPES OF GIFTS OR CHARITY:

That gift or charity which is done with no expectation of any returns, with the feeling that it is one's duty to give , and which is given at the right place and time to worthy people for a good cause, is counted as 'Sattvika' charity.

(20)

The gift or charity, which is given with a view to receive favours in return, or with expectations to receive rewards, or given grudgingly, is called a 'Rajasika' gift or charity. (21)

The gift or charity, which is given at a wrong place or time, to unworthy persons, without respect or with insult, is declared as a 'Tamasika' gift or charity. (22)

"OM-TAT-SAT."....has been declared as the symbolic, threefold appellation of the absolute spirit of God. It means–Truth, Consciousness and Bliss. This triple appellation was invoked by the Brahmanas, while chanting the Vedas and performing Yajnas, in the ancient past. (23)

Therefore, the followers of the Vedas always begin all acts of sacrifice, charity and austerity, by chanting the word 'AUM,' as enjoined in the Scriptures. (24)

By invoking and chanting 'TAT,' all acts of sacrifice, austerity and charity are dedicated to the Spirit of God, by the seekers of liberation, expecting no rewards or fruits, with the feeling that everything in the world belongs to God. (25)

O Partha Arjuna! The invoking, and chanting of syllable 'SAT,' is used for all praiseworthy actions, to denote righteousness and 'TRUTH.' (26)

And steadfast actions of sacrifice, austerity and charity, are also called as 'SAT' or 'True,' when such actions are dedicated to the Spirit of God. (27)

O Partha Arjuna! Remember that whatever acts of sacrifice, austerity and charity are performed without 'faith' or 'Sraddha'; they are declared as 'Asat' or 'Untrue.' Without faith, these acts are of no avail and of no consequence in this life, or the next hereafter. (28)

Bible says, "Do not be quickly provoked in your spirit, for anger resides in the lap of fools. Do not say, "Why were the old days better than these?" For it is not wise to ask such questions. Wisdom, like an inheritance, is a good thing and benefits those who see the Sun. Wisdom is a shelter as money is a shelter, but the advantage of knowledge is this: that wisdom preserves the life of its possessor. Consider what God has done: Who can straighten what He has made crooked? When times are good, be happy; but when times are bad, consider: God has made the one as well as the other. Therefore, a man cannot discover anything about his future?"

CHAPTER 18

THE PATH OF LIBERATION THROUGH RENUNCIATION

MOKSHA SANYASA YOGA

Arjuna said:

O Hrishikesha Sri Krishna! I want to distinctly and clearly understand the truth and facts of both; Renunciation of actions (Sanyasa), as well as Relinquishment of actions (Tyaga). (1)

Sri Krishna said:

The sages declare Renunciation (Sanyasa) as the giving-up of all worldly duties and desires; and relinquishment (Tyaga) as giving-up the fruits and rewards of all actions. (2)

There is a subtle difference between 'Sanyasa' and 'Tyaga.' Renunciation means renouncing all worldly wealth, name, fame, progeny and social status, etc. Whereas, Tyaga means giving up the fruits of actions, while still performing obligatory duties and work.

Some sages declare that all actions should be given up as evil, since all deeds contain a certain measure of taint and blemish. While others say that acts of sacrificial Yajnas, charity and austerity should not be given-up. (3)

O Bharata Arjuna! Hear from Me the truth of relinquishment (Tyaga).–The relinquishment of actions has been declared to be of three kinds–Sattvika, Rajasika, and Tamasika. (4)

Acts of sacrificial Yajnas, charity and austerity should not be given-up, but ought to be performed. For the acts of Yajna, charity and austerity are purifying to the wise. (5)

O Partha Arjuna! But even these acts of Yajna, charity and austerity, should be undertaken without any attachment, and without seeking any rewards and the fruits of action, as dedication to the Spirit of God. This is My definite and firm conviction. (6)

Abandonment of obligatory and prescribed duty is not proper. Such abandonment of bounden duty on the pretext of relinquishment of actions is utter ignorance and of Tamasika nature. (7)

One, who relinquishes work because it is troublesome and causes discomfort to the body, and anxiety to the mind, performs a 'Rajasika' relinquishment (Tyaga). This type of relinquishment carries no merit or rewards, and is useless. (8)

O Arjuna! Prescribed and obligatory duty which is performed with the spirit that it ought to be done without any worldly attachment, and without desiring any rewards; such relinquishment is of the nature of pure Sattvika. (9)

A wise person with a discerning intellect whose doubts have been dispelled, and who hates neither an unpleasant work nor is attached to the pleasant work, is endowed with relinquishment of Sattvika nature. (10)

It is impossible for an embodied being to entirely give up work altogether. But one, who gives up the fruit of actions, is regarded as a true relinquisher (Tyagi). (11)

Threefold fruit of actions; good, bad or a mix of both good and bad, accrues after death to those who do not relinquish; but there is none whatsoever for the true renunciate. (12)

O mighty-armed Arjuna! Learn from Me the five causative factors for the accomplishment of all activities, which is also stated in Samkhya Scriptures. The understanding of this results in neutralization of cause and effect of actions. (13)

The five factors for accomplishment of all activities are; the place of action (body); the doer (agent); the various body senses and the mind as the instruments; different kinds of efforts and energies; and the fifth factor is the Divine Providence. (14)

These five factors are the contributory causes of whatever action a human being performs with his body, mind and speech; irrespective of whether the action is wrong or right. (15)

But an ignorant person perceives the taintless and absolute Self-soul as the doer of actions. Such a person does not view rightly. (16)

One who is free from egoism and sense of doership, and whose intellect is not tainted with any evil motive; even if he kills his opponent as a part of his duties (as in war); he is not considered as a killer, nor does he incur any sin on this account. (17)

Knowledge, the object of knowledge and the knower are the threefold stimulus to perform an action. So also the doer, the body organs of action and the object, are the three-fold constituent factors for performance of actions. (18)

According to the predominance of three types of Gunas; there are three different types of knowledge; three types of actions; and three types of doership, according to the prevalence of Gunas in each individual. Hear about these now. (19)

THREE TYPES OF KNOWLEDGE

The knowledge by which a person perceives One imperishable, all-pervading and Omnipresent Spirit of God present equally and undivided in the entire existence, although apparently looking as divided; understand such knowledge to be of the nature of pure 'Sattvika.' (20)

The Knowledge which divides living beings and Creation into different entities, varying and different from one another, is known as 'Rajasika.' (21)

The Spirit of God is complete and whole. It does not need others to make it full and whole. A car has so many parts and the car runs as a whole. If you open the engine and remove the carburettor, then the car cannot run. No single part is whole.

The Sun, Moon, the Stars, the planets, Earth, Rivers, plant life, oceans, animals and human beings are all the glories of God. If you take away anything from the Universe, then ecological balance is disturbed and human life is adversely affected. Animals, birds, sea creatures and plant life have existence of their own to enhance and support human life.

It is human beings who have polluted and disturbed the ecological balance by industrial pollution, by indiscriminate killing of animals and cutting of forests for their personal motives and benefit. There is thus an emphasis to preserve rare species of animals and wild life, which is becoming extinct due to urbanization of the land areas. Everything constitutes the whole, and everything is important.

The Cosmic soul is whole and complete; and the individual soul is also whole and complete but surrounded by a veil of ignorance. This ignorance separates the individual soul from union with super consciousness, and it longs to unite back with its origin. Knowledge and Self-realization remove the veil of ignorance from the Self-soul, and allows its merger with the Supreme Spirit.

The individual soul comes from the Cosmic soul. The 'whole' comes from the 'whole'; and the 'whole' still remains full and complete. If you add or remove anything from the infinite whole, it still remains full. The oceans are full and complete; the water evaporates from its surface and forms into clouds to shower rains and fill the rivers. The rivers again flow back to the oceans. You cannot add or subtract from the oceans, as the oceans are complete and full, on their own.

The Isha Upanishad explains the insightful meaning of this wholeness and completeness. The meaning of word ***'Purna'*** in Sanskrit means that which is Full, Infinite, Whole, and Complete.

The Isha Upanishad starts with this famous and insightful hymn:— ***AUM***...***Purnamadah Purnamidam***, ***Purnat Purnamudachyate***; ***Purnasya Purnamadaya***, ***Purnameva Vashishyate***. ***AUM***! ***Shanti***! ***Shanti***! ***Shanti***!

There are many translations of this hymn, each of which gives a different slant on its meaning. A sense of complete explanation of the nature of Reality and wisdom on the path of Self-realization is explained in this hymn.

The meaning of this Isha Upanishad hymn is, "***Aum***!....***That is infinite***, ***This is infinite***; ***from That infinite***, ***This infinite emerges***;—***From That infinite, when This infinite is removed or added***; ***That infinite still remains unchanged and whole***."

'That' means the ultimate, the absolute, the hidden aspect of Reality, the invisible, the unmanifest. ***'That'*** has the connotation of the Spirit of God, Truth, Nirvana or enlightenment.—By ***'This'*** is meant the individual souls and the phenomenal world, which has emerged from That infinite Spirit.

The above hymn can also be translated as***, "Aum! God is limitless and infinite, Universe manifests out of the Spirit of God , And merges back into the infinite Spirit of God, The Spirit of God still remains the same, infinite and unchanged. AUM! Peace! Peace! Peace!"***

Another Translation of the verse is***; —"Aum! That is the Whole, This is the Whole; From the Wholeness emerges wholeness,***

Wholeness coming from wholeness, The Wholeness still remains. AUM! Peace! Peace! Peace!"

The knowledge which considers one single effect as if it were the whole, without a reason and without any basis of truth, and which is limited and not complete; is declared as 'Tamasika.' (22)

Partial knowledge can be misleading as the person may think that he knows everything. It is like a person seeing a movie after the interval when half of the movie is already over, and the man does not know the full story. Nobody will accept a pilot to fly a plane with half the knowledge and skill of flying, as he will not be able to handle the emergencies. A surgeon with just a little knowledge of surgery is dangerous for the patients.

Once, a person's eyes, nose, and mouth had a meeting. First the eyes said, "We, the eyes, are the most important part of the body. Everything must be seen by us to know whether one is beautiful or ugly, big or small, tall or short and to see the outside objects to perform the daily tasks in life. Without eyes, life will be extremely difficult. So we the eyes, take precedence above other parts of the face. But we are improperly placed below the eyebrows, which are of no use. It is just not fair!"

Next, the nose said, "I, the nose, am the most important part of the body. Only I can distinguish a pleasant smell from a foul odour. The act of breathing is also dependent on me. If I do not let the breath pass through my nostrils, then there will be no life. So I am the most important part on the face. But I have been unfairly placed beneath the useless eyebrows and this is not acceptable."

Then the mouth said, "I am the most important part of the human body. If I do not speak, then there will be no communication among people. If I do not take the food inside the body then everybody will die. Such an important part as the mouth has been placed in the lowest part of the face. Those useless eyebrows however have been put on the highest part of the face. This is favouritism and there is no logic to it!"

After everybody had spoken, the eyebrows then spoke slowly, "Please do not fight, because of me. The eyebrows, as it seems to all of you are the most useless part of the face; I admit defeat and I am willing to be placed wherever you desire."

Having said this, the eyebrows settled down below the eyes. Unfortunately the person no longer looked like a human being. Next, the eyebrows settled down below the nose. It looked horrible and ugly. The ladies objected that it looked like a moustache on their face, and their beauty is gone. Then the eyebrows settled down below the mouth. Then men objected and said they looked like animals. This is horrible and ghastly!

The eyes, nose and mouth finally huddled together in a meeting, to discuss the situation and find a solution. They concluded that it was best if the eyebrows returned back to their original place on the face. It was the most appropriate place for the eyebrows. The eyebrows thereafter returned back to the original spot, and the appearance of the face was once again as that of a human being.

The attempt by the human beings to dominate others for selfish reasons has created so many complications and perversions in the society. Things have to be viewed holistically as a whole, to get the complete picture. God made human beings in His own image, and everything is just perfect and in the right place. There is no need to alter what God has created.

THREE TYPES OF ACTION:

An action which is done as obligatory duty, and performed without any attachment; without any partiality of likes and dislikes; without seeking any rewards; is known as pure 'Sattvika' action. (23)

An action which is undertaken due to 'egoism' with a longing to satisfy desires; and with great stress and strain, is known as 'Rajasika' type of action. (24)

Skill in 'yoga path' is to tackle problems, and perform work efficiently without undue stress and strain. One should know when to let go, and when to undertake the required work wholeheartedly.

A psychologist walked around a room while teaching stress management to an audience. As she raised a glass of water, everyone expected they will be asked if the glass was "half empty or half full" question. Instead, with a smile on her face, she asked another question, "How heavy is this glass of water?" Somebody said 100 grams, and another said 80 grams of weight.

She replied, "The absolute weight of the glass does not matter. It all depends on how long you hold it in your hand. If you hold it for a minute, it is not a problem. If you hold it for an hour, you will have an ache in the arm. If you hold it for a day, your arm will feel numb and paralyzed. In each case, the weight of the glass does not change, but the longer you hold it, heavier it becomes."

The lady psychologist continued, "The stress and worries in life are similar to the example of holding this glass of water. If you think of a problem in your mind for a while, nothing happens. Keep on brooding and thinking of the same problem again and again, for a bit longer, and stress begins to build up. And if you think and brood on the same problem and start worrying about the problem day and night; then you will feel tired and paralyzed, and will be incapable of doing anything else."

It is important to let go of your stresses, when you return back home from work. In the night before sleeping you should release the burden of your problems from your mind, and undertake the unfinished work on the next day. Do not carry your problems through the late evening into the night. Remember to put the glass down at night, and relax.

An action which is undertaken from sheer ignorance, without heed to the destructive consequences, resulting in loss and injury to others and to oneself; without knowing whether one has the capability to undertake the task; is known as 'Tamasika' type of action. (25)

THREE TYPES OF DOERS OF ACTIONS

A doer or 'agent,' is called a 'Sattvika doer,' when he or she is free from worldly attachments; non-egoistic; and is endowed with perseverance; enthusiasm, firmness; and remains unaffected by success or failure. (26)

A doer or 'agent,' is known as a 'Rajasika doer'; when one is full of passion with a greedy longing to reap the rewards of one's actions; and who resorts to violence to oppress others; has impure conduct and is shaken and afflicted by the joys and sorrows of life. (27)

A doer of actions is known as a 'Tamasika doer' when he or she is unbalanced; vulgar; obstinate; deceitful; malicious; lazy; dishonest; arrogant; gloomy and postpones work. (28)

O Dhananjaya Arjuna! Now listen to the threefold distinction of intellect (Buddhi); and firmness (Dhriti) of mind, according to the predominance of three types of Gunas, which I shall explain exhaustively and separately for each quality (Guna). (29)

THREE TYPES OF INTELLECT (BUDDHI):

O Partha Arjuna! That intellect is of 'Sattvika' Guna, which knows when to refrain, and when to perform actions; the discrimination between right and wrong actions and thinking; and what is to be feared and what is not to be feared; what type of actions bind the soul and what type of actions liberate the soul. (30)

O Partha Arjuna! That intellect is of 'Rajasika' Guna, which wrongly interprets righteousness (Dharma) and unrighteousness (Adharma); and twists and distorts the right and wrong actions. (31)

O Partha Arjuna! An intellect which is surrounded by darkness in utter confusion, and regards unrighteousness (Adharma) as righteousness (Dharma); and interprets everything in a perverted upside down manner; is of 'Tamasika' Guna. (32)

THREE TYPES OF FIRMNESS (DHRITI):

O Partha Arjuna! That firmness and determination (Dhriti) is of 'Sattvika nature'; in which one controls and regulates the functioning of the mind; life-force prana and the body-senses, by regular and unwavering practice of 'Yoga sadhana.' (33)

That firmness (Dhriti), is of the nature of 'Rajasika,' by which one seeks the rewards of one's actions; while at the same time holding fast to Dharma (dutiful work) for enjoyment of sensual desires (Kama) and accumulation of wealth (Artha). (34)

O Partha Arjuna! That firmness, by which stupid men and women, cling fast to lethargy, sleep, fear, grief, despair and deceit; is of the nature of 'Tamasika.' (35)

O Bharata Arjuna! Now listen to three kinds of happiness. That in which a man comes to rejoice by long years of practice on 'Yoga sadhana' on the Divine Spirit of God, and which results in the end of all sorrows. (36)

THREE KINDS OF HAPPENESS:

That happiness is of 'Sattvika nature,' which seems like a poison in the beginning, but is like nectar (Amrit) of pure bliss at the end. It arises due to purification of the intellect and Self-realization of the soul. (37)

That happiness is of 'Rajasika nature"; which arises from the contact of body-senses with their respective sense-

objects; and seems like nectar (Amrit) in the beginning but turns out to be a poison in the end. (38)

That happiness is of 'Tamasika nature'; which deludes the embodied soul right from the beginning to the end, and which arises due to excessive laziness and sleep, heedlessness and false perceptions. (39)

There are no beings on earth, and even among the deities in heaven, who are free from the influence of these three Gunas, born of Prakriti. (40)

O Arjuna! The duties of Brahmins (priest-class); Kshatriyas (warrior-class); Vaishyas (business and agriculture-class); and Sudras (servant and labour-class) have been categorised according to their inborn Gunas and inherent nature (for efficient governing of the society). (41)

Once a king was travelling with his ministers and he heard that a very intelligent boy lived in a village nearby. The king changed his route and went to that village to talk to that boy and asked him, "If you can suggest to me how I can do away with the foolishness and imperfections of the people in my kingdom?" "But why?" asked the boy, "If we flattened the mountains, the birds will have no shelter. If we filled up the deep rivers and the sea, the fish will die and there will be no water. If the madman of the village gets as much authority as the head of the village, then how will the village function? The world is vast enough to accommodate everyone, and the world still moves on."

The qualities of Brahmins (priest class) are calmness of mind, austerity, external and internal purity, forgiveness, simplicity, knowledge of the Scriptures, and belief in the hereafter. (42)

The qualities of Kshatriyas (warrior class) are bravery, vigour, resourcefulness, generosity, lordliness, and firmness in war. (43)

The qualities of Vaishyas are agriculture, cattle-rearing, business and trade. The natural duties of Sudra class are labour and rendering service to others. (44)

Engaged in performing one's respective duty, a man or woman attains the highest good. Now hear how each devoted to one's own duty, climbs up the ladder of evolution. (45)

The power by which this entire cosmos is sustained and which is the origin of all beings, by dedicating one's work and deeds as worship to that almighty power of God, human beings attain the highest good. (46)

Better is one's own duty (Dharma) even if imperfectly performed, rather than the duty of another person well-performed. One, who performs one's work according to one's inborn nature and tendencies, does not incur sin. (47)

O Kaunteya Arjuna! One should not give up one's duties and work for which one is born, even if it is accompanied by some blemish; for all worldly activities are tainted with some blemish, as fire is enveloped by smoke. (48)

One whose intellect and mind is unattached everywhere from worldly objects; who is master of his body and senses; who has outgrown and overcome all desires for sense-enjoyments; such a person by renunciation, attains the highest perfection and freedom from the result of one's actions. (49)

O Kaunteya Arjuna! Learn from Me in brief, how one who has reached this perfection can become One with God-consciousness; which is the highest state of knowledge. (50)

DIFFERENT QUALITIES OF NIRVANA:

Having purified the intellect and having attained union with God-consciousness; with firm control on oneself and all the senses; turning away from all sounds and talking as distraction; abandoning all longing and aversion;(51)

Dwelling in solitude, eating moderately, controlling the body, mind and speech, with constant meditation on Self-soul as the final goal, and dispassion (Vairagya) for the worldly objects; (52)

Then only one is fit to attain Nirvana (Moksha), and become One with the Spirit of God; when he or she is free from egoism, violence, arrogance, lust, anger, greed and worldly possessions, free from notion of 'I' and 'Mine,' and of a peaceful disposition. (53)

The above verses give the road map on the path to 'Nirvana' or 'Moksha.' One who is free from egoism, violence, arrogance, greed, without worldly possessions, living in solitude, turning away from all sounds, master of his senses mind and intellect, having no desires, dispassion, moderate in eating and recreation, and above all one who is cheerful and peaceful. How many saints and holy people possess these qualities to qualify for Nirvana?

Established in union with God-consciousness with a blissful mind, one neither grieves nor desires anything, beholding sameness of Spirit in all beings; thus devoted to My consciousness, he attains My supreme abode (54)

Through deep devotion to Me, he comes to know the true essence of My Krishna-consciousness. With Self-realization, he merges with My infinite Spirit. (55)

Thus continuously performing all actions for My sake, having taken refuge in My Supreme Spirit; by My grace and blessings, you will reach My eternal indestructible Abode. (56)

Mentally dedicating all deeds to My Spirit of God, considering this as the highest goal of life, keeping your heart and thoughts fixed on My Divine consciousness with the discriminative intellect of Self-knowledge (Buddhi yoga). (57)

By keeping your mind constantly absorbed on My God-consciousness; you will by My grace overcome all obstacles; but if due to egoism you will not pay heed, then you will cause your own ruin. (58)

O Arjuna! If due to egoism, you think that you will not fight this war; then in vain is your resolve. Your inborn nature will compel you to fight this righteous war. (59)

O Kaunteya Arjuna! You are bound by your inborn nature and karma. If due to delusion you think you will not perform action, even then you will be helplessly driven to action, against your will. (60)

O Arjuna! The Spirit of God dwells in the hearts of all beings. Maya and delusion created by worldly desires, cause all beings to revolve around in endless activity as if mounted on a potter's wheel. (61)

O Bharata Arjuna! Seek refuge in the Spirit of God alone wholeheartedly. By His infinite grace, you will attain Supreme peace and the Eternal Abode. (62)

Thus this profound secret wisdom has been imparted to you by Me. Think and reflect upon this deeply, and then act as you desire, according to your own free will. (63)

Every individual has the free will to act as he or she chooses, and even God cannot impose His will on others. Various incarnations of God gave guidance and knowledge to the people in the form of Scriptures, but finally the individual himself has to walk the path.

Listen again to My Supreme word, the profoundest of all. You are of steadfast mind and extremely dear to Me;

therefore I declared what is good and beneficial for you and the humanity. (64)

Similar to the above verse, Bible also reiterates the same message by saying, "All Scripture is breathed out by God and is profitable for teaching, for reproof, for correction, and for training in righteousness, so that the man of God may be competent and equipped for every good work."

Unite your mind with My Supreme Spirit, be devoted to Me, sacrifice unto Me, and bow down to My Spirit in gratitude. Thus you shall attain oneness with My Spirit. This is My solemn pledge to you, for you are dear to Me. (65)

Give up the conditioning of all Dharmas (dogmas and doctrines), take sole refuge in My Spirit of God. Do not grieve; I shall liberate you from all sins. (66)

"***Sarvadharman***:—conditioning of all Dharmas (dogmas and doctrines):—***parityajya***:—Give-up:—***mam***:—to Me:—***ekam***:—only My Spirit:—***sharanam vraja***:—take refuge:...***aham***:—I:—***tva***:—your:—***sarva...papebhyah***:—all sins:—-***mokshay-shyami***:—will liberate:—***ma.. shuchah***:—do not grieve."

In this famous verse of Gita, Sri Krishna tells Arjuna and the mankind to take refuge in His Spirit of God. No religion is higher than the absolute Truth. This verse gives total assurance, that if any man or woman will take exclusive and complete refuge in Krishna-consciousness, then He will firmly hold the hand of that person, to deliver him or her from all sins.

A person may be weak due to worldly entanglements and attachments, but God will firmly hold his hand under all circumstances. It is an easy way to get liberated from all sins; but it does require firm faith and total devotion to God, as the foremost requirement.

Once a little girl and father, were crossing a shaky wooden bridge on the hills. The father was worried that his little daughter can fall into the water. So he told the girl to hold his hand. The little girl said, “No, father. You hold my hand.” The puzzled father said, “What is the difference?”

The little girl replied, “There is a big difference. As I am a little girl yet and do not have as much strength as you have, I may let go off my hand. But if you hold my hand, then I know for sure, that no matter what happens, you will never leave my hand.”

Trust the lord and let Him hold your hand, and do not lean on your own strength. To err is human, and we may falter and deviate from the righteous path, but God will still hold our hand.—Sri Krishna says to Arjuna in the above verse: “ Do not grieve I shall liberate you from all sins.”

This secret gospel of Bhagavad Gita is never to be spoken by you to any person who does not want to lead an austere life; nor to one who lacks devotion; or even to one who does not want to lend a willing ear to listen. And in no case to one, who finds faults with My teaching. (67)

Why does the Scripture of Bhagavad Gita lay down this injunction that this teaching is not to be declared to those who lack devotion, and those who do not want to listen or who find fault with this teaching?

One is the way of the critic who is constantly judging, evaluating whether it is right or wrong and whether it suits him or not, and if it agrees with his previous knowledge or not. Such a person is always criticizing and comparing with others. That is not the way to understand the secrets of life and higher truths. Sublime truth is available to only those who are in tune with the teaching with an open heart, and listen attentively without any prejudices.

Those who view the world through cynical and prejudiced eyes, are like a sheet of paper that has already been filled up and on which there is no further space to add or write anything new. This teaching is to be imparted to worthy people who do not find fault with this lofty and sublime Scripture, and are willing to listen and assimilate this profound teaching. A person has to be grateful for what he or she receives. Children learn very fast because they do not have any previous conditioning, or pre-conceived notions and doctrines. They will cling to whatever teaching is imparted to them in full faith.

For a spiritual seeker his whole life is learning, and he is humble to receive the lofty teaching at any age irrespective of whatever profession he or she is following. Rain water does not accumulate on elevated places but flows down to lower levels. Even so the grace of God flows to a person who is humble to bow down, who is devoted to God and is ready to listen to every word of higher truth.

Bible says, "Do not give to dogs what is sacred; do not throw your pearls to pigs. If you do, they may trample them under their feet, and turn and tear you to pieces. If anyone will not welcome you or listen to your words, shake the dust off your feet when you leave that home or town."

Here, the example of dogs and swine indicate those people who will ridicule, reject, and blaspheme the gospel once it has been given to them. The metaphor clearly states that one should not waste one's time and efforts on giving the lofty teachings to unworthy persons, as they will later speak ill of you.

The highest teaching of the scriptures has to be given to worthy people who are grateful to the Lord for the shower of grace and the bounties of life. There are many hypocrites in this world who will ridicule you and find faults in the scriptures because they do not want to understand the true essence of the teaching. Many pretenders and hollow men and women, will try to look wiser and higher than even the Lord, and start their own cult to make money.

Jesus Christ tells the same thing to his disciples in the Bible and says, "I am sending you into the world where you will be like sheep among wolves. Be innocent like a dove but clever like a serpent."

One who with supreme devotion will disseminate and teach this profound gospel of 'Truth' to My devotees;

renders an exceptional service to Me. Such a person shall undoubtedly reach My Abode of Krishna-consciousness. (68)

There is none among mankind who does dearer service to Me than he or she; nor there is another person in this world dear to Me as he. (69)

And whosoever shall study this sacred Gospel and dialogue of Bhagavad Gita; shall gain the merit of worshipping My Divine Spirit as Jnana Yajna (worship through knowledge). This is My declaration. (70)

The above verse says that whosoever studies this sacred text obtains the merit of blessings through 'Jnana Yajna.' This merit as declared in Gita is higher than even the acts of charity and giving away of wealth.

This sacred teaching is imparted by Sri Krishna to his disciple Arjuna in the form of a dialogue. It implies that Arjuna has an open mind, and he is free to clarify his doubts from the teacher without any restraints. According to the above verse, the study of Bhagavad Gita has the merit of worshipping the Divine Spirit; as the teaching is imparted by the God-incarnate Himself.

The readers who happen to be reading this Book have attained the merit of worshipping God through Jnana Yajna. This is a hidden blessing associated with Holy Scriptures. It is to be kept in mind that when Sri Krishna says that this is 'My' declaration; it is not the declaration of Sri Krishna as a human being; but the Spirit of Lord Vishnu as the primal God, talking through the incarnation of Sri Krishna.

One has to read the sacred gospel of Bhagavad Gita again and again as a daily habit to imbibe the true essence of the Holy Scripture. One cannot understand the implied meaning of the verses in one single reading. One is bound to forget the finer points over a period of time, and hence a repetitive reading of this Scripture is called for. Many of the verses are in the form of a metaphor and seed mantras with hidden meanings, and the teaching is applicable in day to day life, in different contexts.

Every time one reads and meditates over a particular verse a new meaning emerges, and that is the beauty of Bhagavad Gita verses. Whenever one needs clarity as to what action is right or wrong, Bhagavad Gita provides the answer.

After repeated readings, the remembrance of the verses settles down in one's mind, and then it becomes a source of inner illumination. It will simply be there to guide a person in all actions, like a beam of light on the path. It shows the way and it helps to avoid the pitfalls. 'The Word of God' is then within the person, and one is like a lotus leaf untouched by the mundane happenings of the world.

And all those who with utmost faith, and without finding faults; will listen to the teaching of this sacred Gospel; they too will be liberated from all evil and shall attain the auspicious regions, equal in merit to those who have performed meritorious deeds. (71)

Faith is a very powerful and essential factor in one's meditation and worship. Action without faith is of no consequence in this world or even in the next.

Adi Shankaracharya extols and praises the virtuous merit of the study and listening to the holy Scripture of Bhagavad Gita and says, "One who has studied the Bhagavad Gita even a little, one who has sipped at least a drop of Ganga water and has worshipped at least once Lord Murari (Sri Krishna); for that person, there is no fear of death and no arguments with Yama, the god of death."

O Partha Arjuna! Has this sacred teaching been heard and assimilated by you with a one-pointed mind? O Dhananjaya Arjuna! Has your delusion and ignorance been completely removed? (72)

One may ask as to why Sri Krishna is asking Arjuna again and again if he has heard this teaching with a one-pointed mind. Arjuna is standing there and listening to Sri Krishna, then why ask him if he is listening? There is a deep reason for asking this question?

In Bible Jesus Christ says again and again to his disciples, "You have eyes but fail to see, and ears but fail to hear? And don't you remember?"

He was talking to people who could see and hear perfectly well. Then what was he implying? He was saying that your eyes are already full of ideas, dreams, preconceived pictures and your ears are full of noises tuned to the outer world. It then becomes impossible to convey anything divine and to touch the inner sanctuary of your heart.

If you are just standing there and listening without full attention, then it is impossible to reach within you with the new knowledge. A human being has to drop his mind and preconceived ideas, to receive the words of wisdom. The words should not fall on deaf ears. One has to open the doors of one's mind to receive the teaching.

Arjuna said:

O Achyuta Sri Krishna! By Your kind grace my delusion has been removed, and I have regained my memory. I am now firm and free from doubts and ignorance. I shall act according to Thy Gospel of wisdom. (73)

Sanjaya said to King Dhritarashtra:

Thus, I have heard this most thrilling and uplifting sacred teaching in the form of a dialogue between Sri Krishna (Vasudeva) and the high spirited Partha Arjuna. This has thrilled me to the very core of my being. (74)

Having been bestowed with a divine vision through the grace of sage Vyasa to view distant happenings; I directly heard the most profound and Supreme Gospel of Bhagavad Gita declared directly by Sri Krishna, the Lord of Yoga. (75)

O King (Dhritarashtra)! As I remember again and again, this most Sacred and wondrous spiritual Gospel of

teaching declared by Lord Sri Krishna (Keshava) to His disciple Arjuna, my joy knows no bounds. (76)

And as often as I recall that most marvellous and Divine Form of Lord Hari (Sri Krishna as incarnation of Lord Vishnu); my astonishment and wonder ever increases, and I am thrilled with bliss to the very core of my being, again and again. (77)

Wherever is Lord Sri Krishna, and wherever is archer Arjuna (to represent humanity); there is prosperity, victory, glory, firmness and right decisions. This is my declaration. (78)